UPON FURTHER REVIEW

UPON FURTHER REVIEW
Sports in American Literature

Edited by
Michael Cocchiarale and
Scott D. Emmert

PRAEGER

Westport, Connecticut
London

Library of Congress Cataloging-in-Publication Data

Upon further review : sports in American literature / edited by Michael Cocchiarale and
  Scott D. Emmert.
     p.   cm.
    Includes bibliographical references (p.) and index.
    ISBN 0–275–98050–2 (alk. paper)
      1. American literature—History and criticism. 2. Sports in literature. 3. Sports stories,
American—History and criticism. 4. Athletics in literature. 5. Athletes in literature. I.
Cocchiarale, Michael, 1966– II. Emmert, Scott D., 1962–
PS169.S62U66 2004
810.9′357—dc22   2004040893

British Library Cataloguing in Publication Data is available.

Library of Congress Catalog Card Number: 2004040893
ISBN: 0–275–98050–2
First published in 2004

Praeger Publishers, 88 Post Road West, Westport, CT 06881
An imprint of Greenwood Publishing Group, Inc.
www.praeger.com

Printed in the United States of America

The paper used in this book complies with the
Permanent Paper Standard issued by the National
Information Standards Organization (Z39.48–1984).

10 9 8 7 6 5 4 3 2 1

For Lisa, who does it all . . . and then some.

For Mike Emmert and Mark Emmert—readers, sports fans, brothers.

Contents

Part II   Leaping Hurdles:
Race, Class, and Sports in American Literature

Part III   Put a Body on 'Em:
Gender and Sports in American Literature

Part IV   What a Beautiful Play!
Language, Aesthetics, and Sports in American Literature

Contents   xi

Acknowledgments

Writing is oftentimes described as a solitary endeavor. Putting together a book is definitely not. While we each put in our fair share of lonely hours copyediting manuscripts and staring at computer screens, we also had several people—family members, colleagues, mentors, friends, and editors—literally and figuratively by our side. Without their help and support, this collection of essays would never have been completed.

Thanks first and foremost to our wives, Lisa Eckley Cocchiarale and Angela Williamson Emmert, for their unflagging support during this long and exhausting (but immensely rewarding) experience. Lisa deserves special thanks for figuring out how to format the manuscript and for proofreading the final product.

Thanks to Widener University for a Faculty Development Grant that provided partial release time at the beginning of the process. Thanks as well to John Serembus, Associate Dean of Humanities, and Larry Panek, former Dean of Arts and Sciences, both of whom provided money to defray the cost of copyright permissions as well as to fund our many long distance phone conversations as we edited the essays. Mark Graybill, in addition to supplying us with a fine essay for this collection, read an early draft of our introduction and gave us excellent suggestions for revision.

The University of Wisconsin–Fox Valley Foundation generously provided funds for travel to academic conferences related to sports literature. In addition, April Kain-Breese, Chris Chamness, and Patricia Warmbrunn of the UW–Fox Valley library provided able and cheerful research assistance.

Bob Lamb and Joe Palmer of Purdue University were especially helpful at the early stages of the process, providing useful feedback and leads for possible contributors. We also wish to recognize the ways these sports and literature enthusiasts helped us immeasurably during our graduate school days. However much we look askance at Bob's undying love for the Yankees and

Joe's worship of the Fighting Irish (these allegiances are especially distressing from our points of view as fans of Cleveland and Minnesota sports teams), we still extend a hearty thanks.

Chris Golden and Gary Jasdzewski had nothing to do with the project itself, but they served the important role of keeping the sports chatter going. In this indirect way, they unwittingly provided significant inspiration.

Last but not least, Suzanne Staszak-Silva, John Beck, and Marcia Goldstein—our Greenwood editors—patiently and quickly responded to our many emails about everything from thorny copyright issues to the correct uses of the underrated en dash. We thank them for all their help.

We learned much during this nearly three-year process. We were delighted to find so many scholars devoted to both literature and sports, and we thank them for introducing us to exciting new works and allowing us to see classic works from new perspectives. As co-editors, we saw each other only a handful of times during the entire process, so we had to do the bulk of the work through email and phone conversations, reinforcing our view that modern communications technology cannot replace direct human interaction. In compensation, we discovered numerous shortcuts we can use while working on such a long distance collaboration again. But most of all, we learned that, even when (especially when) we are most frustrated or discouraged, there are any number of people ready to help us through. Again, many thanks to all of you.

Introduction:
Sports and American Literature

Michael Cocchiarale and Scott D. Emmert

Like fast-food franchises and name-brand coffee houses, sports are virtually everywhere in America. While that, admittedly, is an obvious comment, the very ubiquity of sports (or, more precisely, our mediated encounter of sports as spectacle) tends to create a curious reaction. We take athletic contests for granted, the way we take for granted that water will flow from our taps and electricity will stream from the outlets in our walls. As a result, much about sports seems commonplace, even as (ironically) individual events and athletes receive unprecedented hype and scrutiny. Even the truly special accomplishments of contemporary athletes—Lance Armstrong, the American bicyclist who battled back from cancer to win his fifth straight Tour de France; Ben Curtis, the PGA rookie who won the prestigious British Open; and Annika Sorenstam, who became the first female golfer to play in a PGA event in fifty-eight years, to take just three examples from 2003—seem transitory, the subject of current headlines and passing interest. As with other mass-marketed entertainment, sports exemplify postmodern culture's investment in the current moment. Participation in such a culture—sporting and otherwise—is often less a matter of direct involvement than of detached and enervated spectatorship.

The current climate of omnipresent mediated sports results in noise without meaning, stimulation without reflection. As a result, intriguing issues about the current sporting scene often go unexamined. Have we registered, for instance, the irony that although Americans now have more and better athletic equipment and exercise facilities, we are nonetheless faced with an epidemic of obesity? Have we noticed the fact that intellectual precocity is oftentimes denigrated as "geeky," yet prodigies of the sporting world such as basketball player LeBron James and golfer Michelle Wie are looked upon with awe and wonder? The national obsession with sports in America—evidenced by twenty-four-hour cable channels and sports talk radio outlets—has created much more chatter about the games people play yet has also, paradoxically, led to less critical thinking about them. Awash in sports "news" and entertainment, Americans have fewer and less subtle ways of reacting to one of the richest expressions of human aspiration.

It is not surprising, then, that today's sports stories in newspapers and on radio and TV have all the subtlety of melodrama. The heroes are often clear-cut, as are the villains. When, for example, professional athletes are arrested (e.g., Art Schlichter, Rae Carruth, or Kobe Bryant), most American sports fans—and the print, TV and radio "experts" who feed our nation's sports mania—express perfunctory moral judgments or assign easy blame. When parents become violent at children's sporting events, we tend to dismiss the miscreants as out-of-control individuals or utter clichés about the decline of civility and proper perspective in society. When a lone woman plays golf in a major men's tournament or promotes a lawsuit to require the inclusion of women in an exclusive golf club, most commentators either hail it as a positive action for equal rights or decry it as an erosion of quality in sports or as a threat to tradition.

Along with stories glorifying winners and dismissing "losers," we now have simple morality tales. According to one clichéd narrative, underdogs with big hearts, fierce determination, and a little luck achieve absolute success. This trope is especially evident not only in sports movies such as *Hoosiers* and *Breaking Away* but also in books, such as the best-selling *In These Girls, Hope Is a Muscle* (1995) by Madeleine Blais, which presents the true story of a high school basketball team that loses a playoff game by not playing as a team, and then—with renewed commitment—comes together to win the state championship the very next year. Such an outcome is, to be sure, potentially inspiring; but if "these girls" had again failed to win the state championship, it is doubtful their story would have become a bestseller. Not surprisingly, when Hollywood adapts literary works for the big screen, there is a tendency toward cliché. In Barry Levinson's *The Natural*, for example, Roy Hobbs's career ends not with a loss but with a thrilling (and morally vindicating) pyrotechnic victory.

Variations on the often superficial sports story featuring transcendent success are stories that involve athletes from different cultures or ethnic backgrounds coming together to win (as in the film *Remember the Titans*), suggesting that cultural, economic, or ethnic differences are easily overcome and that all off-field problems can be transcended by on-field success. Again effacing complexity to favor the familiarity of an innocuous narrative trajectory, this suggestion occurs despite, or in conscious opposition to, the fact that in America, the wealthiest nation in the world, many hard-working people live in abject poverty, set apart by class or race (and often by both). The winning-transcends-all sports stories so prevalent in our culture seek, then, to evade rather than confront reality. For that reason, our thinking about sports often has all the subtlety of a Shaquille O'Neal dunk.

If the ephemerality of athletic contests often leads to uncritical interpretations, at the same time for millions of Americans competitive sports may achieve a surprising depth. If a politician fails us, we eventually accept the disappointment with a protective shrug. However, if our favorite player or team loses, the disappointment lingers. One need only speak to Boston Red Sox fans about Bill Buckner's gaffe in the 1986 World Series or to Buffalo Bills fans about Super Bowl XXV, at the end of which Scott Norwood's potential game-winning field goal soared wide, to appreciate how much sports really mean to them. If much of our understanding of sport remains on the surface, these instances of profound emotional investment suggest that sports are something we take very seriously indeed. We place our hopes—not only our own personal hopes but also the hopes of our city and, come Olympic time, the hopes of our country—on the backs of athletes. When they win, our self-worth is confirmed. When they lose, our insecurities are exposed. To many fans, then, sports possess a special kind of density—a complex significance that belies its seeming superficiality. In the same vein, "highbrow" chroniclers of our nation's sporting interests—writers such as George Will and Frank DeFord—subject sports to the same kind of scrutiny one might give to a painting or a novel. Roger Angell, another writer dedicated to raising sports to the level of art, tries to explain this seemingly absurd level of fan commitment. Writing about Boston Red Sox fans specifically, but about all fans in general, Angell comments:

[T]his belonging and caring is what our games are all about: this is what we come for. It is foolish and childish, on the face of it, to affiliate ourselves with anything so insignificant and patently contrived and commercially exploitative as a professional sports team, and the amusing superiority and icy scorn that the non-fan directs at the sports nut . . . is understandable and unanswerable. Almost. What is left out of this calculation, it seems to me, is the business of caring. (83)

For the "ordinary" fan, a sporting event—whether it is the Super Bowl or the Little League World Series or the Women's Figure Skating World Championship—is full of moments and personalities to care about; more important, it is a sublime experience possessing nearly all the attributes of serious theater.

The paradox, then, is that while sports seem frequently to be little more than a feel-good distraction for a disposable culture, it is just as often something in which we invest the deepest parts of ourselves. Deep emotion, of course, is also the province of literary artists—not the chauvinistic and rabble-rousing emotion of sports talk hosts or the feel-good emotion of so many popular artists, but an emotion that requires serious intellectual engagement. Whereas watching sports may or may not engage the mind, the act of reading a work of literature depends on an intellectual investment. To think more carefully and subtly about sports, we may therefore turn to literature to indicate ways to address its multifaceted issues. Far from being a mere diversion or hobby, therefore, sports literature—and a sustained and serious critical attention to that literature—holds up a new and powerful lens to the figures and events that we may passively absorb on a weekend in front of the television set.

* * *

An interest in what might be called athletic exploits shows up in American literature almost from the beginning. Rip Van Winkle in Washington Irving's 1819 tale marvels at the prodigious noise created by the strange bowlers he comes across in the "Kaatskill Mountains." The physical adventuring and woodsman skill of James Fenimore Cooper's Natty Bumppo helped to make his creator one of the most popular authors in American literature. In his often-anthologized "The Big Bear of Arkansas," T. B. Thorpe supplies an early hunting story, one that also displays the advantages of being able to tell of one's sporting prowess after the fact. Indeed, the theme of competition informs the tall tale tradition, for in these tales not only do the characters seek to best each other in some physical activity but their authors also desire the victory in putting one over on gullible readers. Thus, the contest at the heart of Mark Twain's celebrated frog story pits the narrator, the characters he encounters, and the reader in a competition of understanding. Twain was especially impressed by physical skill. In *Life on the Mississippi* his cub steamboat pilots compete avidly with the celebrated river as well as with each other. Much of this literature influenced later writers, to be sure. Twain's emphasis on control as it is manifested in skillful action presages, for example, Jack London, arguably the first "serious" American sports fiction writer (Oriard 9).[1] London wrote stories and novels that reflect an abiding interest in physical ability. Indeed, *The Game* (1905) and *The Abysmal Brute* (1913), London's boxing novels, exhibit the poles of athletic experience, for they portray, respectively, the heartbreak of ultimate defeat and the joy of transcendent triumph. In this latter sense, prevalent in American literature is the notion that physical prowess equates handily to financial, social, and even moral success.

In the decade after London's death, America embraced sports on a mass commercial scale. In the postwar economic boom of the 1920s, Americans found themselves in possession of an unprecedented amount of leisure time—time they spent, in large part, following the exploits of such notable sports figures as Babe Ruth, Jack Dempsey, and Bobby Jones. Not coincidentally, some of the decade's greatest writers found in sports a topic worth exploring. In Ernest Hemingway, for example, sport oftentimes becomes a proving ground for character. In this regard, one thinks of the "grace under pressure" exemplified by bullfighter Pedro Romero in *The Sun Also Rises* (1926). For F. Scott Fitzgerald, sport can become an apt symbol for the corruption of the social and economic elite. In this instance, one need look no further than Tom Buchanan, the truculent former football star of *The Great Gatsby* (1925). More overt in its use of sports is the work of Ring Lardner who, in the spirit of an age that featured scathing cultural critics like Sinclair Lewis and H. L. Mencken, satirized the hypocrisies of American life through the seemingly benign figure of the professional baseball player.

As athletic spectacles gained prominence in America, writers continued in greater numbers to find in sports a rich theme or trope for the representation and critique of American society. From Bernard Malamud's conflation of our national sport and classical myths to Don DeLillo's exploration of the language systems of sports and war, serious literary artists over the last fifty years have continued to be intrigued by how we are defined by the sporting events that clamor for our attention.

More recently, women athletes have begun to be taken more seriously—the result of a focus on "openly promoting competitive sports for women" (Nelson xv) in the 1960s and, not long after, the passing of Title IX, "the 1972 federal law that prohibits sex discrimination in federally funded educational institutions" (Nelson xv). Not surprisingly, the literary interest in women's sports also increases in this era. While the most notable literature of sport by women has taken swimming as its subject (for example, Maxine Kumin's "To Swim, To Believe" [1975], Jenifer Levin's *Water Dancer* [1982], Carol Anshaw's *Aquamarine* [1992]), in recent years, writers such as Lucy Jane Bledsoe have created memorable fiction about women's basketball. What is more, Anne Lamott's *Crooked Little Heart* (1997), a novel about a teenage tennis player, and Jane Smiley's *Horse Heaven* (2001), a novel about the horse racing industry, have achieved bestseller status.

* * *

Our primary intent with this collection is to correct a scholarly imbalance. Despite the long tradition of serious imaginative writing on sports, there has been comparatively very little analysis of the work. To be sure, there are significant scholarly antecedents. Wiley Lee Umphlett, Robert J. Higgs, Michael Oriard, and Christian Messenger have all written excellent studies that examine how sports in American literature are concerned with much more than the games that are played. In addition, exciting scholarship continues to appear in *Aethlon*, the fine journal dedicated to publishing criticism on sports literature, and *Modern Fiction Studies*, which in addition to including individual essays on sports in literature over the years also devoted an entire issue to modern sports fiction in its Spring 1987 number. Adding to this small but distinguished body of scholarship and encouraging additional work in this field are two goals of the present collection.

To these ends, we have sought to collect essays that address sports in literature from a variety of critical perspectives. In addition, although much has been written about the literature produced in the so-called "Golden Age of Sports," we thought that it would nevertheless make sense to go back and attempt, in part, to reread the period and at least some of its key authors. At the same time, we were aware of the need to expand this field of literary criticism by considering contemporary works. While evaluating articles for inclusion, we not only kept in mind the eighty-year time frame but also were wary of the single sport approach. Even though there is certainly more literature devoted to baseball than to any other sport, we (along with many literary artists) do not believe, as Angell claims, that "[b]aseball is the writer's game" (x). To achieve the desired balance, the collection features several essays devoted to baseball out of respect for its prominence in the national imagination, while including a number of essays that extend the examination of sports literature to works foregrounding other sports—everything from basketball (almost certainly the ascendant sport in the United States at this time) to bodybuilding to wilderness adventuring.

To ensure a cohesive collection, we also decided on certain generic restrictions. First, the book does not contain essays that consider sports film, of which there is a rich and wonderful tradition. It was our thinking that, however worthy of analysis such works might be (one thinks of the "literary" qualities of such different films as *Raging Bull* and *Personal Best* and, more recently, the Shakespeare-inspired *O*), opening up the collection in this way would seriously diffuse its focus and thus fail to do justice to either sports in literature or sports in film. Second, readers will notice an absence of drama. Although this restriction had more to do with the kinds of submissions we received than with a specific desire to limit the scope in this way, it is clear that playwrights, like all literary artists, have been intrigued by the possibilities of sport. The works of August Wilson (*Fences*), Lee Blessing (*Cobb*, *Old Timers Game*), Jason Miller (*That Championship Season*), Richard Greenberg (*Take Me Out*), and Milcha Sanchez-Scott (*The Cuban Swimmer*) serve as some of the most notable examples. Finally, the collection features very little on nonfiction from established and insightful voices such as David Halberstam, Roger Angell, Joyce Carol Oates, Doris Kearns Goodwin, or John Edgar Wideman, to name only a few. We feel that collections devoted to any of the above genres would certainly make significant contributions to the field.

* * *

Upon Further Review is divided into four thematic sections featuring essays from a variety of critical perspectives. The essays in the first section, "Who's Keeping Score? Values and Sports in American Literature," treat the significance of sports for both the individual and American society. This section begins with David C. Dougherty's far-reaching essay that surveys baseball novels in post–World War II America, exploring how, through a number of tropes, these works about the American pastime form a "narrative about the ways in which a nation is created by its play as well as its politics." The essays that follow in this section examine the connections between sports literature and our cultural and philosophical values by offering a closer look at individual authors. That three of the essays in this section nonetheless focus on baseball in literature testifies to the ongoing fascination American authors have demonstrated when it comes to defining a national ethos through what may or not may not be America's most cherished sport. In "'War . . . May Hasten This Change in Values': The World War II–Era Writings of John R. Tunis," Ryan K. Anderson discusses the output of one of America's most prolific writers of adolescent sports literature. Anderson's examination of Tunis demonstrates the ways a dominant culture can use such literature for its own political purposes, in the process ignoring the insistent critique of prevailing ideologies present in that literature. In the next essay, Chris York's critical reading of Mark

Winegardner's novel *The Veracruz Blues* (1996) illuminates "the metaphoric relationship between baseball and American culture as a way of problematizing the ideological nature of American myth." Focusing on Mexican League baseball, the novel at once presents an "ambivalence towards American culture . . . the international nature of 'the American dream,' and also, almost paradoxically, a staunch resistance towards American cultural imperialism." The section concludes with an examination of the allusively omnivorous novel *Infinite Jest* (1997) by David Foster Wallace. *Infinite Jest* stands squarely within a tradition of sports writing interested in the theme of personal identity and selfhood, and Stephen J. Burn serves critics by unearthing the novel's source texts in literature, philosophy, and psychology. Among these sources is Don DeLillo's seminal postmodern sports novel *End Zone* (1972), but Wallace also delves deeply into theories of cognitive psychology to dramatize the anxieties surrounding our culture's doubts about originality—in both our sporting life and our ability to communicate individual experience. The desire by authors to use sports to define cultural aspirations and redefine old ways of thinking to express a new set of values is one common theme among the essays in this section.

In the second section, "Leaping Hurdles: Race, Class, and Sports in American Literature," featured essays interrogate the problematic connections between race, social class, and sports in American society. Greg Ahrenhoerster begins this section with an essay that surveys contemporary Native American fiction to examine the subtle ways Native writers use sports references to depict and critique "the profound cultural differences" between white and Native society. Far from offering a convenient escape from conflict, references to sports in this literature express "the struggle waged by many Indians to adapt their culture to the modern industrial world thrust upon them." Next, Tracy Curtis's essay on Paul Beatty's soon-to-be-classic novel *The White Boy Shuffle* (1996) explores the way society creates African American sports stars to serve as symbols that both articulate collective aspiration and erase real differences between blacks and whites, and between individuals of any race, that threaten a socially sanctioned success myth. That the novel's protagonist both participates in and resists this process places him among some of the greatest of American literary heroes who enact a quest for self-definition. At this point the section turns to a canonical writer as A. Fletcher Cole appraises F. Scott Fitzgerald's employment of golf to communicate "his understanding of the effects of America's social stratification," including the social inequities to be found within, and without, the nation's exclusive country clubs. Cole's essay, furthermore, is the first that we know of to examine golf as a consistent thematic element in all of Fitzgerald's fiction. The conflation of race and class can be seen in Lisa Abney's essay on *God Sends Sunday* (1931), a novel by Arna Bontemps. Abney's reading illuminates the ways the novel represents African American and Southern folk life to provide the verisimilitude of literary realism and to evaluate false romantic notions of luck. Because the protagonist is not allowed a comfortable rise from a racially and economically disadvantaged position, for Abney the horse racing and gambling that inform this novel present a skepticism about easy success—luck—that seems as pertinent today as it did when *God Sends Sunday* first appeared.

The third section, "Put a Body on 'Em: Gender and Sports in American Literature," begins with Susan J. Bandy's sweeping essay on sports poetry, fiction, and memoir by women. In addition to documenting a long tradition of women's writing about sports, this survey registers the modulations of a female voice in sports literature, ranging from the poetry of Amy Lowell early in the twentieth century to the fiction of Jenifer Levin at the end of that century, a period of time in which women went from sidelined spectators to full-fledged participants in athletic experience. The essay thus provides a coherent vision of the changes in women's sports literature over the last century.

The rest of the essays in this section analyze the ways literature may depict sports as a challenge to accepted notions of femininity and masculinity. Andrew J. Price locates in Harry Crews's novel about female bodybuilders a conflicted depiction of gender ideologies. On the one hand, Crews's novel critiques traditional notions of femininity for infringing on the individual desire for self-proving and self-improving. On the other hand, Price argues that Crews accepts traditional ideas about femininity to "censor women who build their bodies to the point where they absolve themselves of [femininity's] conventions altogether." The supposedly uncritical display of excessive masculinity in the works and life of author James Dickey informs the next two essays. For Mark S. Graybill, Dickey's novel *Deliverance* (1970) is neglected in discussions of sports literature because it denies the possibility of transcendence through sports, a theme critics tend to prefer. More important for Graybill is the novel's skeptical portrayal of the "exhilarating but destructive power of hypermasculinity and surplus aggressivity" frequently deployed as a defense against a "feminine" incursion into sporting culture. Diederik Oostdijk continues a discussion of Dickey's masculine image by examining the author's employment of a "hegemonic masculinity" to fashion a socially accepted cover for the more sensitive obligations incurred by poets. Dickey's objections to the poetry of Randall Jarrell represent, Oostdijk argues, more than an instance of macho posturing. Those objections may instead be seen as a kind of tribute to Jarrell, a poet who did not share Dickey's unease about seeming too feminine and whose football poem "Say Goodbye to Big Daddy" influenced Dickey's verse. This section concludes with Ron Picard's original comparison of Ernest Hemingway and Leslie Marmon Silko. For Picard, reading *The Sun Also Rises* alongside *Ceremony* (1977) enables a reinterpretation of the concept of competition as a gendered activity. Both novels, Picard argues, suggest the value of "communal competition" as opposed to a traditionally masculine version of competition that seeks a lone winner and that denies intimacy to participants and spectators.

The concluding section, "What a Beautiful Play! Language, Aesthetics, and Sports in American Literature," focuses on the intersection of sports, language, and aesthetics. In the first essay, Derek Parker Royal provides a survey of the novels of Philip Roth as seen through the lens of the satiric baseball fiction *The Great American Novel* (1973). In this and other novels by Roth, Royal examines the "play" of language that "allows the novelist to freely articulate alternative narratives that can tell us volumes about the ways we delineate our national experiences." A particular alternative narrative is the subject of Roxanne Harde's nuanced reexamination of the oft-studied postmodern novel *The Celebrant* (1983). By focusing on author Eric Rolfe Greenberg's particular use of allegory, Harde argues that the novel "ultimately escapes both the Jewish and Christian narratives in order to put forth baseball as a separate temple, a sacred space that invites reverence and insists on justice." In the next essay, Matt Kelley examines Jack Kerouac's recurring use of football and the author's frequent, cinematic shifts in point of view. By tracing Kerouac's inventive use of a "panoramic consciousness" to depict the crowds at football games, a narrative strategy common in the author's fiction, Kelley demonstrates the darkening of vision in Kerouac's treatment of sports, his move from exuberance to pessimism. Rounding off this section is Suzanne Disheroon-Green's essay that explores how sports is embedded in the very structure of our language. By focusing on the "conceptual metaphor" that Life Is a Game, Disheroon-Green reveals the subtle yet deeply rooted ideas about competition and sports that affect the presentation of characters in selected twentieth-century southern novels. More generally, Disheroon-Green's approach suggests the rich critical possibilities to be found in broadening our understanding of sports in literature, thereby providing a fitting conclusion to the collection.

Upon further review, it is clear that many of the most significant American fiction writers and poets of the last century have found sports well worth writing about. It is our hope that the seventeen essays presented here will not only encourage readers to turn (or return) to the literary works under discussion but also inspire further critical inquiry into this captivating field. For the willing reader—for the reader not content with the facile narratives that dominate our movie screens, our popular bookstores, and our sports pages—the literature (and the analysis of it represented in this collection) offers real opportunities for contemplating the deep and lasting significance of sports in America.

NOTE

1. The word "serious" here is used advisedly, for histories of sports literature may make a distinction between writers of juvenile sports fiction and writers of such fiction meant for adults. Michael Oriard asserts that much of today's adult sports fiction originated in juvenile literature, insisting that Gilbert Patten, who wrote juvenile stories under the pen name Burt L. Standish beginning in the late 1890s, is "the real father of American sports fiction" (9).

REFERENCES

Angell, Roger. *Once More Around the Park: A Baseball Reader*. New York: Ballantine, 1991.

Nelson, Mariah Burton. "Introduction: Who We Might Become." *Nike Is a Goddess: The History of Women in Sports*. New York: Atlantic Monthy Press, 1998. ix–xix.

Oriard, Michael. *Dreaming of Heroes: American Sports Fiction, 1868–1980*. Chicago: Nelson-Hall, 1982.

Part I

Who's Keeping Score?
Values and Sports in
American Literature

Batters and Archetypes: Baseball as Trope in Mid-Century American Literature

David C. Dougherty

Baseball, the American pastime, evokes something inherently pastoral, bordering on the mythic. Its very designation as the national pastime suggests a comprehensive narrative, or sys-text, which is not sequential but is surprisingly cohesive, about the ways in which a nation is created by its play, as well as by its politics. Ultimately, baseball suggests a revealing, complex relation between play—an artificial, mythically "green" world—and politics and economics—the real, "gray" world. Many writers and filmmakers have constructed baseball and the athletes who play the game as tropes for the American condition: our politics, our aspirations, our concepts of responsibility, and even our theological concerns.

In her signature poem Marianne Moore, who relished having thrown out the first pitch at a Brooklyn Dodgers' game, pleads for inclusiveness as the proper subject for "Poetry": She includes baseball fans and statisticians as well as critics, toads, gardens, and traditional subjects for poems. Her friend William Carlos Williams, however, saw baseball games as an emblem for the forces of repression and mob violence in *Spring and All XXVI*, or "At the Ball Game." After creating a cluster of positive images celebrating the beauty of the spectators' vicarious, collective participation in the players' grace and skill, Williams introduces a somber trope: He equates this collective mentality with the Inquisition and with revolution in general while imaging the solemn crowd as acting "without thought" (line 36). At mid-century, the youthful protagonists of Philip Roth's short story "The Conversion of the Jews" see Detroit Tigers' star outfielder and fellow Jew Hank Greenberg as their role model, their symbol of cultural assimilation. The hero of Ken Kesey's *One Flew Over the Cuckoo's Nest* (1962) successfully mobilizes the apathetic patients when the Big Nurse refuses to alter her schedule to accommodate the World Series, as close to a tradition as anything McMurphy recognizes. And the embattled "Father" in E. L. Doctorow's *Ragtime* (1975) enjoys a single moment of solidarity with his strange son after a New York Giants' game, although those same Giants show up much later in the novel as uncouth tourists at the Pyramids.

All of these writers identified baseball as a quintessentially American activity, one that yields a trope by means of which artists may explore our creation of cultural, political, and epistemological myths. One comprehensive study goes as far as saying "this body of texts—baseball literature—has the status of a functional modern mythology" (Westbrook 9–10).[1] Although it seems hyperbolic to treat sports as the equivalent of classical myths, and although it is moreover necessary to factor modern and postmodern irony into such an equation, writers have seen sports, particularly baseball, as a useful vehicle for cultural and epistemological analysis.[2]

The focus of this analysis, however, will be certain illuminating crossovers between "serious" literature and film and the popular culture phenomenon of games that appear, when kept pure from the overt commercialism that has infected professional sports over the past half-century, to make considerably more sense than life itself. To develop this theme, we shall explore four ways in which American writers mined baseball's potential as a trope during the quarter-century in which the nation realized that it had lost its innocence—decades of McCarthyism, civil rights struggle and reaction, increasing Vietnam involvement, the Cold War, and the politics of assassination. This representation of a lost Eden, of a game played in what seemed to be the last bastion of innocence, an incongruously green field plunked down in centers of urban decay, serves as constant background among these variations and mutations on the sport's potential as a trope to explore American culture's coming of age. These variations—the "sentimental," the "proletarian and nostalgic," the "political," and the "theological and epistemological"—empower artists to explore personal, social, political, and creative responsibility in an age in which America discovered that its innocence was itself a cultural myth. Moreover, certain of these tropes are self-referential and self-critical, questioning the very power of literature about sports to shape our thinking by telling stories about games and those who play them. In fact, our final two variations on the trope explicitly critique the processes of myth-making and myth-learning itself.

Very close to popular fictions about baseball—adolescent stories, films about heroes like Lou Gehrig—is the "sentimental trope," in which a generally realistic narrative of the fortunes of an athlete or a group of athletes enacts a cliché out of our culture's aspirations, often reinforcing an image of decency or justice we realize we seldom encounter in actual experience. For example, Mark Harris's *Bang the Drum Slowly* (1956) attempts to counter the paranoia and fear plaguing the Cold War and late McCarthy era by suggesting that through sports, and collective effort, men achieve their ethical potential. The novel was the basis for an excellent U.S. Steel Hour live TV presentation and later a feature film, adapted for the screen by Harris.[3] The novel and both dramatizations tell a woeful tale of a dying catcher who had never achieved his modest potential, and thus affiliate with the traditions of literary realism—death comes to all, whether on the field or in the stands. Distinguishing all three versions of *Bang the Drum Slowly* from adolescent literature about baseball is this potentially realistic or mimetic treatment: Bruce is a young athlete, mediocre by major league standards but magnificent when compared with the rest of us. Yet his body, the sole source of his excellence, is at war with itself and nurtures its own destruction. Harris underscores the singularity of Bruce's body as his claim to excellence by presenting him as stupid (he calls protagonist Henry Wiggen "Arthur" because he cannot correlate his teammates' calling Wiggen "Author" with his having putatively authored the book Harris self-references, *The Southpaw* [1953]) and crude (Bruce's favorite pastime is to spit out hotel windows and comment on the direction in which the tobacco-laden saliva drifts). At the obvious level, then, the narrative reminds us of the fleeting quality of human life and glory, as suggested by the cloying lyrics of the cowboy song from which Harris takes his title: "O bang the drum slowly and play the fife softly, / Play the dead march as they carry me on" (249).

A more insidious sentimental trope, however, dominates the narrative and the subsequent films, reinforcing the culture's wish that adversity propels human beings toward meaningful collective effort. As news of Bruce's ailment leaks out among the players, they become his advocates, giving up material advantages so he can remain on the team in his final year. Wiggen himself undergoes a complete transformation as a result of Bruce's dying. The pitcher evolves from the self-absorbed materialist to the cracker-barrel philosopher as a result of his involvement in Bruce's coming to terms with his death. He holds out for a large contract at the novel's beginning, missing most of spring training, to pressure the Mammoths to pay him well. But he eventually agrees to a contract at a salary substantially less than he wanted, on condition that the club accepts a codicil that keeps Bruce a Mammoth as long as Wiggen remains with the team. He also deceives the insurance company he represents in order to prevent Bruce from changing the beneficiary on his policy to benefit a prostitute he is in love with rather than his family. No one interested merely in the commission would place himself in this ambiguous ethical position, to decide for Bruce what Bruce's best interests are. The sentimental trope here is that even a hard-nosed materialist can achieve ethical self-transcendence by participating vicariously in someone else's suffering.

To complete the sentimental trope in a manner later emulated by W. P. Kinsella in *Shoeless Joe* (1982), subsequently filmed as *Field of Dreams*, virtue pays off in material success—the foundational Christian-American myth of virtue rewarded. When the season began, the Mammoths had pennant potential but were torn apart by bickering and self-interest. When Wiggen inadvertently leaks information about Bruce's illness to prevent other players from "ragging" Pearson, the Mammoths begin to play like a team. Striving to win for Bruce, the team surpasses the press's—and its own—expectations by winning the pennant.

Earlier that decade, Bernard Malamud developed the baseball trope in quite a different direction. *The Natural* (1952), notoriously rich with mythic resonance, employs a compound "proletarian-mythic trope." An indication of the abyss between Malamud's handling of the trope and Harris's may be illustrated by examining the watering-down Hollywood imposed on Malamud's narrative to create a commercially successful film. Malamud's hero, named Roy Hobbs to evoke myth and folklore,[4] fails in his final effort to liberate himself from a classic pact with evil (a corrupt owner, a complicit sportswriter, and an enchantress), recalling the contemporaneous popular musical *Damn Yankees*. Hobbs has already sold his soul, and the Shoeless Joe Jackson legend echoes in the novel's final pages, where an anonymous kid begs Hobbs to "say it ain't true, Roy" (217). Adapting the story to film, the producers apparently feared the box office implications of such a negative ending. Therefore, freed of his contamination by a heroic renunciation of his pact with the evil forces, Robert Redford's Hobbs slams a homer and enacts the sentimental cliché of slowly rounding the bases to exploding lights and thumping bass chords of victory.

Malamud, whose novel is possibly the least successfully mimetic baseball novel of the century, represents the sport as a trope suggesting social and cultural responsibility. Malamud regularly sacrifices the "probable" for the mythic, to reinforce this essentially proletarian trope. For example, Hobbs joins the struggling New York Knights as a thirty-five-year-old rookie left fielder. Although a prodigious hitter, he's immediately benched, then pressed into a contest with the team's only outstanding player, Bump Bailey, for the left-field position. It seems never to enter the mind of Pop Fisher (allusively, "Father Fisher King," the Knights' manager) or perhaps Malamud himself that the least competent outfielder at the major league level ordinarily plays left field and that, since Roy excels defensively, he should play right field, where his fine throwing arm could be put to its best use—thereby leaving two productive bats in the line-up. Of course, Malamud's point is the allegorical contest between the comedic egoist Bailey, who does not care about the team's fortunes, and the serious egoist Hobbs, who sees the team's success as an extension and validation of his own. In a final stretching of baseball verisimilitude, Otto Zipp, an obnoxious Bailey fan who never forgave Roy for taking his hero's place, razzes Hobbs during his final game until the guilt-laden protagonist deliberately strikes successive foul balls aimed at wounding Zipp—bat control even Rod Carew would not attempt. The last foul injures Iris Lemon, who has made the journey to New York to support Hobbs and to initiate Malamud's proletarian trope—a scene the filmmakers eliminated.

Through this injured character, Iris Lemon, Malamud asks what athletes gifted with grace and skill, like Roy Hobbs, or even less talented players owe to society—not just the fans, but the entire culture. During his first slump, Iris came out of nowhere to show her support for Roy, although she did not previously know him and does not like baseball. When a Chicago truck driver asks Roy to enact one heroic cliché, to slam a homer for his sick child, Roy sets aside his selfish loyalty to his personal bat Wonderboy, but he feels weak, inadequate to perform the hero's role until he sees a woman standing up in the bleachers. From her show of confidence he gathers the resolve to strike a magical homer that travels between the pitcher's legs before beginning its ascent into the Chicago sky, thereby saving the child's life and symbolically castrating the opposing pitcher.[5] Roy's good angel, Iris articulates Malamud's theme in simple, eloquent, terms: "Without heroes we're all plain people and don't know how far we can go" (139–140). Her belief that Roy's skills are a responsibility to his public contrasts sharply with his selfish goal, to set records and be the best there ever was. This closely resembles the early misadventure that sidetracked Roy's career when, on a trip to try out with the Cubs, he strikes out the Most Valuable Player "the Whammer" at a country fair, thereby winning the attention of mysterious, beautiful Harriet Bird. She condemns the ego-centered goals Roy articulates when she learns what he seeks from the game: fame, money, records, and adoration. But when Harriet asks if there isn't "some more glorious meaning to one's life and activities" (27), Roy is clueless. Malamud implies that her shooting Hobbs, as she has other outstanding athletes, happens because he cannot explain the responsibilities his talent imposes on him.

His delayed rookie season is defined by repeated failures to understand and act on his obligations to the Knights, to Pop, and to his public. Although like the dying Bruce Pearson he energizes the lethargic Knights through his presence, Roy never reflects on his role or his responsibility. After Iris tells him that his skills impose an obligation, Roy continues to try to satisfy his hungers—for food, for wealth, and for the materialistic Memo Paris. When the Knights finish the season tied with the Pirates, Roy conspires with bookies and corrupt owners to throw the playoff game. After his efforts to hurt Otto Zipp result in an injury to Iris, Roy decides to repudiate his agreement and hit a game-winning homer. But in Malamud's variation on the trope, it is too late. One cannot buy back one's soul by willing it, and Roy has already missed several chances to understand the obligations his greatness imposes upon him. Although the film reiterates the sentimental motif by having Roy reunited with Iris and their son, Malamud's novel ends with a man unable even to comprehend his failure to grasp the obligations imposed on his soul by his athletic skills.

Whereas Malamud's version of the baseball trope combines the mythic with the proletarian, Philip Roth's variation is essentially political. The game was a core motif in much of Roth's early fiction, from the adolescents' looking up to Greenberg as a role model in the early short story, through the wealthy, assimilated Jewish family's obsession with sports and competition in "Goodbye, Columbus" (1959), and Alexander Portnoy's paean to the center fielder as the exemplar of a freedom missing in the real world as portrayed in *Portnoy's Complaint* (1968). The motif evolves from athletics as a figure for the problems of cultural assimilation in the *Goodbye, Columbus* stories toward a critique of America's potential for suppressing the politically dangerous *other*—and ultimately into an inquiry into the dangers inherent in the very myth-imposition process to which Roth's novel contributes. In the hubristically, ironically titled *The Great American Novel* (1973), Roth deliberately, with postmodern irony, plays off the vanity of naming a novel in the manner of the cliché about the "great American game" and mentions Hemingway's obsession with writing a great American novel as one model shaping the consciousness of his narrator. Roth, speaking through the voice of a sports writer who lost his job—by extension his voice and his rights under the first amendment—tells the story of the "Patriot" league, which has been deliberately expunged from our history and folklore. Only the narrator, Word Smith (recalling the bardic functions of transmitting sacred or heroic narratives in preliterate cultures) remembers and honors the heroes of that lost league, Luke Gofannon (for whom Smith votes annually to the Hall of Fame) and Mike Mazda, whose names were obliterated from the historical record because of suspicion that other members of the Patriot League were Communist agents. Yet Roth's wordsmith reminds us more of the Ancient Mariner than of Homer, telling a reluctant audience tales that shake their epistemological and political foundations. The novel was written years after the McCarthy era, but its proximity to the events surrounding the Vietnam War, the civil rights struggle, suspicions about the assassinations of the 1960s, and Watergate, confirms that Roth's variation on the trope is to warn us about political power, especially as it is exerted over the press to influence our perception of games—and of political reality. Shortly after *The Great American Novel* came out, Roth wrote about the correspondences between baseball and literature in his youthful view of the world:

Not until I got to college and was introduced to literature did I find anything with a comparable emotional atmosphere and as strong an aesthetic appeal. . . . Baseball, with its lore and legends, its cultural power, its seasonal associations, its native simplicity, its simple rules and transparent strategies, its longeurs and thrills, its spaciousness, its suspensefulness, its peculiarly hypnotic tedium, its heroics, its nuances, and its mythic sense of itself, was the literature of my boyhood. ("My Baseball Years" 35)[6]

Roth's treatment in *The Great American Novel*, unlike those of Harris or Malamud or of Roth's own references to baseball in earlier works, seems cynically deflating. In place of the "heroic/sentimental" narrative of *Bang the Drum Slowly* and its descendants like *Shoeless Joe* or the "nostalgic/proletarian" implications of *The Natural*, Roth paints the players, managers, and owners of the Patriot League as losers, freaks, misfits, scoundrels, and compulsives. Even the more traditional characters, like manager Ulysses S. Fairsmith (modeled loosely on A's legend Connie Mack) are obsessive: Fairsmith believes baseball is a means of Christianizing the world, and in one preposterous digression narrowly escapes cannibalization by an enraged African tribe because he refuses to condone their cultural-religious preference for sliding headfirst into first base. This association of baseball, religious evangelism, cultural imperialism, and political conservatism forms one base of Roth's critique of American society in *The Great American Novel*.

If owners and managers are ignoble, ruthless individuals (though often modeled on recognizable baseball figures), the ballplayers themselves are oddballs, misfits, and freaks, like bitter one-legged catcher "Hot" Ptah, deferential one-armed outfielder Bud Parusha, or heroic midget Bob Yamm and vicious midget O. K. Okatur.[7] Other players are vicious, like John Baal (named for a Canaanite deity associated with fertility and celebratory worship), whose father "Spit" was responsible for getting the spitter declared illegal. Protagonists Roland Agni ("the desperate hero of this great history" [303], whose first name recalls the French epic hero) and Gil Gamesh (the Sumerian god-king) are self-absorbed in ways Roy Hobbs could never be. Although Agni was modeled specifically on Ty Cobb in his obsession with his own greatness and his contempt for foe and teammate alike, most of the novel's characters are vindictive, selfish, vicious, and anything but heroic. Gamesh, once potentially the greatest pitcher in all three major leagues, was banished from baseball but returned during the war years as a trained Soviet saboteur, charged with undermining the game from within. This political sabotage is motivated by his hunger for revenge on a game that repudiated him when he was on the verge of achieving the kind of immortality Roy Hobbs sought in *The Natural*. The only character in *The Great American Novel* who is heroically drawn is Luke Gofannon, whose career mirrors but finally eclipses that of Babe Ruth, without the Bambino's hubris and boozing. "Luke the Loner" was so essential to his team that after the mendacious owners sold his contract, the team went into a decline that culminated with the owners' renting their stadium and placing the 1943 Rupert Mundys in perpetual exile, a team playing all its games on the road (Word Smith defines the era as "A. G.," or After Gofannon, much as the "curse of the Bambino" has haunted the Boston Red Sox since they sold Ruth's contract to the Yankees). Gofannon is, along with Bob Yamm, the only character in the novel who acts in others' interests—one incidence of which costs Gofannon his life.

In a larger context, however, *The Great American Novel* employs organized baseball as a synecdoche for the forces in American society that repress dissent and enforce political hegemony, particularly the information-control by which repressive societies manipulate their citizens' minds. A major element of Roth's indictment is America's tendency to undermine its own best interests. Recalling the zeal of the Joseph McCarthy hearings and the J. Edgar Hoover witch hunts for radicals and sexual "deviants" among the civil rights movement and the Vietnam War protestors, archconservative owner Angela Whiting Trust and League Commissioner Oakhart contribute gullibly to Gamesh's plan to undermine the league, thereby all baseball, and thereby the fabric of American society itself. As a result, the league and all its records, including those of Gofannon and Mazda, are obliterated.

Finally, Roth turns the trope against the very norms he and others have created, against the tendency in American culture to mythicize its institutions. With this metafictive representation of a league of misfits, zealots, spies, scoundrels, and fools, many based on the folkloric heroes of sports history, he warns sternly against our collective wish to view baseball as a fictive, mythic, and political construct. While at the overt level *The Great American Novel* deploys the baseball trope to lament the power of institutions to control information and thereby adjust the definition of reality in the institutions' interests, it also serves as a warning about the tendency of literature (and all "great American novels," hence Word's inclusion of conversations with Hemingway and his commentary on "MY PRECURSORS" [39] Melville, Twain, and Hawthorne) to create dangerous fictions about the nature of our shared experience—to mythologize carelessly.

While Roth was exploring the trope's potential for self-criticism, poet Gregory Corso and novelist Robert Coover were pressing it to what appeared to be its limit by turning it to the theological and epistemological. Corso's "Dream of a Baseball Star" (1960) pitted Ted Williams against an omnipotent deity who could blow the high hard one right by arguably the finest hitter in baseball history, thereby crushing our mythic hero, and with him our aspirations. This scene recalls Malamud's demand that the hero live up to his role, but Corso focuses on the inability of any mortal, even the most powerful among us, to compete with the power of god or fate. His poem represents Williams as a hero in defeat, against the power of a deity that renders even the most gifted among us powerless.[8] Eight years later, in *The Universal Baseball Association, Inc., J. Henry Waugh, Prop.*, Coover created a terrifying metafiction about an accountant who invents, and subsequently populates, an entire baseball league. Ultimately, Coover's handling of the trope questions one compound foundation of American culture as it has evolved from roots in Puritanism and to this day is affected by the forces of religious fundamentalism: the notion of creation and the power of god. J. Henry Waugh, whose name echoes Jehovah, one name for the Judeo-Christian God, invests his statistical sets with meaning, personality, and free will.

At the realistic or psychological level, the novel examines the danger of the obsessive personality, as Henry subsumes his "real" life as an accountant entering into his ledger numbers that symbolize the failures of businesses and their owners' hopes, in the more exciting world of fantasy baseball. When Henry reads in the newspapers about a world that has gone mad, he grouses that the news is "Lunacy: anyway, he sure wasn't inventing it" (131). Instead, despite the fact that he doesn't care much for actual baseball with its spitting and dust, he invents a world that makes sense to him out of the statistics with which sportswriters and fans are obsessed. But his fertile imagination, unsatisfied by the abstractions of the game he has invented, elects to invest certain statistical sets with names and personalities.

At a more subtle level, however, *The Universal Baseball Association* reflects on the power of god and the implications of that power. In this doubly removed artifice—in a game that simulates a game—Henry is creator, overseer, and sole spectator. Logically, his power is either absolute or limited, but even theological power involves responsibility. When Henry tries to impose the order he desires on his creation, he sets into motion a series of events that threaten his creation's belief in his very existence. Henry's problem with creation begins when he becomes overly attached to a single "player," Coover's variation on Luke Gofannon. As a god-man, Henry gets too involved with Damon Rutherford as the game's savior. Waugh feels himself losing interest in the league until Damon promises renewal, and Henry's flagging sexual prowess is reinvigorated through his identification with his creation. So he suspends the logic of his creation to satisfy his appetites. He hungers to see Damon "pitch," before a real baseball rotation would permit, so he invents a celebration of Damon's progenitor, "Brock Rutherford Day," in order to justify the son's pitching out of turn. He reluctantly submits to the statistical inevitability of Damon's death, but he manipulates his creation to punish Damon's killer-antagonist, Jock Casey (whose initials are more than a little suggestive)[9]—to make him pitch against strong teams and ace pitchers. His effort to involve his only friend from the real world, Lou Engle, results in circumstances that, with the manipulation of one die, place Jock on the "Extraordinary Occurrences Chart." Completely aware of the implications of his actions, Waugh chooses between ending the game, and with it his obsession, and making an unretractable commitment to it by sacrificing the anti(?)hero. Quite deliberately, Waugh makes his choice between play and work, between illusion and reality, between creation and submission to the thing created: "Yes, if you killed that boy out there, then you *couldn't* quit, could you? No, that's a real commitment, you'd be hung up for good, they wouldn't let you go" (201).

In the wildly metafictive final chapter, Henry has repudiated his place in the real world of an accountant's ledgers for the artificial world—he's now completely assimilated into his creation. In that chapter eight oblique references to Henry suggest that he has become indeed a *deus abscondus* whose created characters now question whether his creation, interference, and sacrifice have been worthwhile. He has turned his autonomy over to his creation, has mythologized himself virtually out of existence. It is difficult to say exactly what happens in the final chapter, and that ambiguity is critical to Coover's metafictive and tropic intentions. We can be relatively certain that one hundred UBA seasons have passed since Damon's and Jock's deaths, although we have no clue how much actual time this involves, and that during that UBA-time the function of the game to insulate Henry from the real world has failed completely. During those UBA-years, the association has been fraught with political and religious factions; key figures in the association's folklore have been assassinated, others executed. The players wonder if Henry exists, and if he does, whether his existence is benevolent or malign, much as people have wondered about God throughout modern history. One "character," playing the part of another "character" from league history on "Damonsday," concludes that "God exists and he is a nut" (233). Another "character," however, voices the determinist position: The "mortal parable's very message" is that the game is fixed. While political parties, political assassinations, conspiracies, and religious factions seem to be the very thing earlier writers about baseball sought to help us escape, Coover's theme is that no matter how we try to avoid these realities, the game as trope leads us back to the very world we sought to avoid. Although most critics of the novel have emphasized Henry's rejection of a drab, disordered world through his commitment to the logic of play,[10] it is at least equally clear that in this fiction about baseball and the way the mind works, Coover warns about the myth-construction process itself. Baseball is finally an epistemological trope, one that can help to warn us about the dangers of uncritical myth-making and myth-learning.

While generalizations about these several variations on the trope of baseball seem simultaneously tempting and hasty, the works treated here suggest three conclusions. First, the very artificiality of baseball, the game that seems arbitrary in its rules, its customs, and its management of space—and therefore generally removed from the concerns of ordinary life—provides serious writers with a fertile medium for the analysis of "real world" concerns. Second, the directions that serious applications of sport as trope have taken during the middle of the past century suggest a nostalgia for the sense of community, shared purpose, and values that was the intellectual counterpart to the individualism of America's first two centuries. Third, the progression we have traced suggests that the trope became increasingly metafictive and self-critical at mid-century, that writers like Roth and Coover raise important questions about possible problems treating baseball as a mythic subject may entail. What these works suggest collectively is that baseball involves an elegant, but created, order on the field—one valuable to serious writers in examining both the creation and the risks of personal and national myths but one subject in the case of stories and films intended for commercial purpose to be sentimentalized enough to be used to support the very political and cultural complacencies they were designed to challenge.

NOTES

1. Although Westbrook and I discuss many shared texts, I see "postmodern" myth-making about baseball as more of a warning against the process of mythmaking than Westbrook appears to.

2. There is also a vast body of sports literature we may call "escapist," attempting to tell stories about athletes as heroes or victims in our sports-crazed culture, a body of narrative generally in the class of "popular" or "adolescent" fiction. Beyond the scope of the present analysis, this group of narratives serves the purpose of entertaining, in William Carlos Williams's words, "without thought," or more insidiously, of reinforcing unexamined premises behind our political, economic, and social structures.

3. The broadcast was September 26, 1956, on CBS-TV. Albert Salmi, George Peppard, and Paul Newman played the major roles. The live presentation skillfully adapted the novel's point-of-view convention. "Author" Wiggen's dual roles as narrator and character were expressed by having Newman move from a spotlighted intimate revelation to the camera, then join a scene in progress as the lights went up on it. The 1973 feature film, directed by John Hancock and starring Michael Moriarity and Robert DeNiro, while less technically innovative than the stage play, remains one of the finest baseball films ever made—even if DeNiro was less convincing as a batter than as a dying hero or as a cab driver, mobster, Vietnam P.O.W., or boxer in later films.

4. As is often noted in commentaries on *The Natural,* the hero's name itself evokes mythic resonance, roughly translating as "King Rustic." His talisman, a bat he created from a tree struck by lightning, then nurtured and eventually named "Wonderboy," reinforces this association, as does scout Sam Simpson's death-dream of fields full of godlike youths, roaming pastures of innocence, making heroic catches and hits. The

pastoral-urban tension is omnipresent in *The Natural.* After Roy strikes out the Whammer in a country fair contest, the aging superstar returns to the train "an old man," and "in the truest sense of it, out"—an unsubtle allusion to the mythic contest of defeating or killing the old king or father-figure by the aspiring hero. Should any reader miss these rather heavy-handed evocations of myth, Malamud names Roy's team the "Knights" (legendary heroes in the myth tradition) while keeping actual names like "Pirates" for their adversaries.

5. In a striking crossover among the political, the mythic, and the psychological spheres, Wonderboy, which Roy held between his knees while benched, "resembled a sagging baloney" until Iris's show of faith brought potency to the bat and the batter, empowering him to fulfill the heroic-mythic-proletarian role of the deliverer. After Roy has sold his soul, Wonderboy splits when he strikes the foul ball that wounds Iris, and Roy buries it after his climactic and symbolic strikeout—reaching for a bad pitch.

6. See Philip Roth, "My Baseball Years." See also Roth's *Reading Myself and Others,* in which he recalls placing the words "I have written a very wicked book and feel spotless as a lamb" (Melville's famous note to Hawthorne on *Moby-Dick*) on his inspiration board while writing *The Great American Novel.* Roth reflects: "I knew that no matter how hard I tried I could never really hope to be wicked; but perhaps, if I worked long and hard and diligently, I could be frivolous" (87).

7. Small wonder maverick St. Louis Browns owner Bill Veeck embarked with "great trepidation" on Chapter Four, the source for which was his sending Eddie Gaddel to bat during World War II. See Bill Veeck, "Take Me Out to the Ballgame" and "'He Sent a Midget Up to Bat.'" For a discussion of historical figures adapted for *The Great American Novel,* see Ben Seigel, "The Myths of Summer: Philip Roth's *The Great American Novel.*"

8. A somewhat similar variation on the Splendid Splinter as trope is found in "Ted Williams Storms the Gates of Heaven," by Louis Phillips (1996), in which Williams comes out of retirement to salvage the dignity of the institution of baseball but finds himself involved in a labor dispute, in which his prowess is put to good use to aid the workers against the fat cats in a textile mill strike. The story thus recalls both Corso's poem and *The Natural,* but it is unable to follow up on its main premise—that Williams finds the meaning of heroism in renouncing the culture of capitalism and taking up the cause of the oppressed.

9. Although readers of this metafiction initially adopt Henry's point of view that Jock is evil and Damon good, the events of Damonsday (chapter 8) reopen the question of good and evil, and the names of the antagonists create yet another ambiguity in this text rich in ambiguities: First, did Damon and Jock exist? If so, and if their existence transcends or encloses Henry's imagination, was the killing of Damon by Jock, and Jock's consequent, deliberate sacrifice by his creator, a version of the fortunate fall, creating theological freedom within the creation Henry no longer fully controls? Or is this another random behavior by a creator one of the "players" in Damonsday refers to as "a nut"?

10. See for example Neil Berman, "Robert Coover's *Universal Baseball Association*: Play as Personalized Myth"; Roy C. Caldwell, Jr., "'Of Hobby-Horses, Baseball, and Narrative': Coover's *The Universal Baseball Association*"; Jackson Cope, *Robert Coover's Fictions*; Lois Gordon, *Robert Coover: The Universal Fictionmaking Process*; Leo J. Hertzel, "What's Wrong with the Christians?"; and Robert Morace, "Robert Coover."

REFERENCES

Bang the Drum Slowly. Dir. John Hancock. Perf. Robert DeNiro, Vincent Gardenia, and Michael Moriarity. Paramount, 1973.

Bang the Drum Slowly. Perf. Paul Newman, George Peppard, and Albert Salmi. U.S. Steel Hour. CBS. 26 September 1956.

Berman, Neil. "Robert Coover's *Universal Baseball Association*: Play as Personalized Myth." *Modern Fiction Studies* 24 (1978): 209–222.

Caldwell, Roy C., Jr. "'Of Hobby-Horses, Baseball, and Narrative': Coover's *The Universal Baseball Association*." *Modern Fiction Studies* 23 (1987): 161–171.

Coover, Robert. *The Universal Baseball Association, Inc., J. Henry Waugh, Prop*. New York: Signet/Plume, 1971.

Cope, Jackson. *Robert Coover's Fictions*. Baltimore: Johns Hopkins University Press, 1986.

Corso, Gregory, "Dream of a Baseball Star." *The Norton Anthology of Modern Poetry*. 1st ed. Ed. Richard Ellmann and Robert O'Clair. New York: W.W. Norton, 1973. 1259–1260.

Doctorow, E. L. *Ragtime*. New York: Modern Library, 1997.

Gordon, Lois. *Robert Coover: The Universal Fictionmaking Process*: Carbondale: Southern Illinois University Press, 1983.

Harris, Mark. *Bang the Drum Slowly*. New York: Dell, 1973.

Hertzel, Leo J. "What's Wrong with the Christians?" *Critique* 11 (1969): 11–22.

Kesey, Ken. *One Flew Over the Cuckoo's Nest*. New York: Viking, 1962.

Malamud, Bernard. *The Natural*. New York: Pocket Books, 1973.

Moore, Marianne. "Poetry." *The Norton Anthology of Modern Poetry*, 2nd ed. Eds. Richard Ellmann and Robert O'Clair. New York: W.W. Norton, 1988. 457.

Morace, Robert. "Robert Coover." *Critical Survey of Long Fiction*. Ed. Frank Magill. Vol. 2. Englewood Cliffs, NJ: Salem Press, 1983. 617–625.

The Natural. Dir. Barry Levinson. Perf. Kim Bassinger, Wilfred Brimley, Glenn Close, Robert Duvall, Robert Redford. TriStar Pictures, 1984.

Phillips, Louis. "Ted Williams Storms the Gates of Heaven." *Hotcorner: Baseball Stories and Writing and Humor*. Livingston, AL: Livingston Press, 1996. 94–104.

Roth, Philip. "The Conversion of the Jews." *Goodbye, Columbus and Other Stories*. New York: Bantam, 1969.

———. *The Great American Novel*. New York: Bantam, 1974.

———. "My Baseball Years." *The New York Times*. 2 April 1973: 35

———. *Reading Myself and Others*. New York: Farrar, Strauss and Giroux, 1975.

Seigel, Ben. "The Myths of Summer: Philip Roth's *The Great American Novel*." *Contemporary Literature* 17 (1976): 171–192.

Veeck, Bill. "He Sent a Midget up to Bat." *Baltimore Sun* 20 May 1973: D5.

———. "Take Me Out to the Ballgame." *Baltimore Sun* 20 May 1973: D5.

Westbrook, Deeanne. *Ground Rules: Baseball and Myth*. Urbana: University of Illinois Press, 1996.

Williams, William Carlos. *Spring and All XXVI. Selected Poems*. New York: New Directions, 1963. 31–32.

"War . . . May Hasten This Change of Values": The World War II–Era Writings of John R. Tunis

Ryan K. Anderson

Publisher's Weekly tabbed John R. Tunis's 1943 novel *Keystone Kids* as a seminal children's book when it proclaimed that Tunis used the book to translate "the ideals of democracy into the realistic terms of today" ("Keystone Kids" 2098). The author likewise received acclaim for *All-American* (1942), his story of one high school football team's triumph over bigotry. John T. Frederick's Northwestern University radio program, *Of Men and Books*, highlighted the work during its November 18, 1942, episode, "Children's Books and American Unity." Guest commentators picked the story as one that "will make a boy think about a major world problem which is his job to help solve" and added that its "theme . . . is not national but international" (2). Platitudes such as these derived from the role Tunis's books on football, basketball, track and field, baseball, and tennis played in affirming American values during World War II. Ironically, however, Tunis did not support the ideas readers divined from his books.

Tunis used juvenile sports novels to demonstrate the relationship between sports and democracy during the late 1930s and the 1940s. He believed that exposing the corrosive influence of mass sports encouraged his youthful readers to use democratic sport to revive a battered egalitarian society and improve it by including ethnic, racial, and gendered minorities. The democratic spirit of "real sport," he believed, came from player interaction and the desire to succeed. Thus, playing sports helped erode social inequality. Healthy leisure provided the American masses an opportunity to literally "be" democratic. This emboldened their fight against an expanding global problem: totalitarianism.

Educators, parents, and government agencies saw much to applaud in his work, but they hijacked his stories and distorted their messages to support America's involvement in World War II. Individual characters and fictional teams who chose community responsibility over self-interest proved especially useful. By spurning pecuniary opportunities for the good of the community, certain characters accepted appropriate roles on a team governed by just leadership. Their aggregations featured people from a variety of backgrounds in appropriate roles: Whites, blacks, Jews, southerners, native-born Americans, and immigrants all participated. Patriots superimposed the values of racial and ethnic harmony, teamwork, and self-sacrifice onto a successful war effort—and in the process ignored Tunis's real message.

By the 1940s, Tunis enjoyed a career based on the practice of criticizing those aspects of American culture that others took lightly. While many historians consider the 1920s and 1930s to be the golden age of American sports, for instance, Tunis saw only pernicious influences working through athletics to enslave the American people. Instead of glorifying the period's sporting gods, he pointed to "professional" influences that created a nation of spectators rather than participants. On the one hand, he believed the spectacle of mass sport led to totalitarian sport and an unjust society because it encouraged winning at all costs, which excluded the majority of people from participating.[1] His objections dovetailed with those of historians Charles and Mary Beard, as well as a 1929 Carnegie Commission report on college football's detrimental effect on higher education. Tunis argued that fanatics injected improper values into spectator sports. On the other hand, "[e]xperimentally workable, conjugal, and just" games helped democracy progress via the American liberal tradition (Tunis *Democracy and Sport* 2). "Democratic sport" existed as a natural American phenomenon: It remained open to any person regardless of ethnicity, class, or skill; it developed leadership through practice; and it encouraged individuality. People formed teams, appointed officials to run their games, and included the best players possible, regardless of race or religion. Tunis took youth in sports as his subject more often than not because young athletes rejuvenated sport and society with innovation. Playing proved more valuable than watching sports because it taught egalitarianism, opportunity, and social justice—values he hoped they might carry into formal political spheres.[2]

His career in juvenile literature started by accident in 1938 with the publication of *Iron Duke*. The work condemned Harvard society in much the same way that Owen Johnson's *Stover at Yale* took that Ivy League institution to task in 1912. An editor at Harcourt and Brace, however, dismissed *Iron Duke* as a kid's book. Despite his initial misgivings, Tunis recounted in *A Measure of Independence*, that "[t]his was the first time my work counted. . . . From then on I wrote fewer articles and concentrated on sports novels for high school groups" (255). His appointment as a children's author brought newfound notoriety and respect from Americans—despite the fact that his novels presented the same values as his "adult" freelance pieces. The emergence of the juvenile novel genre in the 1940s further encouraged the social critic to accept his newfound role as a children's author. Moralists looked to these works to offset the influence of comic books and present young readers with "real" writing rather than literary garbage.[3] He went on to produce fourteen juvenile novels between 1938 and 1949. As a whole, they reflected the nation's war experience—they took readers from preparedness and mobilization to winning the war at hand for democracy to preparing for postwar America. Despite these shifting utilitarian qualities, the essentials of his theme of democracy and sport stayed the same.[4]

Tunis's first novels educated readers on the nature of the growing German threat. While the period's racist attitudes made the Japanese a clear enemy, Americans wondered: Who was Adolf Hitler, and what did he represent? As a result, the U.S. propaganda machine devoted itself to demonizing Hitler by associating him with the Japanese and disassociating him from German Americans. Franklin Roosevelt, convinced that supporting Britain had become a national security priority, slowly chipped away at a potent late-1930s isolationist sentiment. He used the lend-lease program and bases for destroyers deal to fuel England's defense machine with war materiel, explaining that such actions aided the U.K. without directly involving the U.S. In this period prior to the attack on Pearl Harbor, the American people continued to question the extent of their nation's involvement in the global conflict, wondering why they should bother with a fight occurring on the other side of the world. *Iron Duke* (1938), *The Duke Decides* (1939), *The Kid from Tompkinsville* (1940), *Champion's Choice* (1940), and *World Series* (1941) all tried to help young people solve this quandary.[5]

In *The Duke Decides*, James "Duke" Wellington's trip to the 1936 "Nazi Olympics" provides Tunis with an opportunity to compare American and German sports. Duke discovers that the German people want to play real sports, but a police state abridges that right. Their track stars subsist on government funding and lose the joy of athletics, since their primary function is to act as Hitler's emissaries. As a result, they run methodical races, ignoring the glory of the Olympic experience. Americans hardly prove innocent of similar infractions. Promoters and agents push them to run in exhibitions that compromise their performance. Duke, the lone exception, wins the gold medal in the two-mile run, even though "the games and the military regime surrounding them became distasteful" (218). The book concludes with his monumental decision to leave the "octopus" of organized sport behind in Germany by opting for a vacation in France with a new love interest instead of a tournament of champions and a paycheck in Britain. He announces his retirement from running and his intent to return stateside to coach and teach.

In *A Measure of Independence*, Tunis made clear that he used *The Duke Decides* to introduce readers to the reality of the totalitarian threat in Germany and made a statement on the similarities between that pernicious force and American mass sports. By setting the novel in the recent past, Tunis encouraged readers to look at a time prior to the headlines announcing Nazi Germany's current activities. This prompted readers to ask: If Hitler did such things in 1936, what was he up to by 1939? Duke's experiences in Germany encouraged readers to recognize the danger represented by the images they saw on newsreels and in papers. For instance, he seemed shocked that Hitler looked "[j]ust like his pictures" (163). But an Olympic teammate drove his existence home by snapping, "[w]ell, Foolish, what'd you expect him to look like? Paul

Whiteman?" (163). Readers found not only that Hitler's threat to freedom was real but also that a similar despot plagued the United States through professional sports. Tunis linked sports promoters who infected the American team with the Nazi athletic system's values by having professionalized American athletes act like Nazi athletes. He then has Duke defeat both the Germans and his misguided teammates to prove democratic sport's supremacy. The Olympics, then, represent the battle between democracy and totalitarianism. Americans, furthermore, lose the Games (and a possible war?) because agents and promoters pressure athletes into running in exhibitions that detract from their performance. Duke's pluckiness and ability to stick to his beliefs help him overcome his teammates and the mechanical German runners (Tunis *A Measure of Independence* 213–214, 227–229, 234).

The tenor of Tunis's works adapted to the country's needs once it entered World War II. After two decades of isolation, the nation needed to define its mission abroad. Toward this end, the federal government created the Office of War Information (OWI). Propagandists depicted the Axis governments as absolute enemies (while presenting Germans as good people led astray) by drawing clear lines between "them" and "us." The conflict ahead, the OWI preached, would prove daunting and fraught with setbacks. To assure victory, the nation must band together and put aside selfish goals defined by class, race, and ethnicity. Everyone possessed a unique role to play in a victory that would repay his or her efforts in kind. *All-American* (1942), *The Keystone Kids* (1943), *Rookie of the Year* (1944), and *Yea! Wildcats!* (1944) depicted democratic sport as a way to build community and win correctly. The books feature teams facing both daunting opponents and cleavages within their ranks. A hero steps forward in each to either lead teams to victory or provide a lesson on success off the playing field (Adams 9–13; Blum 15–52; Erenberg and Hirsch 6–11; Shulman 5–8).

Spike Russell's triumph as the Brooklyn Dodgers player-manager in *Keystone Kids* illustrates this theme. Spike and his brother Bob catch on with the Dodgers as a shortstop and second baseman, respectively. The pair soon realizes the talented team is not winning because a despotic manager is breaking their spirit. Young Spike eventually replaces the dictator and commands the respect of his teammates because he lets them play without trying to control their every move and favors reason over intimidation as a rule of discipline. The team's record improves, but they achieve their greatest success when Spike's leadership prompts the acceptance of their Jewish catcher Jocko Klein. Observers considered *Keystone Kids* Tunis's most important work because it highlighted teamwork as a virtue Americans needed to embrace. The Dodgers' acceptance of this value derives from Spike's inherently democratic leadership—something that made accepting his authority natural. He turns the team around, not by teaching them a new strategy or acquiring new talent, but by encouraging them to work with the group's best interests in mind. Klein provides the focal point by suffering through a season of anti-Semitic jibes and assaults. His teammates refuse to protect him until they are struck by the heroism of his fight with an opposing player. In the weeks after the scuffle, the Dodgers realize the contribution he makes to their team and stick up for him when a fan calls him "yeller" and "Jew-boy" (193). Bob Russell leads the Dodgers over the top of the dugout and into the crowd; Klein rests on the bench while a wild melee ensues. After this show of solidarity, the catcher rewards his teammates by smashing a low and outside fastball over the right field fence to win the game and put the Dodgers in position to make a pennant run.

It is important to note that the players do not support Klein's beliefs but merely tolerate them for the sake of victory. They accept him because they realize he is a fighting ballplayer who puts time in day in and day out for the good of the team. Klein, for his part, accepts his role within the unit without challenging the status quo. None of this makes a "new" team but, significantly, it represents a "rebirth" of the aggregation. Indeed, the whole incident represents a tight allegory of President Franklin Roosevelt's New Deal approach to combating racism, which depended on including Jews, blacks, and ethnic minorities for political expediency while preventing them from upsetting the existing social balance. In retrospect, we can see that this policy regulated social change. At the time, however, it advanced the inclusion of minorities into the American mainstream—something Tunis espoused regularly (Cohen 258–260; Franklin and Moss 419–39; Schlesinger 434–438).

Peace hardly brought comfort. A Pandora's box full of problems threatened America's transition to a country at peace: the youth revolt, the role of returning GIs in society, and the nascent Communist threat on a global scale. Tunis's next books—*A City for Lincoln* (1945), *The Kid Comes Back* (1946), *Highpockets* (1948), *Young Razzle* (1949), and *Sons of the Valley* (1949)—all presented readers with answers to the questions their parents raised about postwar America.[6]

The Kid from Tomkinsville introduced Roy "the Kid" Tucker, a Dodger centerfielder, but *The Kid Comes Back* detailed his return to baseball after military service. Roy makes a slow, uncertain comeback due to a back injury sustained in a crash during a bombing run over occupied France. The center fielder wonders if he will fit back in with the team or even play at all. Underscoring this drama are several young rookies who caught on with the team during the war and need veterans to provide leadership. Roy eventually works his way back into shape and replaces a junior teammate, Lester Young, in the starting lineup. When the novice player balks at the move, the manager sits him down for a fatherly talk: "Remember that run Roy Tucker scored for us in that game at home. . . . He risked everything for that one run. . . . He didn't know if he would ruin himself for good, and he didn't care either. . . . That's the way we play on this ballclub" (178–179).

Tunis's postwar novels showed readers that returning GIs had a place in postwar prosperity—the war's mission had been noble and there were benefits to reap. In their absence, the youth of the nation took the opportunity to stretch their wings and threatened to usurp the authority of their elders. With the world made safe for democracy, returning veterans needed to come home and reclaim their rightful place. The end of the war brought other problems—an uneasy alliance with Russia crumbled and revealed a Red Menace that threatened the very way of life America had just secured for Europe. As democracy's crusaders, GIs needed to assert themselves in leadership roles back home to assure democracy's survival.

These novels not only reflected American society during a moment of crisis, but also worked to influence American values. The OWI reproduced Tunis's books for distribution to GIs to reinforce the message their propaganda machine created. This effectively rendered the critical elements of his works toothless. It is important to recognize, however, that he wrote juvenile novels for reasons entirely different from those that made him famous. Imbued in all fourteen books are messages the author developed during the 1920s and 1930s to challenge the mass culture that controlled the war effort (Blum 21–52; Erenberg and Hirsch 1–3; Tunis *A Measure of Independence* 254–255).

The first of these lessons borrowed from a historic belief regarding the preeminence of the individual. The American mind had long revered this myth. But the nature of Tunis's individual, someone he called the "loser," set him apart. This term often confused his supporters, since it implied that his heroes failed. The author argued that shortcomings on the playing field did not matter as much as success in life. Supporters often missed this point; they highlighted the fact that Tunis's protagonists went on to win eventually, glossing over the fact that they achieved greater glory off the field. This mistake prevented them from understanding that his characters learned important lessons in competition that carried over into the real world (Frederick, Litten, and Bontemps 2–3; Holtzman 261–262; Swing 40).

In *Champion's Choice*, the governing bodies of amateur tennis and sport promoters nearly ruin a young athlete named Janet Johnson. The star arises from middle-class anonymity on the basis of talent and the support of monied sponsors from a local country club. She wins national championships at home and abroad, including Wimbledon, but finds the commitments that come with being a champion harrying. Interviews, banquets, charitable events, and the constant grind to remain at the top while spectators root for her to lose take the enjoyment out of tennis. Janet's love interest, a former Yale end named Rodney Davis, offers a release from the tedium heaped upon a tennis champion with a marriage proposal. She declines his offer so that she can defend her Wimbledon crown because of her commitment to her sponsors and tournament promoters. Mid-match, however, she realizes that she can escape the entanglements that weigh so heavily upon her by merely quitting. Despite her lead and the impending defense of her title, she forfeits and chases Davis to accept his proposal. Here triumphs Tunis's "loser." The tennis world considers her a failure since she forfeited her title in the face of sure victory. Tunis thought her a hero, however, because she spurned a tainted championship and its wealth to become a wife. *Champion's Choice* contained a more specific message about the role of women in the war—while they had a role as competitors, their ultimate victory came within the institutions of marriage and the home. Women who worked in war industries should expect to return to their houses once their husbands came home.

Tunis's second theme is that of egalitarian leadership. His protagonists' ability to govern their own teams protected them from outside influences. Since democracy depended on virtuous leaders, Tunis usually made team captains into figureheads rather than coaches for two reasons. First, as active players, he believed that they remained insulated from corruption because they had a stake in the outcome as competitors. Their rewards from the game far outweighed those that promoters or gamblers used to entice them. Second, as the teams' choices for leaders, they received their positions because the body of players-citizens deemed them worthy. Any person chosen this way, Tunis reasoned, must possess the moral fortitude to withstand the entreaties of outside influences.

Two books took Indiana high school basketball as a subject to demonstrate the features of egalitarian leadership. In *Yea! Wildcats!* readers saw Coach Don Henderson make the Kokomo Wildcats into the perfect democratic team. He does this by refusing to overwork them in practice and letting them make important team decisions. Both of these strategies buffer the team from meddling townspeople by giving them a stake in self-governance. The opening chapters of a second book, *A City for Lincoln*, see the team's resolve tested. Henderson suffers a severe case of angina brought on by community pressure minutes before the start of the Indiana high school state basketball championship. Led by their blonde crew-cut sporting captain John Shaw, the team goes on to win the championship on their own. Evident here is Tunis's faith in youth's ability to ensure liberal democratic improvement. New players who join the team in the second book disrupt established lineups and work their way onto the first string, forcing innovation and change, and making new leaders. The creation of new standard bearers carried special significance during the year Tunis published *A City for Lincoln*—the fictional Henderson fell in a book that appeared in late 1945, soon after FDR's death. Like the cage stars of the novel, the nation looked at itself to decide who might carry on as the representative of its ideals. The boys' author pointed a finger back at the American people. By making the Wildcats egalitarian champions, he challenged American youth to take up the task of moral leadership themselves.

These two themes represented liberal virtue in sport, drawn from Tunis's twentieth-century reinterpretation of Jeffersonian democracy. Contests run by individuals and egalitarian leaders forced innovation, which led to an evolution in virtue. When players ran their own teams and played the game they wanted voluntarily, they had "fun." Fun meant value, and in valuing the experience, participants carried their lessons into real life to improve society. This represented the crux of Tunis's reforms—they tried to make sport enjoyable, because doing so encouraged participation. Participation in decentralized political spheres strengthened democracy by assuring responsiveness to ordinary Americans. This, he believed, led to organic change. Improvements in society, then, came from the ground up, thus buffering ordinary people from appropriation by those who looked to use the appearance of progress to dupe the masses (Epstein 56; Tunis *Democracy and Sport* 3).

Time and again his characters experience this phenomenon. Duke's running in *Iron Duke* and *The Duke Decides* carries him through the vicissitudes of the Harvard "machine," makes him a better person, and in the process inspires other classmates to change despite the machinations of the Harvard Athletic Department or the Circle. After setting a new Harvard record in the two-mile, Duke seems a certain pick for induction into the Circle, the elitist social club that controls the Harvard social scene. The snobs pass him over, though; frustrated in the knowledge that he cannot fit in, he quits the track team. When the coach tries to talk him into running in the next meet, he refuses because running for the sole purpose of winning is a hollow pursuit: "All the things they've built up and live for, the clubs and teams and papers and all the rest of it. Unreal, inconsequential" (212–213). Duke exacts his revenge when he is promised membership in the Circle if he runs and wins the next meet. He agrees, but rejects the elitists' offer to demonstrate both his virtue and the fact that they do not control him.[7]

Sports make Ronny Perry a leader on and off the field in *All-American*. After leaving the snobby "Academy" for the public "High School," Ronny learns how to lead after developing patience when he fails to make first string on the football team. He waits until his team needs him to replace an injured player and leads it to a championship. Then, when he learns that the team's black offensive end is banned from a trip south to Miami for an interstate game, he leads a successful player strike and stands up to the coach, who points to the trouble and expense promoters absorbed to arrange the game. Ronny refuses to fold and inspires his compatriots to refuse to go into battle without their black teammate, and eventually everyone wins out. The Miami team finds another opponent, and the high school team is invited to Illinois to play a different rival.

The most important achievements these characters make come in their decisions off the field. Why exclude a catcher who is the best candidate for the job just because he is Jewish? Why play in the biggest game of the year without your first-string end because he is black? By rewarding the Dodgers and the high school eleven with victory, Tunis suggests that there were greater benefits to reap. Most important, these changes do not derive from outside coercion; they come from rational decisions realized through playing sports. Tunis took pains to demonstrate that democratic sport created racial egalitarianism.

Out of his pristine record on race arises a befuddling question: Why did Tunis never include a black character to represent Jackie Robinson on the Dodgers, even though he used the team as a trope in his baseball novels for two years after Robinson broke into the Major Leagues? This omission might have something to do with Tunis's ongoing efforts to carry the promise of reform forward into postwar America. The federal government took its first authentic and tentative steps towards fighting segregation in 1941 when Franklin Roosevelt issued Executive Order 8802, officially ending the division of races in the Armed Forces. Many white Americans assumed that such a move secured the supposed wartime race consensus. In actuality, postwar race relations grew contentious as African American GIs returned home to execute the second half of black America's "Double V" campaign. Tunis's beliefs, of course, shaped his interpretation of Executive Order 8802. Whereas some black Americans discerned an opportunity to break from the past, the children's author might have seen a logical culmination of America's liberal heritage. It is safe to assume that he associated Robinson's acceptance with the executive order. To convince Americans that they craved change instead of security (despite the fact that most people proved willing to flee activism for postwar suburban shelter), he might have avoided the race issue so as not to radicalize his efforts (Ashmore 31–123; Blum 208–220; Franklin and Moss 475–504; Horton and Horton 248–293; Polenberg 216, 227, 244; Voigt 297–298).

Despite the declining popularity of his writing in the 1950s, Tunis continued to use sports to agitate for social reform, labeling the new decade as one of "excitement, of change, of shifting standards of value" (Tunis "Are We Sportsmen, or What Are We?" 41). Despite his pleadings, the American people had reasons not to listen. They listed to retrenchment rather than reform. Many people wanted to enjoy new freedoms and new money with a return to normality. A legacy of misinterpretation, established during the war effort, continued to plague Tunis and his works. This pattern ruled everything he wrote. His readers proved most disappointing of all. After being left on their own and given the experience of work and wealth during the war, young people revolted against the older generation. Liberty shaped the way they read Tunis's novels in ways the author never conceived.

Before World War II, Americans railed against big business. America's success in mobilization, the postwar prosperity following a short recession, and the public's profit from this upswing, excited little incentive to attack a money influence. Americans no longer saw big business's interests as opposed to their well-being. Because people wanted to buy a new car or a television and move to the suburbs, fixing American society faded from the country's consciousness (Erenberg and Hirsch 313–326; Polenberg 6–9; Schlesinger 601–657).

In addition to the loss of moral momentum, Tunis's supporters established a pattern of miscomprehension by the time the war ended. John T. Frederick, as well as children's authors Frederic Nelson Litten and Arna Bontemps, for instance, praised *All-American* for its efforts to instill racial understanding and democratic values but stopped short of examining the aspects of the book that criticized American society. In December 1943, the *New York Times* report of Tunis's Child Study Association of America Golden Scroll Award highlighted his efforts to face children's problems with "honesty and courage." Underlining the praise, however, rested the pundits' failure to recognize his argument on *how* to achieve equality and the nature of the practice of democracy.[8]

The following years brought further miscomprehension. In the mid-1950s, Raymond Swing wrote of a new Tunis basketball novel that Tunis "has contributed . . . to the perpetration of good values" (40). Murray Illson's 1975 *New York Times* obituary painted him as a curmudgeon rather than a critic by writing that he had been "one of the country's most successful freelance writers," and that he exhibited a "disdain for what he viewed as a latter day coarsening of the spirit of sportsmanship." Joseph Epstein and Adam Hammer both agreed in the 1980s that Tunis used heroes to preach bland American values to young readers while arguing that his stories had other appealing features (Epstein 55–56; Hammer 145–146; Holtzman 260; Swing 40).

Adolescent desires rather than democracy may well explain the books' popularity in terms of readership. Not only do Tunis's characters play sports, they enjoy liberty from parental control (Epstein 50, 54–55; Hammer 148–149). Mothers rarely appear on his pages, if at all. When they do appear, they are presented as hen-pecking worriers who treat their sons as though they are still seven years old. Duke Wellington escapes maternal control by going east to school—an escape many readers envied. Fathers appear only slightly more often. They dispense advice on occasion, though they prefer doling out bland pronouncements on the value of work or, even worse, chores. After Ronny quits the Academy in *All-American*, he approaches his father at his office for guidance. Instead, his father puts him off with a chore—picking up his shoes from the repair shop—before agreeing to meet for lunch. Fathers who make sons run errands before helping them in times of need forced Tunis's young heroes to fend for themselves. Without parental guidance, Tunis's heroes are forced to create their own solutions to life's problems. According to the testimonies of two readers writing in their adult years, sports and the subversion of authority in these novels appealed to them. The former appeal is obvious; the latter, though, is intriguing considering the highly proconsensus interpretations put forward by his contemporaries (Epstein 52, 55; Tunis *All-American* 94–99; Tunis *Iron Duke* 3–18; Tunis *The Duke Decides* 107–108; Tunis *The Kid from Tomkinsville* 196–203).

Misunderstandings of his work turned Tunis bitter in the decades leading up to his death in the 1970s. He remained one of America's most celebrated authors of juvenile fiction; many of his books went through reprint editions until his death. His legacy, however, had more to do with the consensus message his supporters created in reviewing his material, not the message of liberal reform that he intended. He wrote a few juvenile novels through the 1950s and 1960s but eventually shed sports as a centerpiece. In an interview a few years before his death, he expressed disappointment with his whole literary effort, noting that "[n]obody paid attention" (Holzman 272).

World War II gave Tunis a special opportunity to make his vision known to the American youth. Fueled by the need for material appropriate for a juvenile market and a home front that presented him with a chance to deliver his message to a young and untainted audience, Tunis poured his efforts into writing juvenile fiction. That his work helped the war effort gained him supporters, but not in the ways he hoped. Unfortunately, the need for propaganda concerning racial cooperation and America's democratic nature clouded his real message. His only hope was that his readers saw the true message in his writings, and in the end he misplaced his faith. Also, while his stories challenged the nation's leadership by urging everyday people to assume a stronger role in their own governance, his ideas suffered from certain moral shortcomings. Equality for ethnic, racial, and gendered minorities, he believed, came slowly and with the guidance of white paternalism. This cautious approach to equality perhaps, at least as much as the misuse of his writings and the changing American social and cultural atmosphere, proved the cause of his ultimate failure.

NOTES

1. For examples of Tunis's writings during this period, the best source is his 1941 collection of essays entitled *This Writing Game*. This work includes a foreword by Tunis that succinctly states his beliefs on the nature of writing, and each piece includes an introduction by the author. See also, John R. Tunis, "Americans Need Play"; "Education without Football"; "Gamelin,"; "Harvard's New Yard"; "Raising a Racket for Germany"; "Sports Return to 1900"; "Tennis Goes Back to the Boys"; "What Price, College Football?"; "What We Do to Our Athletes."

2. See Frederick Lewis Allen, *Only Yesterday: An Informal History of the* 1920s, 206–211; Charles and Mary Beard, *The Rise of American Civilization*, 727–729; Alan Brinkley, *The End of Reform: New Deal Liberalism in Recession and War*, 8–11; Mark Dyreson, "The Emergence of Consumer Culture and the Transformation of Physical Culture: American Sport in the 1920s," 268–271; Epstein, "A Boy's Own Author," 51–52; Louis Hartz, *The Liberal Tradition in America: An Interpretation of American Political Thought Since the Revolution*, 3–32; William E. Leuchtenburg, *The Perils of Prosperity, 1914–32*; Gerald Nash, *The Great Depression and World War II: Organizing America*; Benjamin G. Rader, *American Sports: From the Age of Folk Games to the Age of Televised Sports*, 120–126; John R. Tunis, *Democracy and Sport*, 2–4, 10–11, 38–41; "Faith," 329–34; *Sports: Heroics and Hysterics*; "Tennis Goes Back to the Boys," 35; *This Writing Game*, xxi.

3. This is not to suggest that the juvenile novel did not exist before this. The writings of Mark Twain, Louisa May Alcott, Robert Louis Stevenson, and Jack London laid the groundwork for the juvenile novelists of the 1940s. However, these writers' juvenile works were a "literary accident"; the writings of the 1940s were specifically aimed at juveniles. See G. Robert Carlson, *Books and the Teen-age Reader: A Guide for Teachers, Librarians and Parents*, 41–42.

4. See Carlson, *Books and the Teen-age Reader*, 41–45; Jerome Holtzman, "John R. Tunis," 271; Cornelia Meigs, Anne T. Eaton, Elizabeth Nesbitt, Ruth H. Viguers, *A Critical History of Children's Literature: A Survey of Children's Books in English, Prepared in Four Parts under the Editorship of Cornelia Meigs*, 405–409; John Springhall, *Youth, Popular Culture and Moral Panics: Penny Gaffs to Gangsta-Rap, 1830–1996*, 121–146; John R. Tunis, *A Measure of Independence*, 214–218, 238, 242, 254–255; "Talk to South Carolina High School Library Association, Rock Hill S.C. March 4, 1955," 71–77.

5. *Champion's Choice* presents readers with Tunis's only female protagonist; however, she was not a whole original creation at that time. As Eloise Jones pointed out,

Champion's Choice merely refashioned *American Girl* (1930) for a juvenile audience, proof that the values Tunis expressed in the 1920s and 1930s were the same as those he expressed in the 1940s. See Michael C. C. Adams, *The Best War Ever*, 4, 6–7, 45; Warren Kimball, *The Juggler: Franklin Roosevelt as Wartime Statesman*, 12, 31; Holly Cowan Shulman, *The Voice of America: Propaganda and Democracy, 1941–1945*, 13–25; Ronald Takaki, *A Different Mirror: A History of Multicultural America*, 378–387.

6. Of these books, *Sons of the Valley* is the exception. It is a nonsports book that deals with the acceptance of the TVA among a band of hillbilly farmers in backwoods Tennessee. As to the southern nature of the postwar books, the last three—*Highpockets*, *Young Razzle*, and *Sons of the Valley*—all featured southern protagonists who were taught to be democratic. The first two of these employ the practice of democratic sport to teach the southern baseball players how to assimilate to "mainstream" values of unselfish teamwork. On postwar America, Blum, *V was for Victory*, 301–332; Brinkley, *End of Reform*, 265–268; Erenberg and Hirsch, *The War in American Culture*, 11–12.

7. Michael Oriard notes Duke's transformation into a leader, though he emphasizes the hero's attempts to atone for a degenerate relationship with his father as his driving force. See *Dreaming of Heroes: American Sports Fiction, 1868–1980*, 40–41.

8. "Child Study Association Award Presented for *Keystone Kids*," 1046; Frederick et al., *Of Men and Books*, 1–6; "Selected as Favorite Author by 53,000 Midwest Children," 2179; "*Hobbit* and *Iron Duke* Win Spring Festival Prizes," 1763; "*Keystone Kids* Wins Child Study Award," 2098; Tunis, *A Measure of Independence*, 253.

REFERENCES

Adams, Michael C. C. *The Best War Ever*. Baltimore, MD: Johns Hopkins University Press, 1994.

Allen, Frederick Lewis. *Only Yesterday: An Informal History of the 1920s*. New York: Harper and Brothers, 1931.

Ashmore, Harry S. *Civil Rights and Wrongs: A Memoir of Race and Politics, 1944–1994*. New York: Pantheon Books, 1994.

Beard, Charles and Mary Beard. *The Rise of American Civilization*. Vol. 2. New York: Macmillan, 1972.

Blum, John M. *V Was for Victory*. New York: Harcourt Brace Jovanovich, 1977.

Brinkley, Alan. *The End of Reform: New Deal Liberalism in Recession and War*. New York: Alfred A. Knopf, 1995.

Carlson, Robert J. *Books and the Teen-age Reader: A Guide for Teachers, Librarians and Parents*. New York: Harper and Row, 1971.

"Child Study Association Award Presented for *Keystone Kids*." *Library Journal* 68 (1943): 1046.

Dyreson, Mark. "The Emergence of Consumer Culture and the Transformation of Physical Culture: American Sport in the 1920s." *Journal of Sport History* 16 (1989): 261–281.

Epstein, Joseph. "A Boy's Own Author." *Commentary* 84 (1987): 50–56.

Erenberg, Lewis A., and Susan E. Hirsch, eds. *The War in American Culture: Society and Consciousness in World War II*. Chicago: University of Chicago Press, 1996.

Franklin, John Hope, and Alfred A. Moss, Jr. *From Slavery to Freedom: A History of African Americans*. 8th ed. New York: Alfred A. Knopf, 2000.

Frederick, John T., Frederic Nelson Litten, and Arna Bontemps. "Of Men and Books." Radio conversation led by John T. Frederick. *Northwestern University on the Air* 2 18 Nov. 1942: 1–6.

Hammer, Adam. "Kidsport: The Works of John R. Tunis." *Journal of Popular Culture* 17 (1983): 146–149.

Hartz, Louis. *The Liberal Tradition in America: An Interpretation of American Political Thought Since the Revolution*. New York: Harcourt, Brace and Co., 1955.

"Hobbit and *Iron Duke* Win Spring Festival Prizes." *Publisher's Weekly* 30 Apr. 1938: 1763.

Holtzman, Jerome, ed. "John R. Tunis." *No Cheering in the Pressbox*. New York: Holt, Rineheart and Winston, 1974. 260–272.

Horton, James Oliver and Lois E. Horton. *Hard Road to Freedom: The Story of African-America*. New Brunswick, NJ: Rutgers University Press, 2001.

Johnson, Owen. *Stover at Yale*. 7th ed. New York: Frederick Stokes, 1912.

Jones, Eloise T. "John Roberts Tunis: His Life and Books." M.A. Thesis. Florida State University, 1955.

Kimball, Warren. *The Juggler: Franklin Roosevelt as Wartime Statesman*. Princeton, NJ: Princeton University Press, 1991.

"Keystone Kids wins Child Study Award." *Publisher's Weekly* 4 Dec. 1943: 2098.

Leuchtenburg, William E. *The Perils of Prosperity, 1914–32*. Chicago: University of Chicago Press, 1958.

Meigs, Cornelia, Anne T. Eaton, Elizabeth Nesbitt, and Ruth H. Viguers. *A Critical History of Children's Literature: A Survey of Children's Books in English, Prepared in Four Parts under the Editorship of Cornelia Meigs*. Revised ed. New York: Macmillan Co., 1953, 1969.

Nash, Gerald. *The Great Depression and World War II: Organizing America*. New York: St. Martin's Press, 1979.

Oriard, Michael V. *Dreaming of Heroes: American Sports Fiction, 1868–1980*. Chicago: Nelson and Hall, 1982.

Polenberg, Richard. *America at War: The Home Front, 1941–1945*. Englewood Cliffs, NJ: Prentice-Hall, 1968.

Rader, Benjamin G. *American Sports: From the Age of Folk Games to the Age of Televised Sports*. 4th ed. Upper Saddle River, NJ: Prentice-Hall, 1999.

Shulman, Holly Cowan. *The Voice of America: Propaganda and Democracy, 1941–1945*. Madison: University of Wisconsin Press, 1991.

"Selected as Favorite Author by 53,000 Midwest Children." *Publisher's Weekly* 28 May 1949: 2179.

Springhall, John. *Youth, Popular Culture and Moral Panics: Penny Gaffs to Gangsta-Rap, 1830–1996*. New York: St. Martin's Press, 1998.

Takaki, Ronald. *A Different Mirror: A History of Multicultural America*. Boston: Little, Brown, and Company, 1993.

Tunis, John R. *All-American*. New York: Harcourt, Brace and Co., 1942.

———. *American Girl*. New York: Brewer and Warren, 1930.

———. "Americans Need Play." *Harper's Magazine* Jul. 1941: 200–205.

———. "Are We Sportsmen, or What Are We?" *New York Times Magazine* 11 Jul. 1948: 15.

———. *The American Way in Sport*. New York: Duell, Sloan and Pearce, 1958.

———. *Champion's Choice*. New York: Harcourt, Brace and Co., 1940.

———. *A City for Lincoln*. New York: Harcourt, Brace and Co., 1945.

———. *Democracy and Sport*. New York: A. S. Barnes and Co., 1941.

———. *The Duke Decides*. New York: Harcourt, Brace and Co., 1939.

————. "Education without Football." *Survey Graphic* 30 (1941): 504–506.

————. "Faith." *Horn Book* 19 (1943): 329–334.

————. "Gamelin." *Harper's Magazine* Dec. 1939: 34–40.

————. "Harvard's New Yard." *World's Work* Jun. 1931: 55–59.

————. *Highpockets*. New York: William Morrow and Co., 1948.

————. *Iron Duke*. New York: Harcourt, Brace and Co., 1938.

————. *Keystone Kids*. New York: Harcourt, Brace and Co., 1943.

————. *The Kid Comes Back*. New York: William Morrow and Co., 1946.

————. *The Kid From Tomkinsville*. New York: Harcourt, Brace and Co., 1940.

————. "The Man Looking Over Your Shoulder." *Chicago Schools Journal* Jan.-Feb. 1950: 157–160.

————. *A Measure of Independence*. New York: Athenaeum, 1964.

————. "Raising a Racket for Germany." *Collier's* 18 Jul. 1937: 18.

————. *Rookie of the Year*. New York: Harcourt, Brace and Co., 1944.

————. *Sons of the Valley*. New York: William Morrow and Co., 1949.

————. *Sports: Heroics and Hysterics*. New York: John Day Co., 1928.

————. "Sports Return to 1900." *Harper's Magazine* May 1943: 633–638.

————. "Talk to South Carolina High School Library Association Rock Hill S.C. March 4, 1955." Eloise T. Jones "John Roberts Tunis: His Life and Books." M.A. Thesis. Florida State University, 1955. 71–77.

————. "Tennis Goes Back to the Boys." *Saturday Evening Post* 19 May 1939): 35.

————. "What Price, College Football?" *American Mercury* Oct. 1939: 129–142.

————. "What We Do to Our Athletes." *Nation* 4 Dec. 1937: 623.

————. *World Series*. New York: Harcourt, Brace and Co., 1941.

————. *This Writing Game*. New York: A. S. Barnes and Co., 1941.

————. *Yea! Wildcats!* New York: Harcourt, Brace and Co., 1944.

————. *Young Razzle*. New York: William Morrow and Co., 1949.

Swing, Raymond. "The Boy's Mr. Tunis." *Saturday Evening Review* 19 Jun. 1954: 40.

Voigt, David. *American Baseball: From the Commissioners to Continental Expansion*. University Park: Penn State University Press, 1983.

"Partway There": The Mexican League and American Conflict in Mark Winegardner's *The Veracruz Blues*

Chris York

Richard Slotkin defines myths as "stories, drawn from history, that have acquired through usage over several generations a symbolizing function that is central to the cultural functioning of a society that produces them" (16). Scholars have long identified a number of seminal myths in American culture: the myth of the American frontier, the myth of the American Adam, and the myth of the American dream among them. For Americans, the structures and rhythms of baseball have always been uniquely aligned with the spirit of American myth. According to David McGimpsey, Commissioner A. Bartlett Giamatti saw baseball as "the perfect meritocratic form where essentially virtuous Americans can assert their freedom in an irreplaceable expression of *e pluribus unum*" (28). This belief is part of the lore of baseball. Struggling for the good of the team, but in individual contests, batter against pitcher, is viewed as the perfect statement of an egalitarian meritocracy. That this struggle traditionally takes place on a baseball field, a pastoral landscape that is not urban yet not an untouched natural landscape, engages the myth of the American frontier, another seminal myth of the United States.

Mark Winegardner, in his 1996 novel *The Veracruz Blues*, recognizes this relationship between baseball and American culture. In fact, the novel's first sentence states that baseball and America "are of course mirror and lamp" (1). Baseball, in essence, reflects and further illuminates the patterns of American society. Myth, however, is more complex than it first appears. National myth is a construction of the dominant ideology; and while myth can have a unifying effect on disparate peoples, it can also work hegemonically, "affirming as good the distribution of authority and power that ideology rationalizes" (Slotkin 19).

Winegardner establishes the metaphoric relationship between baseball and American culture as a way of problematizing the ideological nature of American myth. His fictional account of the 1946 "raid" of the Major Leagues by Jorge Pasquel's Mexican League brings issues of race and class to bear on these myths. More significantly, perhaps, he demonstrates how the globalization of corporate capitalism blurs the borders between nations and national cultures. In his depiction of baseball, Winegardner contextualizes selected elements of American cultural myth. In doing so, however, he also brings an international context to baseball. Jorge Pasquel's perception of baseball, its meaning to him as a Mexican nationalist, and his ambivalence toward American culture, show both the international nature of the "American dream," and also, almost paradoxically, a staunch resistance toward American cultural imperialism.

The postmodern era is characterized as a period of fragmentation, a disruption of grand narratives that have defined power relationships during the modern era. Problematizing grand narratives is certainly a positive trend that gives a voice to many historically disenfranchised people. Alfonso Del Toro, echoing sentiments from the likes of Jean-François Lyotard, states that postmodernism allows for "the possibility of a new organization of thought and knowledge in an open form through the relativizing of totalitarian paradigms and the decentralization of Discourse, History, and Truth" (30). Certainly this decentralization is part of Winegardner's purpose in *The Veracruz Blues* in that much of the novel's narration is from the voices of disenfranchised Americans in Mexico.

It is no surprise that disenfranchised Americans make their way south of the border. It is common in both the history and literature of the United States. Octavio Paz, one of Mexico's greatest men of letters, comments that American writers and artists "have not looked for Mexico in Mexico; they have looked for their obsessions, enthusiasms, phobias, hopes, interests—and these are what they have found. In short, the history of our relationship is the history of mutual and stubborn deceit, usually involuntary, though not always so" (115). Winegardner's characters, and indeed Winegardner himself, use Mexico as a site where Americans gain a new perspective on their relationship to the United States.

The season of 1946 promised Americans the return of their baseball heroes who served during the war, but the optimism generated by the returning veterans veiled some very real problems with America's pastime. Black Americans had served in the war in increasing numbers, but their homecoming promised nothing but a return to a continued system of segregation and second-class citizenship. For black baseball players it was no different. Denied access to the Major Leagues through a "gentlemen's agreement" among the owners, African Americans were forced into their own leagues.

Winegardner, echoing Paz, concludes that only in Mexico can black ballplayers find their idea of America. The owners and fans of the Mexican League welcomed the African American players openly. Early in the novel Pasquel declares proudly that the Mexican League will both rival the Major Leagues and also open the door for all races. "Our concern," he proclaims, is "only how well the man plays the game" (25). Theolic "Fireball" Smith, a Negro League pitcher who followed Pasquel's money south, is the primary African American voice in the novel. He confirms Pasquel's claim, stating, "[t]wo years in Mexico changed my attitudes about the U.S.A. We were heroes to those fans. They treated us like they did their own. America was no democracy for a black man" (18). Clearly the equality and liberty that are such a large part of any American myth are undermined in any discussion of opportunity for African Americans. It is only in the Mexican League in 1946 that they experience this equality. Though Smith claims that the 1940 Veracruz Blues (which had Latin and Negro League legends such as Martin Dihigo, Josh Gibson, Ray Dandridge, and Cool Papa Bell on the roster) was the best team in baseball history, it is only in 1946 that those excluded from the Major Leagues were allowed to compete against talent from the Majors. Midway through the novel Max Lanier, a star pitcher with the St. Louis Cardinals, jumps to Mexico and asks Ray Dandridge where all these talented players came from. Dandridge replies, "[m]an, we been here. . . . Been here a while now, just waitin' for you" (144). It is the relative equality of the Mexican League, and the chance to compete against those presumed to be the "best" by white America, that the Negro Leaguers wanted.

Yet Smith is unwilling to abandon the United States entirely and embrace Mexico. After learning that the Negro Leagues, in accordance with the Major Leagues, have agreed to ban every player who jumped to the Mexican League, Smith says, "I don't care what gripes you have against your country, it's still yours and it's still a blow to be barred from making a living there" (75). For Dandridge and Smith, Mexico represents the promise of America.

Wartime replacement players also found themselves in a difficult situation in 1946. They had filled empty Major League rosters during the war but had no guarantee that they would have jobs now that the regulars were returning. The reserve clause, which kept a player bound to a single club regardless of whether that player was under contract, left these players with no leverage in negotiations. As a result, many players found themselves either completely without contracts, or without contracts that represented their true market value. The power of the reserve clause came from the notion that baseball is not like other businesses and is therefore not beholden to the same antimonopolistic rules. As a result, the players were at the mercy of the owners. Frank Bullinger, a troubled American journalist who is given the job of media director by Pasquel, is the overarching narrative voice in the novel. He notes that America's national pastime is "perhaps the least-free enterprise" in the United States (97).

The Mexican League gives the fledgling players union the leverage it needs to gain concessions from the Major League owners. The lack of any real competition to the Major Leagues allowed the reserve clause to remain unchallenged for decades.[1] The competitively and financially viable alternative of the Mexican League gave the owners incentive to negotiate. While in reality only a handful of top players like Max Lanier and Mickey Owen left for Mexico (and only eighteen total jumped from the Major Leagues), the possibility of losing others led Comissioner Albert "Happy" Chandler to blacklist all players who accepted Pasquel's offer. In the novel, Ray Dandridge shares rumors with Fireball Smith that articulate the fears of the Major League owners. He states that blue chip major leaguers like Hank Greenberg had been contacted by Pasquel and that Ted Williams had even been offered a "blank check" to play in Mexico (73). With these rumors circulating, Winegardner suggests that blacklisting alone would not ensure the Major League's continuing hold on the top baseball talent.

It is on the day of Mexican Independence (again, Winegardner is seeing America in Mexico) that the players learn the full impact of their jump to Mexico. Danny Gardella, a wartime player who jumped to Mexico, reads an article wired from Chicago stating that the owners had convinced the fledgling players' union to disband in exchange for instituting a minimum wage and a pension fund. Gardella understands how this came to pass, contending that "[i]t was *us* whose jumping to Mexico gave the players' union credibility" (227). Again, Mexico provides the access to a more egalitarian society, one the United States could not achieve on its own.

Winegardner suggests that one of the reasons the reserve clause was able to survive so long was the connection between baseball and American myth. When confronted with the notion of organizing a players' union, Ace Adams, a Major Leaguer who played in Mexico for a short time, says, "[b]allplayers are individualists" (226). As noted earlier, this American notion of individualism is deeply tied to the lore of baseball. With this notion of individualism embedded in the vision of both baseball and America, the hegemonic effect myth can have on the working class becomes apparent.

Further evidence of the power of myth to overshadow socioeconomic realities surfaces during a party at Ernest Hemingway's cottage in Cuba. The fictional assemblage of characters is mythic in scale. Frank Bullinger joins a party that includes legends like Hemingway, Babe Ruth, the boxer Gene Tunney and his wife, Jorge Pasquel and his brother, the Mexican actress (and Pasquel's lover) Maria Felix, the great Cuban pitcher Dolf Luque, as well as Lou Klein and Fred Martin, two St. Louis Cardinals. After they shoot pigeons at a rifle club and then return to Hemingway's for dinner, "the boozing grew serious and the conversation sank to the level of baseball talk" (41). It is significant, especially considering the number of ballplayers present at the party, that the sport does not come up in the conversation until "the boozing grew serious." Baseball, Winegardner suggests, occupies a part of the American imagination that is not grounded in fact or reason. Its foundation is in nostalgia and idealism. The characters are ready to discuss the game only when the capacity for reason is blunted by alcohol. Thus, when Bullinger comments that the biggest story of the year in baseball is the attempt to organize a players' union, the American members of the party scoff at him.

Bullinger argues the point to the players who are present, noting that they have no pension and no minimum wage. He also observes that they will receive no additional income for arriving at spring training earlier than usual this year and that the unprecedented profits that baseball is sure to earn in the wake of the war will not be passed down from the owners to the players. Lou Klein, however, dismisses him simply by commenting that the "Bawl-playahs don't cotton to unions . . . the American bawl-playah is an individualist" (42).

The myth of American individualism embraced in the lore of baseball bolsters the monopolistic hold owners have over players. It is only in Mexico that disenfranchised players, Major Leaguers and Negro Leaguers alike, approach the promise of American democracy.

The complexity of *The Veracruz Blues* lies beyond issues of race and class, however. While these issues are addressed through the backdrop of Latin America, Winegardner further explores the complicated relationship between the powerful capitalist-imperialist United States and Mexico, which struggles with its own national identity.

As the United States leads the world in establishing an increasingly global economy, the concept of America as an imperial nation has begun to receive considerable attention. Donald Pease notes that while the authority of the United States is based in military and economic power, "it depended for its efficacy on a range of cultural technologies, among which colonialist policies (exercised both internally and abroad) of conquest and domination figured prominently" (22). Attempts at conquest, in whatever form, are always met with resistance, and Pease concludes that, "[a]s an ongoing cultural project, U.S. imperialism is thus best understood as a complex and interdependent relationship with hegemonic as well as counter-hegemonic modalities of coercion and resistance" (23).

This cultural imperialism is evident in the rise of modern sport. Joseph Arbena observes that "[o]ften, though not always, then, the global history of modern sport is characterized by a process of diffusion geographically outward from centers of innovation and hierarchically downward" (2). Latin America, under this framework, has largely been a "recipient region" that has adopted sports from the Western powers. Latin American sport, then, is in many ways a reflection of Latin America's involvement in the global economy and "vividly expresses the ways in which different peoples have reacted to the penetration of the so-called modern models" (Arbena 3). Often these interactions take the form of the imperialist tendencies of assimilation and appropriation.

Certainly these tendencies manifest themselves in the earliest forms of baseball introduced to Mexico. Both in the plantations of the Yucatan Peninsula and in the railroads of Northern Mexico, baseball becomes one element in a larger colonial effort by the United States to co-opt Mexico (Joseph; Klein). The result of this colonial activity is generally a complex interweaving of cultures, and it is this convoluted nature of Mexican-American cultural contact that the novel attempts to explore. At Hemingway's party at his Cuban home, this cultural complexity is evident. Winegarner's choice of Cuba, a site that, within a decade, would become contested by capitalist-imperialist and revolutionary forces, is significant. It will be a frontier between opposing cultures, and this anachronistic spirit of contestation becomes apparent during the party as well. Cultural legends are set in opposition to one another. Latin American icons such as Pasquel, Luque, and Felix engage Hemingway, Ruth, and Tunney. Late in the evening, in fact, Hemingway and Pasquel compete in an impromptu boxing match in Hemingway's living room. They spar ineffectually, tired and drunk, until Hemingway attempts to end the fight by kicking Pasquel in the groin. Luque, who has been slumped in a chair to this point, springs to life, fires a revolver into the air, and shouts, "[f]ight fair!" (45). Hemingway, an American icon and champion of rugged masculinity and individualism, reveals the man behind the façade. His underhanded attempt to win calls into question both the whole myth of American exceptionalism and American dealings with Latin America.

In a reversal of the traditional American western imagery, Luque's gunplay is cowboyesque. Now, however, it is the dark-skinned native who holds the revolver and ultimately deals with the injustices of the frontier. The savage in need of civilization is Hemingway. Interestingly, the bullet Luque fires pierces a novel manuscript that Bullinger brought for Hemingway to read and critique (which has been left on a table and neglected all evening), a book he had hoped would become the great American novel. In each instance, the myth of American exceptionalism is exposed or inverted, and the revisionist tone for the novel is established.

Cuba as a setting is also significant because the Cubans were able to do what Pasquel, in some way, hopes to do: use baseball as a means of resisting the imperial presence of the United States. Milton Jamail identifies in Cuba a baseball tradition reaching back to the nineteenth century that contests the United States' exclusive claim to the game. Fidel Castro himself identifies this tradition, declaring that "[o]ne day, when the Yankees accept peaceful coexistence with our own country . . . we shall beat them at baseball too, and then the advantages of revolutionary over capitalist sport will be shown" (qtd. in Jamail 28). Pasquel, however, tries to create national identity through baseball *while embracing* capitalism. In essence he tries to both embrace and reject the influence of the United States. Paz notes that "[t]he idea the Mexican people have of the United States is contradictory, emotional, and impervious to criticism; it is a mythic image" (115). Certainly we see this in the character of Jorge Pasquel.

In a section narrated by Maria Felix, we learn that on his seventh birthday Pasquel had a baseball diamond built on his parents' polo grounds outside Veracruz on which he and his friend Miguel Aleman could play. His party, however, was cut short by bombings authorized by Woodrow Wilson. Four hundred died from the bombings, and Veracruz was occupied by U.S. Marines. Pasquel says of that day that he "became a man . . . who learned to despise American authority without forfeiting his love for American culture" (151). But separating American authority from American culture is not as easy as Pasquel believes.

Miguel Aleman became president of Mexico in 1946, and the parallel Winegardner creates between the lifelong friends is instructive. The national revolution, which had defined the decades leading up to the Second World War, peaked with the nationalization of the oil industry in 1938. In the postwar years, however, designs for an autonomous national industrial government were abandoned. This was against the best interests of most of the Mexican population (but very lucrative to those aligned with the government), for it established an economic colonialism. Land reform projects begun during the revolution were rescinded, and United States businesses were allowed to return to Mexico. While this trend was established with his predecessor, Avila Camacho, the embracing of foreign investment escalated and became "a virtual counter-revolution under President Aleman" (Niblo 187).

In the novel we see the cultural equivalent in Jorge Pasquel, who sees the Mexican League symbolically putting Mexico on par with the United States. Baseball becomes an arena in which Mexican nationalism expresses itself as it challenges the talent of the American Major Leagues. On the one hand, the attempt to "steal" players from the Major Leagues is certainly a statement of Mexican nationalism. It is a statement of defiance and a move towards equality. In the language Pasquel uses to recruit players, it is clear that he is trying to symbolically establish Mexico as America's equal, if not its superior. The Mexican League, he hopes, will be "a true mestizo baseball" (158), where the only concern is "how well a man plays the game" (25). The nationalist sensibility, implied in the statements above, becomes explicit when he states that the game will be "an egalitarian symbol of the new Mexico . . . a symbol that will ring throughout the world when we defeat the American baseball champion in a true World Series!" (158). There is no mistaking the nationalist tone of those words. On the other hand, Pasquel does not recognize the ways in which America has already assimilated him. Benedict Anderson, referring to a similar, though more intentional effect of formal English education in India, calls this "mental miscegenation" (91). He is referring to the effect the imposition of a culture can have on an individual, an almost unconscious undermining of the native culture.

The impact of American culture is evident throughout the novel. The descriptions of the ballparks attest to the imperial presence of the United States. "Meat" Stephens, a ballplayer who did not enjoy his stint in Mexico, recalls being surprised by the abundance of American products (Coca-Cola, Valvoline, and Seagram's, among others) being advertised on the outfield billboards (91). Even by 1946 national boundaries had become obsolete for large corporations. Another metaphor for the ubiquitous influence of American culture is the railroad tracks that run through the outfield of the stadium in Tampico. Alan Klein notes that railroads served multiple and at times contradictory purposes in Mexico. Toward the end of the nineteenth century, they spurred industrial growth in the country and thus fueled a growing sense of nationalism. However, most of the first railroad lines were direct links to the United States. This led to an increased influence of American culture along these lines, as well as the "wholesale encouragement of foreign colonialism" (Klein 29–32). Trains, then, are a fitting symbol in this novel, expressing Pasquel's ambiguous feelings towards the United States.

Pasquel claims to be both a nationalist and a lover of American culture, but that very culture undermines his Mexican nationalism. He seeks approval in terms of baseball through the acquisition of white players, an element clearly not necessary to quality baseball in Mexico but necessary to gain American approval of that baseball.[2] Even in his defiance of the Major Leagues, he is still deeply entrenched in the culture of the United States.

While he seeks approval from the Major Leagues, he begins to lose the approval of the Mexican fans. His team, the Veracruz Blues, is jeered as it travels through the league. Bullinger asks a Monterrey reporter why the fans whistle when the Blues take the field, and the reporter responds: "They whistle because they resent the Pasquels for stocking [the Veracruz Blues] with all the imported talent, trying to buy a championship. . . . It is no different in your country" (101). As Pasquel tries to make the league more competitive, it becomes less Mexican.

Pasquel attempted to appropriate a symbol of America from America and claim it for Mexico. But the contradictions within the man ran too deep, and the deep ties of baseball with American myth were too well knotted. Nowhere is this more evident in the novel than in Pasquel's relationship with Babe Ruth. If there is a personification of baseball, it is the Babe. Pasquel, recognizing this, tries to appropriate his image for the Mexican League, first by offering him a managerial position and then by inviting him to perform in a hitting exhibition. But Babe Ruth, the man and the myth, cannot be had. At a late season party at Pasquel's Mexico City mansion, Pasquel organizes a ping-pong tournament. Pasquel and Ruth meet in the championship. While Ruth approaches the game lackadaisically, Pasquel struggles feverishly to win. In the end, however, the game is never in doubt, and Ruth wins easily. Gardella says of Pasquel, "you could tell he thought he could win. Ruth didn't look like he could beat anybody, but really there wasn't anybody he couldn't beat" (120). Pasquel's desperate determination and Ruth's matter-of-fact victory illustrate the nature of Pasquel's misunderstanding. He thinks he can beat the Babe and, in doing so, all that he represents. This is true of ping-pong and also of the Mexican League. Gardella, however, states simply and perceptively that "[n]obody overshadowed Babe Ruth" (121).

Maria Felix, speaking of Mexicans in general, but Pasquel in particular, says, "Americans can be hypocrites, but we *are* our contradictions" (152). This, ultimately, is what undermines Pasquel's vision. He does not understand the complexity of American cultural imperialism and the ways in which it had already indoctrinated him in American corporate capitalism. It is the contradictions within himself that lead to his failure.

Winegardner creates a parallel between Jorge Pasquel and Jay Gatsby that accentuates the contradictions in the man. The correlation is explicit early on when Bullinger comments that Gatsby was one of the facets to Pasquel's complex and enigmatic personality (2). The comparison, surprising as it may seem at first, is fitting. Both in many ways embody the qualities of the "American Adam" as defined by R.W.B. Lewis. One of the standard characteristics of the Adamic figure is that he is "bereft of history" (5), and certainly this applies to both Pasquel and Gatsby. Though we are given significant insights into their pasts late in each novel, rumors circulate throughout concerning their histories. The parallels are striking. Gatsby was rumored to have been a German spy during World War I, while Pasquel was rumored to have made his money refueling German U-Boats during World War II. Both were rumored to have killed a man.

Both men rise to positions of power and influence. One guest of Pasquel observes that he "is good at exploiting a guy's crazy dreams" (121). When Bullinger interviews Red Hayworth about his time in the Mexican League, he tells the story of how he was not willing to go until Pasquel presented him with a brand new Cadillac, an extreme rarity during the war and early postwar years and a car Hayworth particularly admired. When Bullinger questions him further, asking him how Pasquel knew of his love for Cadillacs, Hayworth is puzzled: "I always figured you told 'em, Frank." Frank, however, responds, "No. I didn't. I never said word one" (109).

This enigmatic scene is not dissimilar to the way Gatsby is able to manipulate people with the use of his money. One of his guests says, "when I was here last I tore my gown on a chair . . . within a week I got a package from Croirier's with a new evening gown in it," leading another guest to comment, "[h]e doesn't want any trouble with anybody" (47). Both Gatsby and Pasquel are products of capitalism and believe in the power of money to eliminate cultural conflict and cultural barriers.

It is in this belief that the parallel between the two characters is so illuminating. Both are ultimately denied their dream. In the end, Gatsby cannot have Daisy. Class remains a barrier that money alone cannot overcome. Pasquel's dream of a Mexico that culturally and economically rivals the United States is also unattainable. Despite his seemingly endless supply of money, the hegemonic influence of American commerce and industry undermines his project from the beginning.

Furthermore, each character illustrates how money impacts a game that, according to the myth, exists outside regular time and space. This parallel is evident in the narration of Fireball Smith as he relates how he and Quincy Trouppe were saved from the wartime draft by Jorge Pasquel. Pasquel offered eighty thousand Mexican laborers to work for the U.S. war effort in exchange for the services of Trouppe and Smith. Smith reflects that he was never completely comfortable playing for a man so powerful that he "bargained the lives of eighty thousand strangers like they was just so many boxes of cigars" (20).

Smith's narration expresses a similar kind of disbelief to that of Nick Carraway when he discovers that Gatsby's associate, Meyer Wolfsheim, had "played with the faith of fifty million people" when he fixed the 1919 World Series (78). Though the reference here is to Gatsby's associate, what is important is that both novels illustrate the corruptibility of the baseball myth. Baseball is a product of its time rather than a pastoral escape from the workings of time. In *The Veracruz Blues*, baseball is woven into a global economy that is no longer contained within national boundaries and is intricately tied to political and cultural influences.

There are, however, more definitive articulations of Mexican culture than Pasquel's muddy nationalism in Winegardner's novel. Ines, one of Fireball Smith's Mexican lovers, takes him to one of the ancient ball courts of premodern Mexico. She is an artist and an activist who socializes with the likes of Diego Rivera, Frida Kahlo, and other Mexican revolutionaries. Unlike

Pasquel, she is searching for agency through indigenous games, trying to make a connection with the Americans without succumbing to their culture. She is partially successful. She tells the story of how one of the teams would lose their heads when the game was completed. As Ines says, however, it was not known whether the winners or the losers were sacrificed. Smith responds, "I sure as Hell don't understand Mexico" (146). As he reflects on those Mexican ballplayers, on how they lose if they win and win if they lose, he begins to associate their plight with the complex circumstances that brought him to Mexico. If Smith stays in his own country, he is not free; and in experiencing the freedoms of Mexico, he is not at home. Ultimately, he thinks to himself that perhaps he was beginning to comprehend "all too goddamned well" (146).

Arbena notes that the endurance of premodern games like the Mesoamerican ballgame represents "a source of self-respect and even a type of rebellion among people who have seen much of their traditional culture destroyed" (4). Ines, then, stands in contrast to Pasquel. While he tries to appropriate American culture and ends up reproducing many of its prejudices and injustices, Ines expresses pride in her own culture. In doing so, she resists the influence of American corporate capitalism and is able to communicate on a meaningful level with Smith. Homi Bhabha notes that "[t]he 'locality' of national culture is neither unified nor unitary in relation to itself, nor must it be seen simply as 'other' in relation to what is outside or beyond it. The boundary is Janus-faced and the problem of outside/inside must always itself be a process of hybridity" (4). Winegardner explores just how fluid concepts of nationalism can be. Smith and Ines find a tenuous solidarity, one that he does not feel with white Americans and that she does not feel with Pasquel. Identifying the "other," in this tale of two nations, is more complicated than it first seems.

Frank Bullinger reflects on the celebrities that populate his reflections and how he was influenced by their larger-than-life personae. In the end, though, he realizes that it is the forgotten characters like Smith and Gardella who tell more compelling stories and ultimately carry the weight of his narrative. Bullinger, then, finds meaning beyond myth. In telling a story of those who "got partway there" (250), *The Veracruz Blues* reveals what the myths hide, the complex dynamics of race and class, assimilation and resistance, and nationalism and imperialism that are part of the history of baseball and America.

NOTES

1. The last real challenge to the American and National Leagues' monopoly on the top baseball talent was the Federal League, which existed from 1913 to 1915. During that time, most Major League stars received substantial raises to dissuade them from jumping. The Federal League was ultimately unprofitable and was essentially "bought out" by the Major Leagues in December 1915. A succinct history can be found in Charles C. Alexander's *Our Game: An American Baseball History*.

2. As noted earlier, the 1940 Veracruz Blues were regarded by many as the best team ever by many nonwhite baseball men. The 1946 Blues, who, significantly, had the largest percentage of white ballplayers in the league, including the great pitcher Max Lanier, struggled to get out of the cellar of the league all season.

REFERENCES

Alexander, Charles C. *Our Game: An American Baseball History*. New York: MJF Books, 1991.

Anderson, Benedict. *Imagined Communities: Reflections on the Origin and Spread of Nationalism*. London: Verso, 1983.

Arbena, Joseph L. "Sport and the Study of Latin American Society: An Overview." *Sport and Society in Latin America: Diffusion, Dependency, and the Rise of Mass Culture*. Ed. Joseph L. Arbena. Westport, CT: Greenwood Press, 1988. 1–14.

Bhabha, Homi. "Introduction: Narrating the Nation." *Nation and Narration*. Ed. Homi Bhabha. London: Routledge, 1990. 1–7.

Del Toro, Alfonso. "The Epistemological Foundations of the Contemporary Condition: Latin America in Dialogue with Postmodernity and Postcoloniality." *Latin American Postmodernisms*. Ed. Richard Young. Amsterdam: Rodopi, 1997. 29–51.

Jamail, Milton H. *Full Count: Inside Cuban Baseball*. Carbondale: Southern Illinois University Press, 2000.

Joseph, Gilbert. "Forging a Regional Pastime: Baseball and Class in the Yucatan." *Sport and Society in Latin America: Diffusion, Dependency, and the Rise of Mass Culture*. Ed. Joseph L. Arbena. Westport, CT: Greenwood Press, 1988. 29–61.

Klein, Alan. *Baseball on the Border*. Princeton, NJ: Princeton University Press, 1997.

Lewis, R.W.B. *The American Adam: Innocence, Tragedy, and Tradition in the Nineteenth Century*. Chicago: University of Chicago Press, 1955.

McGimpsey, David. *Imagining Baseball: America's Pastime and Popular Culture*. Bloomington: Indiana University Press, 2000.

Niblo, Stephen R. *War, Diplomacy, and Development: The United States and Mexico, 1939–1954*. Wilmington: Scholarly Resources Inc, 1995.

Paz, Octavio. "Reflections: Mexico and the United States." *New Yorker*. 17 Sep. 1979: 136–153.

Pease, Donald. "New Perspectives on U.S. Culture and Imperialism." *Cultures of United States Imperialism*. Eds. Amy Kaplan and Donald Pease. Durham, NC: Duke University Press, 1993. 22–37.

Slotkin, Richard. *The Fatal Environment: The Myth of the Frontier in the Age of Industrialization, 1800–1890*. New York: Atheneum, 1985.

Winegardner, Mark. *The Veracruz Blues*. New York: Penguin 1996.

"The Machine-Language of the Muscles": Reading, Sport, and the Self in *Infinite Jest*

Stephen J. Burn

With one of its multiple narrative lines set in a Boston tennis academy that models its academic curriculum on the Oxbridge Trivium and Quadrivium, David Foster Wallace's *Infinite Jest* (1996) intertwines sport with questions of learning and memory that ultimately shade into a larger meditation on contemporary identity. But while Wallace observes that the dynamics of "competitive tennis [are] largely mental" (269), the foundations of the novel's synthesis of sport and study only partly derive from cerebral elements intrinsic to the game. Instead, Wallace uses tennis as a focal point around which larger arguments about the self are generated by the precision of the novel's structure, by its network of allusions to earlier works, and by the position of its mini-essays on tennis amid a spectrum of other intellectual concerns.

The techniques and themes Wallace uses to articulate these arguments are presented in miniature in the novel's opening scene, and one of the most immediately striking is the broad intellectual territory in which Wallace locates his discussions of tennis. *Infinite Jest* opens in 2010,[1] with a set piece that is carefully orchestrated to provide an unusually eclectic intellectual context for the novel's treatment of sport. In this initial narrative strand, which is really one of three unifying threads, the reader is introduced to eighteen-year-old Hal Incandenza as he faces an admissions panel at the University of Arizona. Hal is a continentally ranked junior tennis player and prodigious reader, but in the opening scene he has been accused by the panel of plagiarising application essays to mask the limited academic skills that they suspect accompany his undoubted athletic abilities. As part of his first monologue in the novel, Hal defends himself against this jock stereotype with an account of his extensive reading: "'I *read*,' I say. 'I study and read. . . . I consume libraries. I wear out spines and ROM-drives. . . . But it transcends the mechanics. I'm not a machine. I feel and believe. I have opinions. Some of them are interesting. . . . I believe Hobbes is just Rousseau in a dark mirror'" (12). Hal's defence neatly delineates his intellectual range, but it also introduces one of the mysteries of the novel because, despite his precise diction, all the admissions panel hear of Hal's speech are noises that sound "[l]ike some sort of animal with something in its mouth" (14). Concerned for his well-being, they wrestle him to the ground while Hal plaintively intones: "I'm in here . . . I am not what you see and hear" (13).

This introduction is important to the rest of the book (which chronologically precedes it, being set mainly in 2009) in part because it stimulates the reader to search through earlier time to trace what exactly goes wrong for Hal, given that in 2010 he can play high-level tennis but cannot connect internal thoughts with external expression. But it is also important because it introduces two characteristic strategies of the novel. The first is the tendency of characters to draw on their wider reading when they require an explanation. Reading is an unusually important activity for characters in Wallace's novel and, as will become apparent, it is significant that Hal tries to explain himself in the opening scene by claiming to have read the work of the seventeenth-century political scientist Thomas Hobbes. The second, connected strategy is the tendency of sporting environments in the novel to seek to reduce the complexity of open systems to the simplistic workings of a closed system.

In his earlier fiction, Wallace has described how individual lives are located amid a complex "interplay of forces probably beyond the comprehension of everything and everyone involved" ("Order and Flux" 94), but the urge to simplify this sort of complex interaction is already apparent in the admissions room where Hal's potential contribution to Arizona's tennis squad is weighed. This environment is precisely reduced, as the novel's third sentence stresses with clauses cataloguing the room's three defences (it is "wood-walled . . . double-windowed . . . insulated" [3]) against the external world. By contrast, however, the sporting environment that produced Hal—the Enfield Tennis Academy, founded by Hal's father James—was deliberately set up to escape the restrictions of this philosophy. In fact, the academy's head coach and athletic director, Gerhardt Schtitt, was specifically hired because he perceived that real tennis was not "reducible to delimited factors" but instead thrived on a more complex "*not*-order . . . the places where things broke down, fragmented into beauty" (81).

Schtitt tries to teach that tennis is an "infinite system of decisions and angles and lines" (84), and so acts as a kind of antidote to reductionist sporting strategies. But in spite of his teaching, the legacy of closed system thinking is still evident at the heart of the academy. Hal, for example, sums up his delimited existence by telling his brother that at the academy he is "out of all loops but one, by design" (1016 n.110), and closure even seems to be expressed in the academy's architecture. The academy grounds are laid out as a cardioid, which partly reflects the intended path of the young players, pumped from one isolated chamber to another. They are part of a closed circuit designed to route them from raw potential to accomplished professionalism. Like almost everything else in the novel, however, hearts appear in multiple contexts, and a further reference to hearts suggests that circulation is not the only interpretation that may be attached to the academy's topography. In a digression that catalogues the impact of addiction, Wallace claims that "chronic alcoholics' hearts are . . . swollen to nearly twice the size of civilians' human hearts" (200), and this seems to connect to the academy's cardioid because the stresses of academy life drive so many of the young players to alcohol. The linear route mapped for the players is, in fact, part of a more complex system where the simple goal of tennis success is complicated by obsession, loneliness, and envy. Struggling under these pressures, the young players take paths that branch into alcohol and recreational drugs, where they seek relief from the strains of academy life. A narrowed down life at the academy, Wallace suggests through its architecture, contains one route to the bloated heart of an alcoholic.

This critique of narrow, linear thinking connects to the tendency of characters to draw on their wider reading, because *Infinite Jest* itself imitates an open system by layering its plot with allusions that send the reader outward to trace connections to other novels. In particular, the book has a strong intertextual relation to Don DeLillo's 1972 novel of football and nuclear terror, *End Zone*, which several characters in *Infinite Jest* seem to have read.[2] When Schtitt, for example, argues against linear approaches to sporting success by exclaiming "straight ahead! Plow ahead! Go! This is myth . . . they assume [in America] always the efficient way is to plow in straight" (80), he seems to be critiquing *End Zone*'s assistant coach, Tweego, whose philosophy is to think "in one direction, straight ahead" (49).[3] Similarly, Marlon Bain from Wallace's novel seems to have read and learnt from *End Zone*, if we are to judge by the extent to which his letter to "Helen" Steeply paraphrases the earlier book. Bain explains, "pay no attention to Orin's defense of football as ritualized substitute for armed conflict. Armed conflict is plenty ritualized on its own, and since we have real armed conflict . . . there is no need or purpose for a substitute" (1047 n.269), a refutation that strongly echoes *End Zone*'s Alan Zapalac, who claims, "I reject the notion of football as warfare. Warfare is warfare. We don't need substitutes because we have the real thing" (64).

These connections are important not just as a footnote to Wallace's postmodern heritage but also because they offer a particularly good example of the way allusion works in *Infinite Jest*. The intellectual texture and dense allusiveness of Wallace's prose are not (as Michiko Kakutani charged in a review of the novel) simply an excuse for Wallace to "show off his remarkable skills as a writer and empty the contents of his restless mind" (B2) but are, rather, a scrupulous attempt to illustrate how people interact with books. Like most readers, characters in the novel are swayed and influenced by their reading and react according to those readings and misreadings. This leads to a heightened anxiety about where words come from (a theme introduced in the accusations of plagiarism that dog Hal in the opening scene and extend throughout the book) that complicates the reliability of many statements in the novel. In the previous example featuring Marlon Bain, for instance, it is worth noting that nowhere in the novel does Hal's brother Orin offer the defence of football that Bain attributes to him. This could simply be Wallace economically implying a conversation so he need not include it; but given that he *does* include an account of Orin outlining a defence of his part in football that is different from Bain's (Orin claims punting is something "emotional and/or even, if there was such a thing anymore, spiritual: a denial of silence" [295]), it seems that Wallace is showing how Bain has confused his reading with "reality" and extended lessons absorbed from books into the "real" world.

Elsewhere in the novel are similar instances where identifying a book that a character has read can help clarify a scene. The most important example of this reveals the essential connections the novel maps between sport, reading, and the self, which can be discerned by following a chain of clues that Wallace has embedded in the names of different locations in the postmillennial landscape of his novel.[4] As the cardioid architecture of the academy subtly suggests a path to addiction, so the philosophical topography of the novel's landscape also suggests interpretations. One of the ways young players like Hal escape the pressures of institutional existence is by drinking in The Unexamined Life, a Boston club. The club's name, of course, recalls Socrates's observation in Plato's *Apology* that "the unexamined life is not worth living" (38a), and so is darkly appropriate in the context of the academy where the whole tennis program is intended as "a progression toward self-forgetting" (635). The Platonic allusion subtly implies a critique of the human worth of their training as Wallace suggests the ease with which athletic transcendence can edge into the alcohol-doused oblivion of self. But it is a different philosopher whose name is hidden in another tavern that eventually reveals the books behind the academy. The important location, here, is Ryle's Jazz Club, an "upscale pub-type bar" in Inman Square (479).

Visited at different times by Poor Tony Krause, Rémy Marathe, and Kate Gompert, Ryle's Jazz Club provides a node where a number of narrative connections cluster. But while none of the academy players visit it, Ryle's Jazz Club is subtly connected to the academy's founder, Hal's father James Incandenza, by a strange comment from "Helen" Steeply. While watching Hal play, Steeply remarks of him that "[t]he son described his father as 'genre-dysphoric'" (682). The phrase is dismissed by an academy tutor, Thierry Poutrincourt, as "not sound[ing] like Hal," but it does sound like the "Gender-Dysphoric Night" (691) that Ryle's hosts every second Wednesday. But why should this confusion emerge in a discussion about James Incandenza? Perhaps it is because Incandenza's own tennis career began with a combination of alcohol, tennis, and another Ryle—the English philosopher Gilbert Ryle, who at mid-century was one of the leading advocates of philosophical behaviourism.

Given that Wallace's previous novel, *The Broom of the System* (1987), draws heavily on Wittgenstein and features a character who is persuaded (by a grandparent who knew Wittgenstein) that her life is "told, not lived" (119), it is not surprising that his next work refers to Gilbert Ryle. The two philosophers were friends; and like Wittgenstein, Ryle is often considered one of the central thinkers behind the development of Linguistic Analysis. It is, however, the argument of Ryle's most influential work, *The Concept of Mind* (1949), that is embedded into Wallace's narrative.

Ryle's book is an attack on what he calls the official doctrine which, deriving from Descartes, asserts that "with the doubtful exception of idiots and infants in arms every human being has both a body and a mind" (13). Ryle argues that this doctrine is the result of a category-mistake that leads us to mistakenly differentiate between the outward actions of the body and the internal actions of the mind. But, he argues, there is no privileged nonspatial realm of mind separate from a mechanical body, and so he mockingly refutes the official theory as "the dogma of the Ghost in the Machine" (17).

Ryle's argument with Cartesian dualism is important to sport in *Infinite Jest* because, just as Marlon Bain and Gerhardt Schtitt seem to have read *End Zone*, Hal's grandfather seems to have read *The Concept of Mind* and incorporated its message into the first tennis lessons he gives James in 1960.[5] In this account, tennis basics merge with a monistic account of the self that even includes an inverted quote from Ryle:

Son, you're ten, and this is hard news for somebody ten, even if you're almost five-eleven, a possible pituitary freak. Son, you're a body, son. That quick little scientific-prodigy's mind she's so proud of and won't quit twittering about: son it's just neural spasms, those thoughts in your mind are just the sound of your head revving, and head is still just body, Jim. Commit this to memory. Head is body. Jim, brace yourself against my shoulders here for this hard news, at ten: you're a machine. . . . Today, Lesson One out there, you become, for better or worse, Jim, a man. A player. . . . A machine in the ghost, to quote a phrase. (159–160)

Like Ryle, Hal's grandfather effectively dismisses the idea of dualism by correcting the logical geography of language ("head is body"). But it is also significant that Wallace follows this lecture by cutting to 2009 when one of the academy's young players, Michael Pemulis, is leaving Inman Square where Ryle's Jazz Club is located, because forty-nine years after the grandfather's early lesson, his brand of Rylean materialism has become the dominant philosophy of the academy.

Despite the fact that Schtitt, in his efforts to counter reductive sport philosophies, insists that the young players remain in the open air for as long as possible so that they can distinguish a separate "world inside" themselves (459), the prevalent mode of self-conception is mechanistic materialism.[6] The top players are described as "grim machines" (438); and at the sessions where older players offer advice to the younger academy students, the ephebes are schooled to see themselves as machines for whom the accretive weight of repetitive training will make the movements "sink and soak into the hardware, the C.P.S. . . . The machine-language of the muscles . . . wiring them into the motherboard" (117–118). In the year 2009 Hal also flourishes as an athlete, and appropriately at this point he recognises that he has become "robotic" and that "inside . . . there's pretty much nothing at all" (694).

And in an ironic twist on Ryle's dismissal of Cartesianism as the "official doctrine," in Wallace's postmillennial future, it seems that a version of Ryle's doctrine has been adopted by a whole range of officials outside the academy: Government agents in *Infinite Jest* base their judgements on "the boys in Behavioral Science" (420), and in the novel's opening scene Hal tries to stop the admissions panel basing their judgement on behaviourism when he argues, "I'm not a machine . . . I'm not what you see and hear" (12–13).

In placing this plea at the start, Wallace stresses the importance of Ryle's account by the temporal arrangement of his narrative. The scene featuring Hal's grandfather is the earliest action dramatised in the novel, while Hal's claim that he is not a machine is from the chronologically latest section, so the novel is structured so that arguments concerning Ryle chronologically bracket the entire novel. But the structure of *Infinite Jest* is also precisely arranged to place Ryle's critique of dualism in a longer historical context, and this partly explains why Hal claims to have read Thomas Hobbes in the opening scene.

Despite the fact that Hobbes does mention tennis in his vast study *Leviathan* (1651),[7] his importance to *Infinite Jest* lies in what Bertrand Russell calls his "thorough-going materialism" (570); two of the three references to him in the novel are tied up with this. After the reference to Hobbes in Hal's opening monologue, his name appears next on page 44 in a section that fully introduces Orin for the first time in which he recalls watching a documentary about materialist accounts of schizophrenia.[8] So the first two times Hobbes is mentioned are both in a sporting context, and both have to do with materialism, which subtly suggests that Orin's sports career has been dominated by the same kind of materialist reductionism as Hal's.[9]

At the same time it also prepares the ground for Hal's attempted movement against the Rylean tennis tuition of his grandfather. In his introduction to *The Concept of Mind*, Daniel Dennett argues that prior to Ryle's work, philosophy had been involved in a "centuries old pendulum swing between Descartes's dualism ('para-mechanical' hypothesis) and Hobbes's materialism (mechanical hypothesis)" (xx). So it is appropriate that as Hal seeks a counternarrative to a mechanical hypothesis, he turns to his reading, and this leads him (via Shakespeare) to Ryle's target: René Descartes. In this move he is following Wallace himself who told an interviewer not long after the publication of *Infinite Jest* that Descartes's *Meditations on First Philosophy* and *Discourse on Method* were among the "stars you steer by" when writing (27).[10]

On 4 November 2009, Hal reads *Hamlet* and, typically for the novel, this reading experience resonates and influences his subsequent thinking. Sixteen days later when, drawn out from withdrawal and depressed over his own nebulous selfhood, he reflects: "It's always seemed a little preposterous that Hamlet, for all his paralyzing doubt about everything, never once doubts the reality of the ghost. Never questions whether his own madness might not in fact be unfeigned" (900). But like the other characters in *Infinite Jest*, Hal absorbs the lessons of his reading and seems to question whether he is himself mad. But how is madness to be defined? In *Hamlet* Polonius offers the rather unhelpful example that "to define true madness, What is't but to be nothing else but mad?" (II.2.93–94), but Descartes offers a clearer example in his *First Meditation*: "And how could I deny these hands and this body belong to me, unless perhaps I were to assimilate myself to those insane persons whose minds are so troubled and clouded by the black vapours of the bile that they constantly assert that . . . they have a body of glass" (96).

Late in November 2009, Hal is suffering an increasing disjunction between inner emotion and external expression that may make him doubt his connection to his body, and so he evidently explores the possibility that he may be mad, because by 2010 he is presented as the author of an essay that adopts Descartes's metaphor for madness: "A Man Who Began to Suspect He Was Made of Glass" (7).[11] Equally, Hal's emphasis on Hamlet's doubt is relevant to a Cartesian reading of his own situation. Descartes's philosophical investigations move outward from himself to seek certainties by dismissing as false everything that can be doubted until there remain two certain foundations: mathematics and theology. And in many ways, these provide the poles for belief in Wallace's novel, too. The first is abundantly present in *Infinite Jest*, and it even includes a minilecture from Pemulis on how "you can trust math" as a reliable certainty in life (1071 n.324). The second is less tangibly articulated in the novel, but Wallace apparently "got religion" (Moore 102) while writing the book, and it is clear that the search for a solid foundation for belief is a unifying thread throughout the different narrative strands.[12]

For all his precocity as a reader, however, Hal finds little support in Descartes's foundations. Hal has been dependent on mathematical tutorials from Pemulis, and both (significantly falling back on mechanistic language for the self) accept that he is not "hardwired for" more advanced mathematics (852). As the end of the novel approaches, Hal can find only emptiness not just in theological belief, but in any kind of belief:

It now lately sometimes seemed like a kind of black miracle to me that people could actually care deeply about a subject or pursuit, and could go on caring this way for years on end. Could dedicate their entire lives to it. It seemed admirable and at the same time pathetic. We are all dying to give our lives away to something, maybe. God or Satan. (900)

In the *Second Meditation* Descartes takes "as assured that the proposition: *I am, I exist*, is necessarily true" (103), but as Hal falls away from the foundations of Descartes's theological and mathematical certainties, he questions even this axiom as he falls into ontological doubt. The last time he is seen in 2009 he is preparing for a challenge match, and questions whether he only exists in "call-uppable for rebroadcast" format (966). For all its expertise in philosophy and tennis, Wallace's excavation of sport and "the soul's core systems" (692) effectively finds its boundaries in a reading of *Hamlet*. The play's opening line, "Who's there?" introduces the search for identity that preoccupies Hal throughout the novel, while the dying words of Hamlet underscore his inability to communicate in the latest sections: "[T]he rest is silence."

NOTES

1. The year 2010 is known as the "Year of Glad" in the twenty-first century America of Wallace's novel because the Gregorian calendar has been obscured by a sponsorship program that renames years after the highest corporate bidder. The key to the novel's temporal setting, however, is hidden between the main text and the footnotes of the novel and (as I outline in *David Foster Wallace's Infinite Jest* [25–26]) the Year of Glad can be identified as 2010.

2. These references are perhaps unsurprising because Wallace has stated his admiration for DeLillo on several occasions and described him as a "true prophet of . . . U.S. fiction" in his essay collection *A Supposedly Fun Thing I'll Never Do Again* (47).

3. The verbal echoes here are compounded by a number of other similarities between the two sports novels. On the most superficial level, both novels obviously interweave sporting events and apocalyptic war games, but the novels also share young players who are training to be sportscasters, coaches who oversee practice from a position of godlike omniscience in a tower, and players who were lured to their respective colleges by dreams of self-transcendence (compare *End Zone*'s Taft Robinson, promised he will "get past his own limits" [237], and Wallace's Kyle Coyle, lured by "promises of self-transcendence" [453]). An unkind reader might even suspect *Infinite Jest*, with its 96 pages of footnotes, to be "the drowsy monologue . . . [on] the modern athlete as commercial myth, with footnotes" (3) that Gary Harkness imagines at the start of *End Zone*.

4. While names of places provide critical clues here, there are also clues hidden in some characters' names, and one of these goes some way to explaining Hal's problems in the opening scene. It is strongly suggested that they are the result of a meeting with Luria Perec, a terrorist in the novel who shares his name with the Russian neurophysiologist, A. R. Luria, to whom Wallace refers in his 1997 essay collection *A Supposedly Fun Thing I'll Never Do Again* (144). In this collection, Wallace cites Luria's 1972 case history *Man with a Shattered World*, a volume that traces the efforts of a Russian soldier to recover from an injury to the parieto-occipital regions of the left hemisphere of his brain. As a result of this injury, Luria's patient lost what Luria calls the attribute that makes us "distinctly human—the ability to use language" (86), and the book charts his attempts to escape his diminished selfhood. By naming the terrorist who may be to blame for Hal's problems after Luria, Wallace subtly links the two, while also suggesting that Hal's problems result from a problem with the language capabilities of his brain. As Luria's study suggests, language skills are located in the left hemisphere, but since Hal is left-handed (260), he is likely to be right-brain dominant. An impairment to his left hemisphere, then, would explain why Hal can still play high-level tennis but cannot even type his thoughts out (he tells the Arizona Admissions panel that had he tried to write in the last year "it would look to you like some sort of infant's random stabs on a keyboard" [9]). In previous criticism of the novel, this issue of Hal's problems hasn't been fully addressed. In fact, in her essay on the novel Catherine Nichols goes so far as to suggest that Hal has no problem in the opening scene and instead sees his condition as a reflection of his success in connecting "his inner feelings and outward expressions" (13), with any failure of interaction indicating a failure on society's part. This fits her argument well, but it is somewhat idiosyncratic and doesn't explain why Hal is unable to type. It is perhaps also worth noting in this context that Wallace presumably chose the distinctive surname Perec to evoke the innovative French novelist Georges Perec. The combination of Luria and Perec in the

name of a terrorist, then, suggests Wallace's resistance to certain strands of brain research and innovative fiction.

5. I discuss the following passage and its relation to both the novel's scattered chronology and to addiction in *David Foster Wallace's Infinite Jest* (43–51).

6. As noted in The Unexamined Life example, Wallace links athleticism and addiction, and the addict's narrow desires seem to parallel the increasingly refined specialism of the modern athlete. It is appropriate, then, that at a nearby halfway house a character insists that most of the addicts there are also "metal people" with "heads full of parts" (733).

7. Intriguingly, one of the two times Hobbes uses the word *tennis* is in a context that combines two of *Infinite Jest*'s other obsessions, the union of countries and mathematics: "The skill of making, and maintaining Common-wealths, consisteth in certain Rules, as doth Arithmetique and Geometry; not (as Tennis-play) on Practise onely" (261).

8. Orin watches a documentary entitled *"SCHIZOPHRENIA: MIND OR BODY?"* and reflects that "the documentary's thesis was turning out pretty clearly to be *SCHIZOPHRENIA: BODY"* (47).

9. Inasmuch as any statement from the unreliable Orin can be trusted, it is at least revealing in this respect that he attributes his decision to quit tennis to the fact he had become "an empty withered psychic husk" (288).

10. Dualism and Descartes also come up in *The Broom of the System*, which refers to the pineal gland at the centre of the brain where "Descartes thought . . . mind met body" (148), while Wallace's *Everything and More* discusses both Descartes and Hobbes, though the latter is described as "something of a mathematical crank" (19).

11. This title, of course, echoes a film attributed to Hal's father entitled *"The Man Who Began to Suspect He Was Made of Glass"* (989 n.24) which suggests that Hal's struggle with his grandfather's materialism was his father's before him. As the holder of a "doctorate in optical physics" (63), James is also likely to have been drawn to Descartes as the philosopher explains the properties of light in his treatise "Optics" through a detailed discussion of a tennis ball. James's Cartesianism was apparently more obvious in the first draft of the novel, as Steven Moore has observed in his invaluable essay that James's motto for the academy was originally *"LARVADUS PRODEO*—a slip for *Larvatus Prodeo*, 'I advance masked,' which was the young Descartes' motto" (30). In addition, Moore observes that the first draft of the novel also included a passage on "the principle of induction, Descartes and St. Augustine" (93).

12. In *David Foster Wallace's Infinite Jest* I outline how religious hope is suggested in the novel through the elusive young player Dymphna, who shares a name with a Catholic Saint (59–61). In the context of this essay's attempt to trace some of the source texts for Wallace's novel, it may be worth noting that Wallace probably came across Saint Dymphna in DeLillo's *Americana*, where a school in southwestern New Hampshire is named after "The Nervous Breakdown Saint" (156).

REFERENCES

Burn, Stephen. *David Foster Wallace's Infinite Jest: A Reader's Guide*. New York: Continuum, 2003.

DeLillo, Don. *Americana*. New York: Penguin, 1989.

———. *End Zone*. Boston: Houghton Mifflin Co., 1972.

Descartes, René. *Discourse on Method and the Meditations.* Trans. F. E. Sutcliffe. Harmondsworth: Penguin, 1968.

————. "Optics." *The Philosophical Writings of Descartes.* Trans. John Cottingham, Robert Stoothoff, and Dugald Murdoch. Vol. 1. Cambridge: Cambridge University Press, 1985. 152–175.

Hobbes, Thomas. *Leviathan.* Ed. C. B. MacPherson. Harmondsworth: Penguin, 1985.

Kakutani, Michiko. "A Country Dying of Laughter. In 1,079 Pages." *New York Times* 13 Feb. 1996: B2.

Luria, A. R. *The Man with a Shattered World: The History of a Brain Wound.* Trans. Lynn Solotaroff. London: Cape, 1973.

Moore, Steven. "The First Draft Version of *Infinite Jest.*" *The Howling Fantods.* 161 pars. 28 May 2003. 18 Oct. 2003 <www.thehowlingfantods.com/ij_first.htm>.

Nichols, Catherine. "Dialogizing Postmodern Carnival: David Foster Wallace's *Infinite Jest.*" *Critique* 43 (2001): 3–16.

Russell, Bertrand. *History of Western Philosophy, and Its Connection with Political and Social Circumstances from the Earliest Times to the Present Day.* London: Allen, 1946.

Ryle, Gilbert. *The Concept of Mind.* Harmondsworth: Penguin, 2000.

Shakespeare, William. *Hamlet.* Ed. T.J.B. Spencer. Harmondsworth: Penguin, 1996.

Wallace, David Foster. *The Broom of the System.* London: Abacus-Little, 1997.

————. *Everything and More: A Compact History of* ∞. New York: W.W. Norton, 2003.

————. *Infinite Jest.* London: Abacus-Little, 1997.

————. "Order and Flux in Northampton." *Conjunctions* 17 (1991): 91–118.

————. "The Salon Interview: David Foster Wallace." Interview with Laura Miller. *Salon* 9 (1996): 42 pars. 16 Dec. 1997. 18 Oct 2003 <www.salon.com/09/features/wallace1.html>.

————. *A Supposedly Fun Thing I'll Never Do Again.* Boston: Little, Brown and Co., 1997.

Part II

Leaping Hurdles:
Race, Class, and Sports
in American Literature

White S(ox) vs. Indians: Sports and Unresolved Cultural Conflict in Native American Fiction

Greg Ahrenhoerster

Perhaps the most common theme in Native American fiction is the conflict felt by American Indian characters who try to succeed in white-dominated American society without abandoning or betraying their Native traditions. Many characters in these works search for a middle ground where the two cultures can coexist peacefully, but time and time again, this middle ground proves to be at best elusive—and at times intrinsically impossible—because of fundamental differences in the way whites and Native Americans view the world. This unpleasant reality frustrates not only the characters but also the well-intentioned reader who is often puzzled by this barrier separating the two cultures. One of the places that both whites and Native Americans have looked to (both in fiction and the "real world") as a potential common ground is the sports arena or ball field. Certainly the fact that all players are theoretically competing on even terms, coupled with the success of a few Native American athletes like Jim Thorpe and Billy Mills, suggests that the field or arena is a place free of cultural bias; however, this does not often prove to be the case. In two important articles about young Native American basketball stars who try to make the leap from the reservation to Division I college basketball, *Sports Illustrated* writer Gary Smith demonstrates that the arena walls are not thick enough to keep out the profound cultural differences that separate these two groups and weigh heavily on every step these young athletes take. It is, then, little surprise that many Native American authors have used sports references to try to explore this cultural conflict that haunts their characters.

The symbolic use of basketball by Native American authors has been discussed by a few critics, most notably Peter Donahue in "New Warriors, New Legend: Basketball in Three Native American Works of Fiction." In this essay, which focuses on the works of James Welch and Sherman Alexie, Donahue suggests that basketball has been both a blessing and a curse in Native American culture. Donahue astutely points out that one important cultural difference suggested in Alexie's *The Lone Ranger and Tonto Fistfight in Heaven* is the Native Americans' lack of emphasis on statistics and the final score (48). Whereas white culture often emphasizes box scores and statistics (often tied to money during contract negotiations), for Native Americans it is the playing of the game that is supposed to matter. Like some other aspects of traditional Native American culture (such as dancing, singing, and story-telling) sports and games were historically more than a simple pastime but were, in fact, an integral part of their spiritual life.

Native American sports, says Joseph Oxendine, are "steeped in tradition and intimately related to all phases of life, especially to ceremony, ritual, magic, and religion" (xii). Not only do sports appear in the stories and mythology of Native cultures—lacrosse, for example, "occurs in a surprisingly large number of traditional American Indian legends" (Vennum 301)—but sport is also frequently one of the ways in which Indians "create a bridge between themselves and the forces of nature" (Nabokov 9).

Obviously, it would be an overstatement to suggest that all Native Americans see sports as the means to some grand connection with nature, but certainly there is evidence in the sports references used by Native American authors that their characters are involved in much more than just a game. A clear example of this is Alexie's description of reservation-hero Silas Sirius, "who made one move and scored one basket in his entire career" (47). In the other characters' description of Silas, it is obvious that, though his final statistics are unimpressive, through basketball he got in step with the movement of the universe: "[H]e grabbed that defensive rebound, took a step, and flew the length of the court, did a full spin in midair, and then dunked the fucking ball. And I don't mean it looked like he flew, or it was so beautiful it was almost like he flew. I mean he flew, period" (47).

Such basketball references are deserving of critical attention, but it is also useful to analyze references to the more traditionally "white" sports of baseball and football, which are often used by Native American writers to emphasize the stark differences between white and Native American culture and to symbolize the confusion and angst felt by Native Americans who try to bridge this cultural gap.

Football and baseball are particularly powerful symbols because of their association with the boarding schools that young Native Americans were forced to attend in the early part of the twentieth century when the American government decided to solve the "Indian problem" by kidnapping Native children and indoctrinating them into white culture at boarding schools.[1] At these schools, the young boys were often forced to play both baseball and football, with the "best" schools, such as the Haskell Institute and the Carlisle Indian Industrial School, often parading their teams around the country to play grueling exhibition schedules. As some sports fans know, this is how the great Jim Thorpe got his start.

At the age of six Thorpe and his twin brother Charles were forcibly sent to a missionary boarding school twenty miles from their home. After his brother died, Jim was sent first to Haskell Institute in Lawrence, Kansas, and later to

Carlisle Indian Industrial School in Pennsylvania. Both Haskell and Carlisle were known for their successful sports teams, and at Carlisle Thorpe was subject to the coaching of Glenn "Pop" Warner, who had little regard for the Indians' cultural or spiritual beliefs about sports and who put his young athletes through notoriously grueling training and schedules (Oxendine 206–207).

As a result, it seems likely that even today for many Indians, white sports like football and baseball may be consciously or unconsciously linked to boarding schools and assimilation, one of the sadder chapters in the history of Native Americans. Gary Smith notes that the excitement felt by the friends and family of Crow basketball sensation Jonathan Takes Enemy over his college scholarship offers was somewhat tempered by the fact that almost every one of them "had a close relative who had been forcibly taken from his home by white government agents in the early 1900s and sent off to a faraway boarding school, where his hair was shorn, his Indian clothes and name were taken away, and he was beaten for speaking his own language" ("Shadow" 69). How many of them, Smith asks, "could chase an education without feeling an old pang in their bones?" ("Shadow" 69). This association, as well as the stark difference in the way the two cultures view sports, may explain why many Native American authors associate white sports with characters who have abandoned or been lured away from Indian culture.

An example of this is Rocky, Tayo's football-hero cousin, in Leslie Silko's *Ceremony*. Prior to the novel's opening, Tayo had abandoned his Native culture for the white world, and the novel describes what he must go through in order to return and be healed. Rocky is Tayo's foil, illustrating one alternative path Tayo could follow: reject his heritage and embrace white culture. Rocky's abandonment of Indian ways is illustrated both by his rejection of native ceremonies—such as his scoffing at Robert for placing cornmeal in the nose of a deer after killing it—and by his success in and understanding of white culture, specifically school and football: "He was an A-student and all-state in football and track. He had to win; he said he was always going to win. So he listened to his teachers, and he listened to the coach. They were proud of him. They told him, 'Nothing can stop you now except one thing: don't let the people hold you back.' Rocky understood what he had to do to win in the white outside world" (51). Indeed, it seemed as though Rocky was on track to succeed in the white world by following the white-sanctioned formula of fulfilling "the American dream" through sports: "He would be the first one ever to get a football scholarship, the first one to go with no help from the BIA or anyone" (91). But, as it does to the other young Indian men in the novel who try to embrace it, white society destroys Rocky; he is killed in the war.

Through one of the stories within the novel, we learn, along with Tayo, that whites are not intrinsically evil; they are the pawns of a despicable witch who cast an evil spell over the world at a witching contest a long time ago. The witch commanded that these men would, among other things, "grow away from the earth . . . the sun . . . the plants and animals" (135). One of the results of this "growing away" from the universe is the abandonment of Indian sports, which keep one in step with nature; just as the development of this new, white, way of looking at sports encourages individual success and, as "Texas roping" illustrates, a turning against nature. In this "sport of aging cowboys," the riders cruelly jerk down the steers as they flee, often resulting in the animals' injury or death. The anger of witnessing this horrible sport "made [Tayo] light headed," we are told, "but he did not talk about this other dimension of their perversion which, like the hunting of the mountain lion, was their idea of 'sport' and fun" (212–213). Clearly, Silko is associating the white conception of sports with the other "evil" things that, under the witch's spell, they brought to this land.

Louise Erdrich makes a similar connection between white sports and the negative aspects of the white world in *Love Medicine*. Although she refers to sports much less frequently than Silko, the undertones of Erdrich's few sports references echo those of *Ceremony*. When describing the events that lead to his journey to Hollywood, Nector Kashpaw reminds us that he, like Jim Thorpe, is a product of boarding school sports programs: "I got out of Flandreau [boarding school in South Dakota] with my ears still rung from playing football, and the first thing they said was 'Nector Kashpaw, go West! Hollywood wants you!'" (122). The reader is thus invited to associate boarding school football with the Hollywood Westerns in which Nector is brutally killed over and over again on the screen in the same way that Indians were destroyed by both bullets and boarding schools for decades.

Likewise, when Beverly "Hat" Lamartine, the urbanized Indian who has left the reservation for a job selling books door-to-door in the Twin Cities, proudly describes the son he has fabricated to con his customers into buying his product, he emphasizes the fact that the boy plays baseball: "His son played baseball in a sparkling-white uniform stained across the knees with grass. He pitched no-hitters every few weeks" (110). This association with baseball makes Hat's fictitious son less Indian and more white, indicating that he has lost touch with his heritage. This loss of understanding is made clear when Hat returns to the reservation and tries to retrieve the boy he believes is his son from Lulu and is completely dazzled by her boys' actions: "[T]hey moved in dance steps too intricate for the noninitiated eye to imitate or understand" (118). Ultimately, he is forced to retreat to the white world without a son, suggesting that the two worlds are incompatible.

In a chapter entitled "Crown of Thorns," Erdrich details the downward spiral of Gordie Kashpaw's life. We know that Gordie used to beat his wife June, probably because he drank too much, but Erdrich curiously associates the beatings with the sport of boxing: "He'd been a boxer in the Golden Gloves. But what his hands remembered now were the times they struck June." (213). This reference implies that it was corruption by the white world—through both alcohol and the white idea of violence as a sport—that, at least in part, led to Gordie's downfall. Admittedly, these sports references are not one of the primary focuses of Erdrich's novel, yet one cannot ignore the fact that Erdrich associates white sports with other, more clearly negative aspects of the white world.

A much less subtle denunciation of the white sports mentality is seen in Jack Forbes's vignette, "Only Approved Indians Can Play: Made in USA." In this tale, a basketball team from the Great Lakes region is awarded a victory over a team from Tucson in an all-Indian basketball tournament. Before the game can even begin, the Great Lakes team protests that the Tucson players are not all "real" Indians. The Great Lakes players "all had their BIA identification cards, encased in plastic [which] proved they were all real Indians, even a blonde-haired guy" (262). Most of the Tucson players do not have BIA cards, and one of them, a Tarahumara Indian, came from a people who lived off in the mountains, resisting the government's control (263). This makes it clear to some that he is not officially an Indian, because "all official Indians are under the whiteman's rule by now" (263). Finally the tournament directors agree that because they are not in the dictionary, "Tarahumaras don't exist," and they award the Great Lakes team the victory on the technicality (263). Just in case Forbes's message is not yet clear, after the Great Lakes team is declared the victor, a white BIA agent in the crowd gets tears in his eyes, saying to a companion, "God Bless America. I think we've won" (263).

Obviously, this story is filled with irony and satire, but it is making an important point about Native Americans adopting the white "win at all costs" mentality. It is significant that the players never even get to play the game—the whole point from the traditional Native standpoint—and are simply awarded an end-result, the win. The fact that the Indian mentality has been Anglicized is driven home when the Tarahumara man remarks that "his father and uncle had been killed by whites in Mexico and that he did not expect to be treated with prejudice by other Indians" (263).

As Donahue and others have discussed, there are at least two likely explanations for Native American authors' fascination with basketball. The first is the questionable origin of the sport. Although most whites will claim that basketball was invented in 1891 by James Naismith in Springfield, Massachusetts, many Indians contend that it is a traditional Native sport—usually in reference to the Southwest, Mexican, and Central American Indian sport Pok-Ta-Pok. Such is the belief of Sherman Alexie's character, Victor, of "Jesus Christ's Half-Brother Is Alive and Well on the Spokane Indian Reservation," who contends that "basketball was invented by an Indian long before that Naismith guy even thought about it" (127).

Another possibility is the fact that basketball does not carry the boarding-school stigma the way football and baseball do. Basketball has not been forced on Indians the way so many other aspects of white culture have been. In the last few decades, Indians have been drawn to the sport, and particularly in Montana and the Southwest they have been remarkably successful, especially at the high school level.

In his two articles about young Indian basketball stars, Gary Smith makes no secret of the wealth of basketball talent on reservations, with Indian schools winning ten Montana state high school basketball championships between 1980 and 1990 ("Shadow" 64). This remarkable dominance of a small segment of white society is not only satisfying but reminiscent of days gone by when their people thrived in other ways:

Of all the perplexing games that the white men had brought with him—frantic races for diplomas and dollar bills and development—here was one that the lean, quick men on the reservation could instinctively play. Here was a way to bring pride back to their hollow chests and vacant eyes, some physical means, at last, for poor and undereducated men to reattain the status they once had gained through hunting and battle. ("Shadow" 64)

Unfortunately, most Indians have not been able to gain any long-term reward from this high school success.

Whereas a significant number of African Americans have ridden college basketball scholarships out of the ghetto, Native American athletes seldom last more than a year at a university before returning to the reservation. This pattern has been so consistent that many college scouts refuse to even look at an Indian player, regardless of his or her reputation, for fear of yet another let-down ("Shadow" 65). Part of the problem is certainly white resistance and racial prejudice, but black athletes obviously face these obstacles as well yet manage to overcome them. Ultimately, Smith suggests, it is the Native American culture and belief system that dooms these young people.

One obstacle is the social structure of the tribe, which is very close knit. In most tribes, individuals are taught to look to friends and family for advice when making decisions ("Shadow" 70), hardly good training for the solitary life of an Indian at a large white university. Coupled with this is the elders' reluctance to lose their children to the white world. The case of "Sis" Becenti illustrates this problem. Becenti's father expected her to return to the reservation after her four years at Arizona State University, because the tribe needed her and she needed them. All of the Dine elders wrestled with the same problem: "Television sets were luring their children to a different dream, grant money from the tribal scholarship office was luring them off to college. If the covenant was broken between the land and the People . . . the tribe was doomed" (Smith "Woman" 57). For these reasons, the tribe expects, and almost encourages, the athletes to fail and return home. Dell Fritzler, a high school basketball coach at Plenty Coups High where Takes Enemy went to school, assesses the situation bluntly: "Like crabs in a bucket, that's how we are . . . whoever tries to get out, we yank him back down" ("Shadow" 70). Indians who do get out are viewed as traitors, as Fritzler again notes: "We want our young people to go off and show the world how great a Crow can be . . . but as soon as anyone starts trying or studying too hard, a lot of us say, 'Look at him. He's trying to be a white man'" ("Shadow" 70).

Not only is basketball not a solution for the Indians, it has, in fact, developed into something of a problem. Because so much attention is focused on high school basketball successes, the people develop what Dale Old Horn calls "pseudo pride" ("Shadow" 65). A victory on the court helps the tribe temporarily forget everyday misery, poverty, and racism; but it does not solve anything ("Shadow" 65). Smith puts it gently when he calls the Crows "the tribe that loved basketball too much" ("Shadow" 63), but former high school basketball star Myron Falls Down is more pessimistic. Like the alcohol and marijuana that have held his people back for decades, Falls Down suggests that *"basketball*, the way the Crows were using it, had become a drug too" ("Shadow" 70).

Through all of this pessimism, Smith paints the portraits of two Indians who are attempting to bridge the gap between cultures and succeed in the white world without abandoning their cultures. Takes Enemy had failed once but in 1991 was trying again to play college basketball. Becenti, thanks in large part to overwhelming support from her tribe (who, by the hundreds, drove five and a half hours to watch her play every home game), was the starting point guard on the Arizona State women's basketball team in 1993. Both attempts were seen as highly experimental. Becenti, Smith reminds us, is "a litmus test" ("Woman" 57). She and Takes Enemy will show whether it is possible to "learn the Anglos' strange ways and still return home" ("Woman" 57). Through these two examples, one can see why basketball is the ideal sport for representing both the violent clash and harmonious melding of cultures.

Alexie's fiction illustrates a less harmonious but still significant blending of white and Indian cultures through basketball. Alexie makes it clear that "Indians need heroes to help them learn how to survive" (49) and that on the reservation basketball is a source of heroes. Unfortunately, Alexie's characters exist in a world in which success is measured by white standards; this is what gives his stories their subtle sense of tragedy. Despite the fact that these heroes live on in reservation mythology, the reader is constantly reminded that, like Smith's real-life high school heroes, they never actually "make it" (to college? to the pros? off the reservation?). Even Julius Windmaker, who has "that gift, that grace, those fingers like a goddamn medicine man" (45), ends up drunk and washed up before he gets out of high school. Significantly, though, almost immediately after Julius's last game, in which "he just wasn't the ballplayer we all remembered or expected" (51), even as people are talking about the younger players and who looks promising, Julius is already being mythologized: "Everybody told their favorite Julius Windmaker stories too" (51). These tragic basketball heroes, who live on in stories and contribute to the culture in ways arguably more meaningful than they could as graduates of white colleges, are one of the most poignant literary symbols of the conflict between white and Native cultures.

Similarly, in James Welch's *Indian Lawyer* basketball is used as a symbol of a Native American's return home; however, in this case it is also, ironically, the instrument of his initial departure. Welch—a member of the Blackfeet tribe of Montana who, Smith reminds us, share "the Crows' tragedy" of loving basketball too much ("Shadow" 65)—creates a protagonist, Sylvester Yellow Calf, who does what few real-life Indians have done: He rides a basketball scholarship off the reservation. Sylvester does not just get by in the white world either; he dominates it. The owner of a law degree and a partnership in a prestigious law firm, Sylvester has a realistic chance to become a United States congressman. Sylvester is an intelligent and thoughtful man, deserving of his good fortune; but there is no question that his success in the white world results directly from his success on the basketball court. He was welcomed at college because of his basketball ability, and his reputation as a sports hero opens doors for him in the business world. Eventually, due in part to a scandalous affair and blackmail plot, Yellow Calf symbolically rejects the white world when he withdraws from the political race and takes a leave of absence from his job to handle a pro bono water-rights case on the Standing Rock Reservation in North Dakota. Few Indians get an opportunity to make such a decision themselves.

Despite the fact that basketball is Sylvester's ticket off of the reservation, the sport is primarily associated with his life back home. Through flashbacks we learn that as a child Sylvester was seldom without a basketball in his hand. Most of his childhood memories, good and bad, are tied to the sport. Although his basketball talents led to his position on the state parole board, he understands that things could have turned out differently. He recalls, after approving the parole of the brother of one of his old friends, Donny Little Dog, that Little Dog's parents were killed while driving to one of his basketball games. Their deaths marked the end of Donny's basketball career and the beginning of his life's decline. Furthermore, it was on a basketball court that Sylvester broke Stan Weintraub's nose, an event that marked the end of the special relationship between Sylvester, Stan, and Lena Old Horn, the guidance counselor who befriends and encourages Sylvester and whom both men love.

After using the sport as a means to a college degree and high standing in the "white" world, however, Sylvester curiously abandons it. Early in the novel he reveals to an admiring fan that he had not "touched a basketball in years" (47). Instead, he has taken up handball, which he plays with Ed Vance who epitomizes the white American lifestyle: wife, kids, mortgage, and all the other trappings. Although Vance is clearly jealous of Sylvester's success and exciting bachelor life, he is not about to give up his stability. Sylvester, however, seriously ponders settling down and marrying Shelly, his respectable white girlfriend, and essentially becoming another Ed Vance. Ed and their weekly handball games are as much a part of white culture as Sylvester's business suits, law degree, and political aspirations; and Welch implies through a sports reference that this culture is unhealthy for Sylvester. As he stands up to meet Patti Ann Harwood, the white woman who lures him into the scandal that almost destroys him, Sylvester grimaces because he had injured his back playing handball. "In all his years playing basketball," we are told, "he had never hurt his back" (72). This physical injury represents the damage that has been inflicted upon Sylvester's sense of culture. Basketball, we may well infer, is the sport he should be playing.

Yet this is not simply a matter of Indian culture (basketball) being clearly superior to white culture (handball). In fact, Sylvester is revered as a sports hero primarily by his white friends; at home he is respected "not because he had been a basketball player . . . but because he was Little Bird Walking Woman's grandson" (48). Sylvester's grandmother, a tribal elder, raised him after his parents abandoned him. She tried to teach him about his people, but he was "more interested in basketball and cross-country and girls" (156). Through most of the novel, Sylvester maintains only a distant interest in his culture. Although he wishes to help his people as a congressman, he remains strangely removed from them. This separation began when a white sportswriter, Ray Lundeen, wrote an article decreeing that Sylvester was a "winner" who would go on to better things, unlike his teammates who "will have had their brief moment in the sun and will fall by the wayside, perhaps to a life of drink and degradation" (103). As soon as Lundeen put these words on paper, it was as if Sylvester's course was set: He would be a "winner." Unfortunately, the words also caused him to become estranged from his teammates, whose "failure . . . [was] guarantee[d] . . . by his success" (105).

In this respect, basketball is another tool used by the white man to disrupt the lives of Native Americans. Just as his grandfather had been taken away to Carlisle Indian School years earlier, Sylvester was removed from his people by this white sports reporter and a college scholarship. Sylvester eventually adapts a "white" way of thinking, about both business success and sports. His new attitude toward sport is seen in his reminiscences about his last college game. He remembers the exact time on the clock when he fouled out and exactly how many points more than he (twenty-eight to seventeen) his rival Al Childers had scored—a fact that haunts him even though "he out-rebounded and out-assisted Childers" (98). Such attention to final statistics, with little regard to the actual quality of play, is a product of the influence white sports journalists have over Sylvester. Thus it is significant that after he rejects white culture he is seen playing basketball by himself back on the reservation, "going one on one with the only man who ever beat him" (349). The motion and action of dribbling and shooting a basketball for no purpose other than the enjoyment of the sport is clearly a cleansing ritual, washing away the white, capitalistic notions of winning and losing and "putting up good numbers."

Although some may prefer Welch's optimistic ending to Alexie's bleaker vision, it is clear that both men, like the other Native American authors discussed, see some connection between the struggle waged by many Indians to adapt their culture to the modern industrial world thrust upon them—a struggle they yearn to explain and explore—and sports. Of course they express this conflict in other ways as well, but given the complex history of white–Indian interaction through sports, these references are a most appropriate choice. It seems these writers have found that the best way to explain the tragedy and success, sorrow and joy of the Native American people is through these hero-traitor sportsmen and women.

NOTE

1. I have further discussed the symbolic use of baseball in American literature, including Native American literature, in "'I just hit .300—time to renegotiate my

contract': Baseball as a Symbol of Capitalism in Non-Sports Literature," in *Baseball/Literature/Culture: Essays 1995–2001.* Ed. Peter Carino (New York: McFarland, 2003).

REFERENCES

Alexie, Sherman. *The Lone Ranger and Tonto Fistfight in Heaven.* New York: HarperCollins, 1994.

Donahue, Peter. "New Warriors, New Legends: Basketball in Three Native American Works of Fiction." *American Indian Culture and Research Journal* 21.2 (1997): 43–60.

Erdrich, Louise. *Love Medicine.* New York: HarperCollins, 1993.

Forbes, Jack. "Only Approved Indians Can Play: Made in USA." *Earth Power Coming: Short Fiction in Native American Literature.* Ed. Simon Ortiz. Traile, AZ: Navajo Community College Press, 1983.

Nabokov, Peter. *Indian Running.* Santa Barbara, CA: Capra Press, 1981.

Oxendine, Joseph. *American Indian Sports Heritage.* Champaign, IL: Human Kinetics Books, 1988.

Silko, Leslie. *Ceremony.* New York: Penguin Books, 1977.

Smith, Gary. "Shadow of a Nation." *Sports Illustrated* 18 Feb. 1991: 60–74.

———. "A Woman of the People." *Sports Illustrated* 1 Mar. 1993: 54–63.

Vennum, Thomas, Jr. *American Indian Lacrosse: Little Brother of War.* Washington: Smithsonian Institution Press, 1994.

Welch, James. *The Indian Lawyer.* New York: W.W. Norton, 1990.

Basketball's Demands in Paul Beatty's *The White Boy Shuffle*

Tracy Curtis

The vigorous pace of basketball makes describing its action while also including a sense of the game's historical and social aspects challenging. Unlike baseball or football, basketball has a pace that requires broadcast commentators to delay observations on players' history or past games until official breaks in the action. Conversely, descriptions of basketball in literary or historical settings often feel too ponderous to convey the game's dynamism. In his memoir *Hoop Roots*, John Edgar Wideman remarks that writing in general focuses on "the alienating disconnect among competing selves," leading to writing about basketball that often "describes ball games the reader can never be sure anybody has ever played" (Wideman 10). Even in his tale about basketball's role in his life, he argues that the game's speed makes it antithetical to traditional reflection. Commenting on the place history has in basketball he says, "[t]he past is not forgotten when you walk onto the court to play. It lives in the Great Time of the game's flow, incorporating past present and future . . . a past that's irrelevant baggage unless you can access it instantaneously" (Wideman 9–10). He sets up a tension between the history that is useful in playing basketball and that which provides material for narrative.

If history is to be used in the game, the player must recall and react almost simultaneously. A split second later, the next play will have a different story. In contrast to this practical history, the written version is often linear, formal, and driven by cause and effect. Within a game, linear narrative is neither present nor relevant. Written history requires pause and reflection. Narration of these reflections typically follows familiar patterns. Yet writing about basketball by nonplayers indicates the inefficacy of explorations of the sport through traditional narrative. Players often frustrate reporters' attempts to explain trends within a season. Questioners ask whether an incident in a previous game will affect the next game with that team. The players' cliché that mistakes were made then and that this game is a different one seems to explain nothing (Shields 207–208).[1] However, this is true only in terms of the cause and effect found in traditional narrative. Wideman's description of basketball history clarifies why the typical questions garner unsatisfying, nonnarrative responses from players. The questions do not reflect players' experience of the game. Yet readers demand the stories that traditional narrative enables. To satisfy those expectations, writers often attempt to explain players' actions through recollection of other plays. Past game trends or players' personal histories substitute for elaborate explanations about play itself. For readers, the narrative arc needs to be logical and relatively clear.

Paul Beatty, in his 1996 novel *The White Boy Shuffle*, writes about the sport in a way that captures its dynamic moments while acknowledging the social and historical contexts that shape basketball and basketball players. He uses satire to critique basketball's place in the protagonist's life. Satire works well for such a treatment because its use of the absurd allows different historical moments to be juxtaposed. Satire also allows a mixture of realistic elements with those purely fantastic. Even with absurd images and ideas, satirical narratives are coherent; however, their unity lies in the points they emphasize rather than in the method of the telling. Using satire, Beatty flows easily between basketball history and individual games. Beatty's antihero is a black kid named Gunnar Kaufman. The book follows his development from junior high school through young adulthood, marriage, and fatherhood. As the book begins, Gunnar's mother moves him and his sisters from predominantly white Santa Monica to a West Los Angeles black neighborhood Beatty calls Hillside. The culture shock and the ridicule he suffers continue until he learns to play basketball. Then his fortunes change miraculously. Having formed a tentative friendship with a boy in his junior high school, Nicholas Scoby, Gunnar finds himself on a basketball court at recess. Never having played before, Gunnar surprises everyone except Scoby with his skills. Trying to defend himself, Gunnar inadvertently dunks (Beatty 74). After having been afraid of making a fool of himself, being a detriment to the team, and getting hurt, Gunnar takes to the game as though it is his destiny.

This idea of fate infuses Beatty's depiction of Gunnar, who describes himself as destined by his family of "coons, Uncle Toms, and . . . boogedy-boogedy retainers" (5). In addition to the pressure from his lineage, Gunnar feels himself steered by the school system, by his friends, and perhaps most of all, by the expectations that he comes to realize people have of him. Soon after the playground dunk, strangers begin telling him how they look forward to his next game. For a time, basketball serves him well. However, others' investment in his play changes its effect on him. Gunnar becomes a commodity. Though he sees the process, he cannot interrupt it. For a short time, he has compelling reasons to love the game. Then the possibility of his neighbors' vicarious pride and his own profit saddle him with the weight of the community's hopes.

His friend Scoby is similarly burdened. Unlike Gunnar, Scoby focuses intensely, almost obsessively, on things that interest him. He is a jazz aficionado, whose way of ensuring that he misses nothing is to listen to all jazz in alphabetical order. His gaming obsession takes a similar form. He tells Gunnar that when he discovered hopscotch as a younger boy, he fell in love with its process (119). He became perfect at that game, which he played until the boys who chased him home daily caught him and beat him. When his mother made him play basketball with the boys who tormented him, Scoby developed into the skillful player Gunnar meets. By seventh grade, he has become a one hundred percent from the field shooter. Beatty exaggerates his skill to portray Scoby as a basketball miracle; however, not everyone responds without suspicion. After enjoying a time of admiration, Scoby finds himself accused of using magic or evil to maintain his on-court perfection. His skill makes him the target of extremes of admiration and envy.

Beatty shows how futile and how dangerous a community's hoop dreams can be. He lampoons basketball from the very beginning, marking both Gunnar's on-court success and the first time Scoby calls Gunnar "nigger" as his points of entry into the community. This parallel scripts ambivalence into Gunnar's basketball success, as "nigger," whether it comes from friend or foe, remains historically loaded. Beatty expresses both an appreciation for the game and an awareness of its danger. His work fits into an African American satirical tradition, which Darryl Dickson-Carr describes as having begun as a way to protest the illogic of slavery that evolved as a means to comment on the slowness of the progress toward equality (Dickson-Carr 3, 9–10). Dickson-Carr also cites John R. Clark's definition of degenerative satire "as a means of exposing modalities of terror and of *doing violence* to cultural forms that are overtly or covertly dedicated to terror" (qtd. in Dickson-Carr 17). In *The White Boy Shuffle,* Beatty comments on both limited progress and abject institutional terror in a number of social, economic and political arenas. He uses various methods in his satire, including absurdity, the grotesque, historical allusion, and shifts in genre. Although the book is not about basketball primarily, an examination of Beatty's satirical treatment of the game yields an understanding of how the sport acts as a social force that can exert dangerous levels of control over the lives of young black men.

From the first moment Gunnar grabs a basketball, the game's process and history collapse. Gunnar's assimilation to basketball and the neighborhood involves achieving the proper look. Soon after his playground demonstration, he replaces his skate shoes with basketball sneakers, plain white Adidas ones costing nearly $200. As he enters the "Tennies from Heaven," he faces credit checks, "shoes sewn by eight-year-old Sri Lankans" and shoes called "Air Idi Amin Fire Walker" that are made to resemble an African mask (88–89). In this brief account, Beatty shows how socioeconomic and cultural exploitation unite as basketball is packaged and sold. The store's name invokes Hollywood fantasy while the exposition notes how those who make the shoes are exploited. Gunnar constructs an identity for himself using the labor of children who remain largely anonymous. His age and relative apathy make him a perfect target for the sneaker manufacturers' marketing. Companies employ various gimmicks, such as the Idi Amin sneaker, to appeal to African American consumers. They play on superficial cultural interest in objects that invoke Africa while relying on consumers' ignorance of the history of African suffering that the reference to Idi Amin invokes. Beatty critiques these marketing and manufacturing practices along with consumers' willingness to spend money for the latest trend presented to them. While Gunnar remains much more empowered than the children who make his shoes, his power is nothing compared to that of the companies that target him. He and his community are complicit in his disempowerment because they embrace the trappings of basketball as signs of success.

As his skill increases, so does his vulnerability to sneaker corporations. By the time he reaches high school, Gunnar has become a well-known player. His reputation garners him a spot in Nike's legendary basketball camp. This episode illustrates how young athletes become subjects of commodification while believing corporate outreach is purely beneficent. For the few pages that camp occupies, the novel becomes epistolary. Beatty's use of the form, which traditionally conveys unbridgeable distances, illustrates the gap that opens up between him and his community once he becomes protomarketable. In the neighborhood, scoring matters, but so do aesthetics and personality. Statistics govern the camp, which is strictly hierarchical. Players are ranked. Gunnar is number one hundred, last, which means that he showers and eats after every one else. In an e-mail home, he assures his mother that "the condescending white people are feeding" him (143). Gunnar's commentary emphasizes both his caustic wit and his awareness of his position. At camp, his value is only as a player. He views his treatment as unprofessional, unethical, and racist. Gunnar's contact with staff seems limited to their gestures and yelling. With no words exchanged, one coach shows him thousands of dollars that he could take for an agreement to matriculate (148). His only other report of direct contact with a coach occurs when one from Wyoming Tech yells at him for a reckless pass. To his first high school coach, Shimimoto, Gunnar writes, "I put my nose on his forehead and told him if he ever raised his voice in my direction again I'd kill him" (150). This is Gunnar's first attempt at intimidation; it works. Aware of Gunnar's skill, the coach begs for forgiveness.

With the exception of the time he bests one of the camp's stars, Gunnar is treated badly. The fact that he notices the staff's poor behavior differentiates him from his fellow campers. Joking, Gunnar lets Scoby know of the coaches' interest in him, saying they want to know "your quickness-to-speed ratio. Shit like that. . . . [T]hey really want to get to know you as a person" (144). His sarcasm illustrates his awareness that the camp does not exist for the young players' benefit. However, his fellow campers adjust to their poor treatment with sheepishness or compliance. Gunnar remains amazed at his roommates' ability to focus on basketball during their spare time after a day of nothing but the sport. He is nearly alone in recognizing how they are being groomed for sale.

Beatty comments on the permutations of this commodification. The neighborhood has a stake in the reputation of its basketball team. "People who didn't give a fuck about anything other than keeping their new shoes unscuffed all of a sudden had meaning to their lives" (116). Unlike that of the coaches, the community members' interest in the team has no connection to their employment. Beatty conveys the seriousness of the investment by depicting Gunnar's friend, a dedicated gang member called Psycho Loco, parading in front of the opposition's bench using a sawed-off shotgun to threaten anyone who fouls Scoby. The image is wildly exaggerated and implies that in a community whose members receive little respect from outside, basketball affords possibilities for power and acclaim largely unavailable in other arenas. Although most neighborhood residents do not bring weapons, they do treat basketball as more than a mere game. Once Gunnar and Scoby begin representing their neighborhood, their play, which had been a means of self-definition, enjoyment, and bonding, becomes their primary responsibility to their neighbors. As this responsibility grows, the community pressure becomes as dangerous as that from outside. For people outside the community, Gunnar is a commodity long before he ever plays in a televised game. For those within the neighborhood, both Gunnar and Scoby represent a success they can all share. While basketball is not the only realm in which people from the neighborhood can be transcendent, it is one of the most visible. People praise their achievements and encourage their focus on basketball, often ignoring other aspects of the boys' lives.

Scoby, the jazz aficionado, fantasizes about one day climbing high enough to see his shadow on a cloud. His dreams inspire Gunnar to create dreams of his own. Although he is initially shy, Gunnar develops into a poet. Both are intellectually curious and good students. Yet other than their Phyllis [*sic*] Wheatley High School coach Shimimoto, no one involved in their playing takes interest in the rest of their lives. Scoby continues his jazz listening, which for the most part people ignore. At the same time that he becomes a ball player, Gunnar begins writing; his work becomes public when he sprays his first poem, "Negro Misappropriation of Greek Mythology or, I know Niggers That'll Kick Hercules's Ass" on a wall soon after he moves into the neighborhood (85–86). Although it takes some time for everyone to connect the poet to the poem, Gunnar cultivates two public personae at once. Scoby, on the other hand, has no public persona outside basketball. Their neighbors' pride depends upon the attention the boys receive. This factor is another that differentiates the boys' attachment to the sport. Both Gunnar's community and wider audiences grow to respect his poetry, giving him an alternative to basketball that serves his neighbors' needs. Although Scoby appreciates jazz, he is no musician. Only his closest friends know of his interest. Even they see it as a peculiar personality quirk and not something that inspires their bragging as basketball and Gunnar's poetry do. No one encourages Scoby's nonbasketball interest.

Early in high school, the exclusive attention paid to their basketball skills hurts both boys. However, Gunnar's lackadaisical attitude about basketball protects him. Unlike Scoby, Gunnar feels little pressure to play well. When the coach praises him for maintaining his cool, Gunnar refuses to disappoint him by telling him that his cool is due to lack of investment. At the free throw line, in response to the local crowd's cry of "we need these," Gunnar thinks, "[w]e?

I didn't even need these free throws" (117). Neither schoolmates nor neighbors nor coplayers consider his style to be caused by anything other than a steely demeanor. The bragging rights surrounding the game are so important to everyone else that no one can imagine Gunnar's true lack of interest. Because Gunnar remains unconcerned, he has energy left over after he plays.

While Gunnar plays well without giving much thought to the game, Scoby pays a kind of constant attention. His shooting game is perfect. The fact that Scoby never misses makes people worship and fear him. The scrutiny disturbs Scoby from its onset; as observers grow more hostile, the pressure's effects become more obvious. Fans go from tattooing "Nick Scoby is God" on their chests to throwing "bananas, coconuts, nooses, headless dolls" because by the time the two play for Boston University together, Nicholas inspires fear (118, 193). He has no models for being a person of his temperament and for handling this strange attention. His mother, Beleeta "Queen Nairobi" Scoby, could have provided a model had she been as flawless or as hated as her son. Before Scoby's birth, she was the go-to person for the Los Angeles Thunderbirds, a roller derby team (68). She watches her highlight reels and revels in those days, cheering for her younger self while watching crowds at the Los Angeles Forum do the same. Scoby inherits her athleticism and ability to fascinate a crowd while never gaining her enjoyment for the attention. His renown brings with it a great deal of pressure.

The attention overwhelms Nicholas so much by early high school that Gunnar advises him to miss a shot occasionally and the coach tells him to get used to the attention or quit basketball. Scoby can do neither. To Gunnar's suggestion, he replies, "I can't even try. Something won't let me" (118). Gunnar assesses the situation:

[S]ometimes the worst thing a nigger can do is perform well. Because then there is no turning back. We have no place to hide . . . no reclusive New England hermitage for xenophobic geniuses like Bobby Fischer and J. D. Salinger. Successful niggers can't go back home and blithely disappear into the local populace. American society reels you back to the fold. "Tote that barge, shoot that basketball, lift that bale, nigger ain't you ever heard of Dred Scott?" (118–119)

The use of "nigger" is important here because it defines a social role. Scoby performs well; but his performances are, in a sense, not his property. Beatty invokes Dred Scott, whose lawsuit for his and his wife's freedom stretched on for years and ended in failure. Scoby resembles Scott in that his protestations for others to end their investments in him fail. In this instance, "nigger" marks him as a member of a class rather than an individual. Despite his perfection, he is not considered a genius as J. D. Salinger and Bobby Fischer are; instead, people attribute his success to evil. Fischer, the chess prodigy, and Salinger, the reclusive writer, are legends yet live in relative obscurity. Through the use of these two figures and Scott, Beatty points out that no black community is sacrosanct. While Fischer and Salinger can hide undisturbed because the areas where they choose to live are free from prying eyes, Scoby has no such place to disappear. "American society" does not grant black neighborhoods freedom from surveillance. To mistake momentary neglect for privacy is to have been lulled into complacency. However, the inability to escape attention also comes from within the black community. Because both Scoby and Gunnar act as emissaries for those who either cannot or will not leave the neighborhood, the boys continue playing for longer than it benefits them. Without the two friends' public lives, their neighbors would have to face the profundity of their isolation from mainstream society. Eventually Gunnar and Scoby serve the same function for people they do not know. When they play for Boston University, most of the teams and fans they encounter are white. However, black people with little traditional connection to the teams attend games to cheer for them. About a Columbia game Gunnar notes, "all of Harlem was in the gym" (193). During their basketball careers, their African American fans increase their investment in the two friends' playing.

The responsibilities placed on them become so excessive that neither wants to continue playing basketball. Beatty's satire works particularly well in considering an aspect of basketball seldom mentioned in sports narratives—how to get out. In many basketball tales, the narrators age out either early or late.[2] Little is written about going out at the peak of one's game, which is what Gunnar and Scoby want. Beatty makes this desire entirely reasonable while painting the expectations put upon the two as excessive at best and absurd and dangerous at worst. While both realize that they are being asked too much, Beatty uses Gunnar as the more active objector. The signs that he will leave the game appear while he is still in high school. Fed up with administration, fellow students, and the coach at El Campesino Real High School, Gunnar makes his first basketball exit in dramatic fashion. His new school, with the three other bused-in starters, plays his neighborhood school. Local media play up competition between Gunnar and Scoby, referring to Scoby's success as voodoo induced and touting Gunnar's return from the Valley as a civilizing force. Gunnar alters the roster to highlight his and the other bused students' positions. The unwitting announcer reads the revised card which contains the names, "Anthony 'Rastus' Price," "Anita 'Aunt Jemima' Appleby," and "Tommy 'Nigger T' Mendoza." The reading ends with, "first team all-city, second team all-American, Hillside's own Gunnar 'Hambone, Hambone, Have you Heard' Kaufman" (164). Gunnar's redubbed teammates chuckle, clearly in on the joke. After the card is read, Gunnar exposes his formerly hidden face and performs a minstrel routine. He has cold cream around his lips and wears white gloves. His stoop and shuffle draw a roar from the crowd and ire from his coach. Gunnar's performance brings critical attention to his function on that team. His invocation of black-face minstrelsy provokes both an in-group appreciation of how ridiculous the tension in this situation is and a pointed critique of how he is viewed and used by the Valley school.[3] In addition to helping the team improve its record, he and the other students make the school appear fully integrated. At the game described above, Gunnar burns his uniform and abandons his team. As he takes a seat beside his former coach, the fans take his behavior as an affirmation of his commitment to them rather than a rejection of basketball. Beatty scripts an absurd scene to show how players are made spectacles even at the high school level. Gunnar can escape his basketball obligations momentarily by exchanging one kind of performance for another, which leaves most of his audience satisfied.

Scoby, on the other hand, has fewer visible nonbasketball skills than Gunnar and does not have an opportunity to return home triumphantly during high school. These factors lead people to take his playing for granted even more. Their reliance on him causes Scoby to internalize the pressure, leaving him little route for escape that is not self-destructive. In many ways, Scoby is more typical of high-profile basketball players than Gunnar, in that fans are interested only in his playing and in any controversy that surrounds him. By the time the two begin college, the differences in their treatment have serious impact. Although both boys do well academically, only Gunnar is recruited. In a scene that burlesques college interviews, a Boston University recruiter joins Gunnar, his mother, Scoby, and their friend Psycho Loco in the Kaufman kitchen for a game of spades. The recruiter woos Gunnar with the promise that Boston University's recent purchase of an Ivy League membership will pay off for him. Scoby, whose nonbasketball life has been ignored, produces his SAT scores and a copy of his transcript, saying "[w]hat about me? Can I go?" (161). His actions surprise the others who are present, and may even surprise the reader, as Scoby's academic skill is seldom mentioned after the boys leave junior high school. The scene is notable because of the two boys' positions. Everyone speaks on Gunnar's behalf. Although they treat him as though he is an older version of the hapless child he was when he moved to the neighborhood, Gunnar has started making independent decisions, including turning down Harvard because of his disdain for its culture. Yet when they meet with the recruiter, his mother wants him to go to Boston where his paternal ancestors lived during the Revolutionary War. Scoby asks about the social atmosphere that Boston has to offer a black student. Psycho Loco asks about married student housing. Ms. Jenkins, the recruiter, gives Gunnar the first indication that his poetry has a following in Boston. The people closest to him and a woman he has just met consider various aspects of his life. Yet Scoby, who also has exceptional grades and test scores, has been ignored. He gets to college because of his presence during the recruiter's visit with Gunnar but again receives little encouragement to explore interests beyond sport.

At Boston University, Gunnar's poetry makes him famous; his dissatisfaction with that fame leads him to act out more forcefully than he had with basketball. On the first day of classes, fellow students in his poetry workshop behave obsequiously toward him when they learn that he is the "unknown street poet" whose works they have read (178). Having already responded to his classmates' presentation of their idols with derision, Gunnar literally flees the classroom, stripping himself naked along the way. The feeling that he has no common ground with these kids, who are like him in so many ways, causes an immediate crisis (179). While the episode is absurd, it shows Gunnar adjusting his role in the world. The changes he makes here are crucial. He stops attending classes, focuses on his relationships with his wife and his friend, and returns to basketball because its familiarity is comforting. Yet he conforms less and less to basketball-based expectations. His classmates' bizarre behavior spurs Gunnar to contend with his power as a poet and to become self-directed.

Scoby has no similar outlet. In fact he has little other than basketball and his friendship with Gunnar and Gunnar's wife Yoshiko. The latter provides less succor as Gunnar settles into his marriage and the relationship with his wife becomes primary. While Gunnar suddenly finds himself pulled in several directions, Scoby seems committed only to basketball. Even his alphabetical journey through jazz suffers. He skips several letters in the alphabet to get to Sarah Vaughan, who in his words is "not one of those tragic niggers white folks like" (194). This break in Scoby's systematic approach to life signals a crisis. One might expect him to neglect his hobby or change his methods as the activities of adulthood take more of his time. Yet he has no such distractions. As Gunnar contemplates his purpose in life, Palomino, the college coach and Bobby Knight parody, tells him that his purpose is to make free throws and return to play defense. Gunnar can respond with "[f]uck that" (190). Scoby seems to neither trust the coach's assessment of basketball's importance nor express his frustrations. He does not try to leave the game. As Gunnar has his wife as a confidante, he expresses to her his worries about Nicholas, with whom he is unable to talk. In one letter home, he questions Nicholas's sanity three times, writing about the puppetry under which Scoby toils: "Nicholas sees the strings. . . . Every now and then the puppet-master hands him a pair of wooden scissors—Charlie Parker, Thelonious Monk, Sarah Vaughan, an open jump shot—and Scoby thinks he's free" (194). Although much of this novel is flippant, Beatty changes tone here, contrasting this observation with many of Gunnar's wry ones. He predicts that Scoby's own methods will fail to help him escape others' control over him. As Gunnar's writing leads him to become a reluctant student spokesman at a campus antiapartheid rally and as a result more famous around campus, Scoby spirals further downward. Diagnosed with homesickness, he tries to recreate Los Angeles in Boston. Beatty returns to the absurd in his description of Scoby's behavior. For example, "[h]e plants palm trees [and tries] to pay some Puerto Ricans to act Mexican for a day" (203). The bizarre nature of his attempts both indicate his insanity and predict his failure. Faced with extreme alienation on the East Coast and an inability to get home to the West, Scoby commits suicide.

His failure to thrive is tied to Gunnar's successful escape. Gunnar abandons his concern for the game as his talent and notoriety as a poet grow. At the aforementioned rally, he questions African Americans' commitment to antiapartheid work and suggests a willingness to die as the truest indicator of dedication. Although Gunnar explains to Scoby that he does not mean to suggest suicide literally, instead wishing to prompt people to care more deeply about one another, Scoby sees words as directions (204). He jumps off the law school roof and becomes one of many black people whose suicide notes Gunnar receives. After Scoby's death, Gunnar returns to Los Angeles for the funeral and drops out of school. Although predictably his attempts at an anonymous life fail, no one expects him to play basketball again. Scoby's death enables both of them to leave the game, a feat that they seemed unlikely to accomplish as long as their skills kept them competitive. Only after such a dramatic separation from the sport does Beatty's text point to possibilities for life outside it. When Gunnar goes home again, his position as a spokesperson, albeit a reluctant one, replaces his public basketball persona. He creates a forum for his neighbors to testify about their lives, an opportunity that they, along with those strangers who send Gunnar their suicide notes, embrace. Still, he must contend with his neighborhood's constant surveillance by the state and with his neighbors' investment in him. He was right about the jeopardy in performing well. Obscurity is not an option. Instead Gunnar's and Yoshiko's lives become a protoreality show. Each night, helicopters from police and television stations hover above the motel where Gunnar and Yoshiko live. She gives birth on live television. The neighborhood never frees itself from surveillance. Nor does Gunnar escape his duty to the neighborhood. By garnering attention and returning to the neighborhood, he still bridges the gap between his neighbors and the outside world.

Beatty's novel portrays the hold that basketball can have over young African American men. Both his main character Gunnar and Gunnar's best friend Scoby seem destined for on-court success. Although their participation in organized ball affords them educational opportunities, it also damages the pair by limiting what is expected of them and tolerated from them in other arenas. When they step on to the court, Gunnar and Scoby take with them the responsibility to make up for a history of the community's exploitation. Gunnar notes that Scoby doesn't realize that he remains a puppet no matter what strategies he employs to alleviate his suffering. This observation reflects one of the book's primary themes. Although people try to escape their scripted roles, external control remains intact, especially when others have a stake in the performance. Beatty's satire portrays connections between a moment on court and the indefatigable pursuit of fugitive slaves. His use of minstrelsy comments on the racial spectacle that organized basketball can be. His work successfully presents the game as a microcosm of what the world will offer Gunnar and Scoby, eventually showing how each young man, their families, friends, and neighbors would have been better served had they never moved their game from the outdoor local courts.

NOTES

1. David Shields follows the Seattle Supersonics through a season as a reporter for the *Seattle Weekly*. As part of his work, he analyzes coverage of the team.

2. The writers of basketball narratives noted here are no exception. John Edgar Wideman writes his memoir in part because he feels that his body is getting too old for playground ball. Shields writes that he has always loved basketball but was never good enough to play competitively after adolescence.

3. For a discussion of minstrelsy's effects on various audiences, see Mel Watkins, *On the Real Side: Laughing, Lying, and Signifying—The Underground Tradition of African-American Humor That Transformed American Culture, From Slavery to Richard Pryor* (New York: Simon and Schuster, 1994) 393–394.

REFERENCES

Beatty, Paul. *The White Boy Shuffle*. Boston: Houghton Mifflin, 1996.

Dickson-Carr, Darryl. *African American Satire: The Sacredly Profane Novel*. Columbia: University of Missouri Press, 2001.

Shields, David. *Black Planet: Facing Race during an NBA Season*. New York: Crown, 1999.

Watkins, Mel. *On the Real Side: Laughing, Lying, and Signifying—The Underground Tradition of African-American Humor That Transformed American Culture, From Slavery to Richard Pryor*. New York: Simon and Schuster, 1994.

Wideman, John Edgar. *Hoop Roots: Playground Basketball, Love, and Race*. Boston: Houghton Mifflin, 2001.

"Fairways of His Imagination": Golf and Social Status in F. Scott Fitzgerald's Fiction

A. Fletcher Cole

F. Scott Fitzgerald famously remarked in his short story "The Rich Boy" that "the very rich . . . are different from you and me" (317). And Ernest Hemingway famously retorted: "Yes, they have more money."[1] Hemingway might also have said that they play more golf. Through a number of his writings, Fitzgerald posits golf as a marker of success and social elitism. The importance of tradition and "fair play" in golf and its sharp division between amateurism and professionalism help inform his masterpiece *The Great Gatsby* and the stories "Winter Dreams" and "What a Handsome Pair!" The country club often occupies the center of its community, and it provides a gate that both excludes the lower classes but also admits them for mingling with their superiors. Membership in a particular club acts as a determiner of social—even moral—acceptability in "Bernice Bobs Her Hair" and "A Freeze-Out." Golfing prowess is occasionally mentioned to establish quickly a character as a member of the elite class. Thus the reader finds golf intertwined with some of the class-related themes that concern Fitzgerald most: social position and acceptability, mobility, and the interclass romance. This interest in the sport and the choices Fitzgerald makes about when to employ golf—even as a minor detail—reveal that he saw the sport as a reflection of his understanding of the effects of America's social stratification.

A few critics have considered Fitzgerald's work in light of sports, and others have mentioned golf as part of a broader explication of particular texts. Christian Messenger devotes a section of *Sport and the Spirit of Play* to Fitzgerald, and Michael Oriard's *Sporting with the Gods* gives Fitzgerald several pages, but both focus mainly on his obsession with football.[2] Alice Hall Petry and John Kuehl each mention "Winter Dreams" but only in passing as part of broader readings. In a 1984 article, Richard Lessa deals with sports in *Gatsby*, including a helpful section on the role of golf in defining Jordan Baker's personality, but does not examine the short stories. Neil Isaacs's

"'Winter Dreams' and Summer Sports" places the short story into a context of American sporting life in the 1920s but does not examine other works. "What a Handsome Pair!" inspired an interesting article by James L. W. West, but though he recognizes the role of athletics and competition in the story, the significance of golf as the principal sport goes without comment. In short, no major work specifically traces the role of golf throughout multiple Fitzgerald writings, which is the basic goal of this study.

Even when "Bernice Bobs Her Hair" appeared in 1920, golf was already associated with class-based exclusivity. The expensive equipment and substantial leisure time required by golfers had given the sport the reputation of elitism (Wind 46). And the expansion of public courses encouraged private country clubs to invest in lush clubhouses to lure wealthy golfers—and even status-seeking nongolfers—to purchase memberships and therefore provide financial stability (48–49). Thus golf was widely seen as a game for the wealthy and the country club as a private enclave, despite a growing base of popularity. It is at a private club that the story opens at "the first tee of the golf-course," from which the clubhouse looks like a "yellow expanse over a very black and wavy ocean" ("Bernice" 25). This ocean turns out to be a human one, comprising "curious caddies, a few of the more ingenious chauffeurs, the golf professional's deaf sister"—people unwelcome inside (25). If the reader misses the point, Fitzgerald makes a contrast between this crowd and those "stray, diffident waves who might have rolled inside had they so desired" (25). The divide between the members and nonmembers is emphasized by his sharp concluding shift of attention from the "gallery" outside to the participants inside (25). Thus, the difference between inside and outside is not merely one of physical position but of social position.

In this introduction, Fitzgerald uses golf explicitly to establish two important themes he will explore: social inclusion/exclusion and play. By referring to the crowd outside as an "ocean," he obscures any individual characteristics. Who these people are is not important; what they do for a living is, because it explains why they are excluded. They are all service providers for the wealthy: caddies who carry their bags, chauffeurs who drive their cars, and pros who provide personal instruction. They are at the country club because of their menial professions, which also ensure they will not be admitted to the private clubhouse reserved for the social elites. They become spectators, like the gallery at a golf tournament, and the real game is not outside with them but "inside" where the young men and women of the privileged class look for romance. Two themes, exclusion and play, are therefore quickly introduced through golf and prepare the reader for a story about a girl trying to fit into an unfamiliar circle of elites, to "play the game."

Like "Bernice," other stories provide instances in which golf is used to develop themes or establish character. In *This Side of Paradise*, Fitzgerald calls Rosalind "a delight to watch . . . move about a room, walk along a street, *swing a golf club* [italics mine], or turn a 'cartwheel'" (196). Rosalind's golfing prowess places her among a privileged class and inevitably she leaves poor boy Amory in the rough. In "The Captured Shadow," Basil's rival for lovely

Evelyn Beebe is Andy Lockhart, the "handsome," and "successful" Yale baseball captain who also happened to be "winner of the Western Golf Championship at eighteen" (418). When Basil finds him at Evelyn's house—cutting a dashing figure "in golf knickerbockers" (418)—he is as intimidated as any of Andy's golf rivals. Jim Powell, who opens an academy for rich kids to learn slumming in "Dice, Brassknuckles, & Guitar," is crushed to realize that to his patrons he is like a "golf professional who, though he may fraternize, loses his privileges with the sun-down, [who] may look in the club window" but not dance (249). But, of course, the golf pro, "being English, holds himself proudly below his patrons" because he is accustomed to social class stratification (249). Powell, contrarily, is profoundly disappointed—a comment on both his personal pride and the false presumption of America as a classless society. Fitzgerald subtly uses golf's elitist associations to underscore class distinctions.

Fitzgerald's best-known work, *The Great Gatsby,* introduces Jordan Baker, the best-known golfer in Fitzgerald's work. Because of the massive criticism *Gatsby* has generated, her character has been examined more rigorously than that of other golfers. For example, she fits in nicely with autobiographical studies of *Gatsby.* Although narrator Nick Carraway does not at first recognize the famous golfer, upon Daisy's announcement that Jordan is in town to "play in the tournament . . . over at Westchester," he recalls seeing her face "look[ing] out at me from many rotogravure pictures of the sporting life at Asheville and Hot Springs and Palm Beach" (23).[3] Jordan, like many of Fitzgerald's characters, was based upon a real-life acquaintance. In this case, she was Edith Cummings, a schoolmate of love interest Ginevra King and, at the time *Gatsby* was published, an acclaimed golfer (Lehan 66).[4] She was also, like Jordan, a child of privileged upbringing and an active socialite.

The Baker–Cummings connection is helpful for scholars who wish to place Fitzgerald—and his characters—into a proper historical sporting context. Though largely forgotten now, Edith Cummings was not just a star in the 1920s but added glamour to her sporting achievements. She was the first golfer to appear on the cover of *Time* magazine, gracing the August 25, 1924, issue (Stevens 1). The related story was a preview of the upcoming women's national championship tournament, which featured Cummings, Glenda Collett, and Alexa Stirling, among others ("Providence" 28). The key to victory, according to the article, would not be Cummings's game—which was "loosely constructed"—but her temperament, "bursting with boyish energy and spirit" (28). The author then tantalizingly adds, "[h]er interests are not confined to golf alone" (28). In short, she is wealthy, sexy, and glamorous—much like Jordan.

Jordan and Cummings also had other qualities in common. The description Fitzgerald gives of Jordan—"slender," "erect," "throwing her body backward at the shoulders like a young cadet"—is the "perfect caption for the cover picture of Cummings" (Stevens 3). And when Nick comments that the "jauntiness" of Jordan's movements is as if "she had first learned to walk upon golf courses" (*Gatsby* 55), he could be memorably—and accurately—describing Cummings's privileged upbringing; the daughter of "Chicago socialites," she grew up in a mansion, enjoyed private schools and tutors, and became a "charter member" of an American "elite whose families belonged to the nation's great old private clubs" (Stevens 4–5). Off the links, Cummings kept a high social profile; in 1934, long after her competitive career, her marriage to a successful businessman garnered coverage in newspapers across the country (6). For her unique combination of talent, beauty, star power, and social advantage, Cummings was the ideal choice for a character in a novel about wealth, privilege, and glamour.

Making Jordan Baker a golfer also helps Fitzgerald establish her as a privileged, unscrupulous character, similar to Tom Buchanan and therefore crucial to *Gatsby*'s rereading of the American dream. Richard Lessa makes the point that, much as Tom is defined by his football past, Jordan is defined by her athletic skill. Both Tom and Jordan are "prototype[s]" for their particular sports; just as establishing Tom as a brutal physical presence helps the reader understand his character, so also does Jordan's "cool detachment" make sense for her profession (71–72). Tom may leave physical bruises, but Jordan never does; it would require a level of personal attachment that she lacks. Golf is an individual sport, and the object is to lift oneself to victory. Thus the self-centeredness that marks Jordan's character is understandable; she could never be a "team player" (72).

The drive for individual glory is also expressed in an even less attractive way. Jordan's past is revealed after her theft of a car and subsequent lying jog Nick's memory. He recalls that when Jordan won her first major tournament, there had been "a suggestion that she had moved her ball from a bad lie in the semi-final round" (*Gatsby* 62). Though the matter had blown over, the incident leads Nick to remark of Jordan, "[s]he was incurably dishonest [and] wasn't able to endure being at a disadvantage" (63). In this keen moment of character revelation, critics have seized upon the importance of her cheating.[5] But I think they miss an essential point; after all, Jordan Baker could have cheated at most any sport. Even Tom did not (as far as we know) cheat at football. The author's decision to cast Jordan specifically as a cheating golfer has significance greater than the chance relationship between Fitzgerald and Cummings.

If any sport is obsessed with the purity of its rules, it is golf. Like the strict insistence on the purity of amateurism in the early tournaments, golf course etiquette also has been an important tradition of the game. The original thirteen rules for golf established in 1754 allow for a bad lie to be altered with a one-stroke penalty attached, the same rule that exists today (Nickerson 111). Traditionally, though, any hand contact with the ball has been considered dubious; for many golfers, "the spirit of the game" decried wiping muddy balls or altering a bad lie in any way (Wind 29). Because there are no on-site officials, the integrity of the sport depends upon the integrity of the players, who are trusted to police themselves. Players are responsible for their own scoring and for submitting the correct score at the end of a round; there are no umpires, referees, or judges watching them. Had Jordan Baker altered the lie without assessing herself the penalty, she would certainly have been disqualified.

Because Jordan Baker is a golfer, the reader knows that she is a woman of privilege who has a professional duty unheard of in other sports to honor the integrity of the game. But as a golfer who cheats, Jordan is the perfect model for Fitzgerald's statement on the corruption of the American dream: Even with wealth, talent, and social advantages, Jordan Baker stoops to breaking the rules to get what she wants. And while Jordan's character is frequently read this way, few critics observe that the particular integrity required of golfers makes her misdeed more profound than it would have been if she had cheated at, say, tennis or polo. Therefore, the choice of golf as the sport she cheats at is at least as significant to the novel's theme of corruption as Meyer Wolfsheim's World Series fix.

Perhaps the strongest textual clue that golf plays a more significant role in *Gatsby* than is usually acknowledged is Jordan's last scene, when Fitzgerald uses golf to explore Nick's disillusionment. After realizing the corruption of the Buchanans' circle and of Gatsby himself, Nick decides that the East has become "distorted beyond my eyes' power of correction," and returns to the Midwest (185). But his desire to "leave things in order" leads him to Jordan one last time (185). For no plot-related reason, she shows up "dressed to play golf [and] look[ing] like a good illustration" to hear and accept Nick's explanation for leaving (185). Dressed as she is, Jordan is the very model of the leisure-class woman. When he walks away from her, Nick leaves behind the segment of society she represents and demonstrates his newfound ability to resist the allure of the glamorous leisure class. Jordan could, of course, have worn anything, but her golf attire is an outward marker that clearly places her in the elite social circle with which Nick has become disillusioned. Again, Fitzgerald effectively uses Jordan's golfing, this time to demonstrate Nick's evolution as a character.

Unlike *Gatsby*, Fitzgerald's short fiction has been neglected by critics. Indeed, the author himself once listed only four to be "worth reading." One was included among a recent collection titled *The Greatest Golf Stories Ever Told*: "Winter Dreams," published in 1922 and the most significant and complete golf story in the Fitzgerald canon. John Kuehl thoroughly examines the "Dreams"–*Gatsby* relationship: the themes (rich–poor, past–present, dreams–disillusionment), characters (Dexter Green–Jay Gatsby, Judy Jones–Daisy Buchanan), and plot (poor boy falls for rich girl, is rejected, leaves, makes his fortune, tries to win her back) are all shared, though in embryonic form (64–65). However, one element of "Winter Dreams" was reduced rather than expanded in *Gatsby*: the crucial position of golf.

The class implications of Dexter Green's position as a caddy are brought to the fore immediately. As in "Bernice," the country club is a place of social stratification; there are the "poor as sin caddies [who] lived in one-room houses," and then above them is Dexter, who caddies for "pocket-money" because his father is a successful grocer ("Dreams" 217). His winter dreams clearly conflate success on the golf links (becoming "a golf champion [by winning] a marvelous match played a hundred times over the fairways of his imagination") with entering the upper class (arriving at the Sherry Island Golf Club in a Pierce-Arrow and entering "surrounded by an admiring crowd")—presumably the golf championship comes first (218). Therefore, Dexter's sudden decision to quit his job is a function of his class position; as newly moneyed middle class, he is secure enough to quit, but quitting also is an act of disgust with the patronizing upper class that would never treat a caddy as an equal regardless of his finances. While Dexter admits that he will miss the "thirty dollars a month" earned by a top caddy, his pride and impulsiveness prevail. For plot purposes, the scenario makes perfect sense; the country club is a plausible place to arrange the meeting between Dexter and spoiled rich kid Judy Jones in a clearly class-marked relationship. But for thematic purposes, the club is also the ideal place to reveal this wealthy, spoiled girl's character and lay the foundation for Dexter's ruthless quest for status.

Aside from setting the class context, golf serves to reveal character. When Judy first appears on the links as a spoiled eleven-year-old who threatens her nurse with a golf club, the reader immediately sees her as the reckless, self-centered person she will prove to be as a young woman. When she reappears later—again on the links—hitting one of Dexter's playing partners with a drive, Judy acts unconcerned, remarking to her partner, "I'd have gone on the green except I hit something" (222). She is completely unconcerned with both the traditions of golfing etiquette and whether the struck man suffered any injury. We learn that Judy lives life the way she plays golf—selfishly and recklessly. Consider her repeated seductions of Dexter followed by rejections; her intrusion into his life that pulls him away from his fiancée and ends with a broken engagement to Judy; her eventual disastrous marriage to an abusive man and subsequent decline. The lack of self-control that makes Judy a demon on the golf course also ruins her life; like Jordan, she could never be a team player.

The golf setting also reveals two important facets of Dexter's character: his ability to succeed (he is acknowledged as "a favorite caddy" for his skills) and his pride and impulsiveness (Dexter quits his job rather than serve Judy though "[t]he enormity of his decision frightened him") (218, 220). The first trait will make him upwardly mobile, and the second will corrupt him. When he later becomes a successful businessman who engages in impulsive flings with Judy, these decisions make sense in light of the character we see on the links. Though the narrator assures the reader that Dexter is not "merely snobbish," he also reveals Dexter's acquisitiveness, his unappealing obsession with "glittering things" (220–221). After all, the club has brought Dexter into contact with his superiors, the sort of people who have the glittering things he wants to acquire. And when the now-successful businessman returns to play golf rather than caddy, Dexter encounters Judy, "arrestingly beautiful" in her "blue gingham dress" on the links (222). Despite her bad behavior, there is no question what glittering thing Dexter wants next: "[H]e had wanted Judy Jones ever since he was a proud, desirous little boy" (226). It is on the golf course, then, that Dexter's impulsive fetish for glittering things reaches its peak: He wants Judy, for all the wrong reasons.[6] Dexter's prior experience mingling with the upper class in a position of subservience no doubt contributes to this most audacious act of pride.

Unlike Gatsby, who becomes wealthy through corruption, Dexter actually seems to fulfill the stereotypical American dream. Golf is not simply a marker of class status in "Winter Dreams"; it is also the tool of Dexter's social mobility. Using his knowledge about golfers, Dexter joins the booming golf industry, investing in a chain of laundries that specializes in "catering to the trade that wore knickerbockers" (221). Dexter goes from finding their lost balls to cleaning their socks and sweaters and thus becomes a wealthy young man (221). This is the prototypical success story: boy starts at entry-level job, learns the trade, takes advantage of a capital investment opportunity, and becomes a self-made man. Isaacs points out that Dexter's name is a play on both his youth and his line of work (204). I submit his name also charts his rise: Dexter starts out "on the greens" and winds up "in the green."

But like Gatsby, Dexter becomes corrupted in the sense that he loses a part of himself. As Jay Gatsby leaves behind farm boy Jimmy Gatz, Dexter has so distanced himself from his modest past that he spends his foursome "glancing at the four caddies who trailed them, trying to catch a gleam or gesture that would remind him of himself, that would lessen the gap which lay between his present and his past" ("Winter" 221).[7] The result of this estrangement from his past is an unappealing Dexter Green who is "at bottom hard-minded" (233). Like Judy, Dexter seems well suited for an individual sport. Even after throwing over his fiancée Irene—the night before a golf date, no less (232)—for Judy, Dexter seems as uncaring about the hurt he caused her as Judy is about the hurt she caused him (233). When he learns of Judy's fate, picturing her at the country club, in "gingham on the golf links" proves impossible—these things "existed no longer" (235). This is the final estrangement of Dexter from his winter dreams. Isaacs recognizes the fading images of the country club from Dexter's memory as part of a greater loss of "youth" and the illusions that accompany it (207). Through golf, Dexter Green finally attains the wealth he always wanted, but at the expense of his character, leaving him intangibly poorer.

The major role played by golf in "Winter Dreams" is anomalous in Fitzgerald's work, but the country club consistently acts as a place of both excluding and mingling. "A Freeze-Out," a romance that has received scant critical attention, is, like Gatsby or "The Rich Boy," a study in the decayed morality of the wealthy. Pierce and Eleanor Winslow represent old money, the Rikkers the Jay Gatsby nouveau riche. Chauncey Rikker has not exactly fulfilled the American dream; he declared bankruptcy and moved to Europe, returning later to a contempt of court charge (651). This entire history is presented by the Winslows to explain Pierce's determination to blackball Rikker from the exclusive Kennemore Club. Membership in the country club therefore seems to demand a moral standard as well as a financial or class standard. Because the exclusion of Chauncey Rikker is not presented as an act of class politics but a moral obligation, inclusion in the club becomes equivalent to moral acceptance.

At first, this standard seems persuasive, or even admirable, to young Forrest Winslow, who, though unwittingly smitten that very afternoon with Alida Rikker, "sympathized passionately with his father's refusal to second Rikker for the Kennemore Club" (652). Tradition is at stake. Forrest's grandfather had personally founded the club; his family had been upstanding citizens in town for five generations; and, as his father said, "certain people were without the pale" (653). He convinces himself to blackball the Rikkers. Then, while searching for a ball that has (unsubtly) gone in the rough, he overhears a conversation between Alida and Helen Hannan, a member's daughter. For Helen, the thought of poor Alida having to play on a public course is unsettling; "I'd feel so silly" having to play there (653). But after the scorn she and her family have suffered, Alida claims, "I wouldn't care. . . . It wouldn't touch me at all" (654). Suddenly sympathetic, Forrest decides Alida is "a lady" regardless of what her father did and decides not to blackball them (654). The separation of Chauncey's past from Alida, however, does not change the role of club membership in the story. For Forrest Winslow, a scandalous past is still apparently a disqualification; he does not say that Alida's father should be admitted. He merely believes the sins of the father should not be visited on the child.

Ultimately, though, this definition of club membership as moral acceptance falters under social and economic pressures. After hearing the sordid gossip, Forrest's grandmother, old Mrs. Forrest, sees through the bluster. "Are they rich?" she asks; after an affirmative answer, she asserts, "[t]hey'll get in all right" (652). She is right, of course; money overcomes morals. Pierce admits that in exchange for a business favor he did not intervene, allowing the Rikkers to be admitted. Stunned by the placement of money above morals, Forrest realizes Pierce's true priorities, and "some old childhood faith in his father died at that moment" (654). Pierce is not the only one who does not practice what he preaches; when echoes of the scandals surface in the local papers, they elicit "angry talk and threats of resignation" from the club members but no action (654). Forrest follows their lead; when the Rikkers arrange a dance, he stubbornly refuses to attend. But, since "[h]is father had weakened on the Kennemore Club," he eventually sees no point in boycotting (655). The dance, of course, is the next step in the inevitable Forrest–Alida romance that ends in marriage, and his father can only disapprove while "feeling guilty" for having opened the door with his concession on the membership (659). Though the ending is a rather happy one, "A Freeze-Out" is yet another Fitzgerald exposé of the moral corruption of the rich. And golf plays the central role in demonstrating how selectively moral the rich can be.

Marriage, class, and golf also work together in "What a Handsome Pair!"—a story James West calls "a thoughtful meditation on the institution of marriage" (220). West recognizes the biographical context, observing that the story appeared in 1932, when the Fitzgeralds' marriage was largely over, "probably . . . irreparably damaged by internal competitiveness" (220). But the sporting context also proves crucial. The story traces the lives of two couples, Stuart and Helen Oldhorne and Teddy and Betty Van Beck. Once engaged to unathletic Teddy, Helen believes that Stuart Oldhorne, whom she met while visiting Southampton, is more her style (682). "She rode nearly as well as Stuart and gave him a decent game in tennis. He taught her some polo, and they were both golf crazy" (684). The pairing of two wealthy, athletic young people seems perfect, but they have no idea just how intense their golf craze will become.

As often is the case in Fitzgerald's stories, money comes between the Oldhornes. Stuart inherited a company from his father and managed it into the ground, making Helen the provider. This naturally leads to conflict, as Stuart is reduced to parlaying two amateur golf championships into a job as a lowly golf pro "at a club which his father had helped to found" (692). Golf marks Stuart's social decline and failure while creating a basis for Helen's growing contempt. His new status as a teaching pro irritates his still-competitive wife: "I just keep wishing you and I could play together like we used to. And now you have to play with dubs, and get their wretched shots out of traps" (693). But because of his financial decline, Stuart must sacrifice the amateur career that once attracted Helen to him. Meanwhile, Helen is still pursuing and winning amateur championships that, as a pro, Stuart is ineligible for. Even when Helen wins an important amateur title, Stuart—as a pro—is not allowed into the clubhouse to congratulate her (694). A humiliated Stuart tries to regain his manhood by joining the Canadian Air Force during the war, but he is refused because of an eye injury suffered when "a dub cracked me with a brassie" (695).[8] Golf thus strips Stuart not only of his competitive manhood but also of any chance to regain it.

Fitzgerald's major theme in the story is what makes a good marriage, and simply choosing a mate with common interests is clearly not it. In direct contrast to the struggling Oldhornes, the Van Becks are succeeding even though Teddy has proven a gifted musician and Betty "doesn't know a note" (685). But by not sharing a common interest, they also avoid potential competition. Marriage requires complete partnership, but the Oldhornes allow themselves to become competitors through their obsession with sport. They play their favorite sports as opponents, golfing as individuals or against each other as mixed foursomes, playing polo on gender-segregated teams, and confronting one another on the tennis court. As athletes, the Oldhornes are in extreme danger of falling prey to their competitiveness. Particularly by using golf (and polo, another sport with class implications), Fitzgerald charts three related and simultaneous movements in the story: marriage (from vibrant to shaky), class (from governing the riding club or founding the golf club to taking care of the horses and giving golf lessons), and competitiveness (from winning amateur titles to being excluded from the clubhouse). And not polo but golf is the sport that marks most strongly the final decline of the Oldhornes' marriage. This authorial decision fits perfectly into Fitzgerald's pattern of charting status and success using the sport as a backdrop.

Even if Fitzgerald never was a golf aficionado, it is easy to see why he employed the game so often in his writing. Consider his favorite themes: class conflict, social mobility, the inner workings of the very rich versus the poor, the relationships between people of different classes, the pursuit of the "American dream." Golf, a sport marked by a commitment to tradition and honor but also by class implications, is exceptionally well suited to exploring these themes. It is a game of leisure played on exclusive oases for the few wealthy and important enough to belong. The country club is a microcosm of F. Scott Fitzgerald's materialistic, class conscious, sports-crazed America, defined by who gets in and who is left out and reflecting the mobility—and the rot—of the American dream.

NOTES

1. There is some question about where this quotation originated and in what context, but Hemingway unquestionably was the first to print it publicly, in his short story "The Snows of Kilimanjaro."

2. Oriard mentions Jordan Baker's cheating at golf only briefly as part of an overall comment about "the cynical world" rejecting a "spirit of play" (425).

3. Compare to the itinerary in "What a Handsome Pair!": "Stuart and Helen visited friends in Asheville, Aiken, and Palm Beach" (692). These cities were strongly associated in Fitzgerald's mind with the wealthy leisure class.

4. Richard Lehan quotes a December 1920 letter from Fitzgerald to Maxwell Perkins that states: "Jordan Baker of course was a great idea (perhaps you know it's Edith Cummings)" (66). Jordan's role as Daisy's confidante leads Lehan to reread *Gatsby* as an altered retelling of Fitzgerald's lost romance with Ginevra, which would of course put Fitzgerald in Gatsby's position (68).

5. Lessa reads Jordan's dishonesty as proof of a conflict between her air of detachment and her inner drive (72). Oriard goes further, linking Jordan's cheating to the novel's two other important sports ties—Tom's football-hero brutality and Meyer Wolfsheim's World Series fix—to show that the degradation of sport fits into a greater pattern of corruption in *Gatsby*'s America (425).

6. Isaacs makes a convincing case that the conflation of athleticism and wealth lures Dexter to Judy (206); golf, of course, combines those elements as well as, or better than, any sport.

7. Petry picks up nicely on this, noting that "in pursuing his goal of wealth," Dexter also becomes estranged from himself. By making his fortune serving the golf crowd just as he did as a boy, "he would always remain fundamentally at the level of a caddy" in the eyes of those at the country club—fit to be a guest but never a member (130).

8. A brassie is an archaic golf term for the two wood, made with a brass plate underneath.

REFERENCES

Bruccoli, Matthew J., ed. *The Short Stories of F. Scott Fitzgerald: A New Collection.* New York: Scribner, 1995.

Fitzgerald, F. Scott. "Bernice Bobs Her Hair." Bruccoli. 25–47.

———. "The Captured Shadow." Bruccoli. 412–430.

———. "Dice, Brassknuckles, & Guitar." Bruccoli. 237–258.

———. "A Freeze-Out." Bruccoli. 648–666.

———. *The Great Gatsby*. New York: Scribner, 1995.

———. "The Rich Boy." Bruccoli. 317–349.

———. *This Side of Paradise*. New York: Modern Library, 2001.

———. "What a Handsome Pair!" Bruccoli. 680–697.

———. "Winter Dreams." Bruccoli. 217–236.

Isaacs, Neil D. "'Winter Dreams' and Summer Sports." *The Short Stories of F. Scott Fitzgerald: New Approaches in Criticism*. Ed. Jackson R. Bryer. Madison: Wisconsin University Press, 1982. 199–207.

Kuehl, John. *F. Scott Fitzgerald: A Study of the Short Fiction*. Boston: Twayne Publishers, 1991.

Lehan, Richard D. "*The Great Gatsby* and Its Sources." *Critical Essays on F. Scott Fitzgerald's The Great Gatsby*. Ed. Scott Donaldson. Boston: G.K. Hall and Co., 1984. 66–75.

Lessa, Richard. "'Our Nervous, Sporadic Games': Sports in *The Great Gatsby*." *Arete* 1.2 (1984): 69–79.

Nickerson, Eleanor. *Golf: A Women's History*. Jefferson, NC: McFarland and Co., 1987.

Oriard, Michael. *Sporting with the Gods: The Rhetoric of Play and Game in American Culture*. Cambridge: Cambridge University Press, 1991.

Petry, Alice Hall. *Fitzgerald's Craft of Short Fiction*. Ann Arbor, MI: UMI Research Press, 1989.

"Providence Ho!" *Time*. 25 August 1924: 28.

Stevens, Peter F. "The Fairway Flapper." *Golf Online*. 1999. 12 Jul. 2003 <http://www.cnnsi.com/golfonline/womensgolf/ cummings0799.html>.

West, James L. W., III. "'What A Handsome Pair!' and the Institution of Marriage." *New Essays on F. Scott Fitzgerald's Neglected Stories*. Ed. Jackson R. Bryer. Columbia: Missouri University Press, 1996. 219–231.

Wind, Herbert Warren. *The Story of American Golf*. New York: Simon and Schuster, 1956.

Dualism and the Quest for Wholeness in Arna Bontemps's *God Sends Sunday*

Lisa Abney

Arna Bontemps's popular novel *God Sends Sunday* (1931) is a *bildungsroman* profiling the life of an African American jockey named Augie. Bontemps uses horse racing and the sporting life as vehicles for Augie's escape from his poverty-ridden existence on the banks of the Red River near Alexandria, Louisiana. The character's occupation becomes a point of entry into a world of wealth and power for him. Despite the success the character obtains as a jockey and professional gambler, he remains unfulfilled, moving from place to place in search of that which will complete him. Augie lives within a framework of dualities not unlike those addressed by W.E.B. DuBois in his groundbreaking 1903 work *The Souls of Black Folk.*

Bontemps, in both his poetry and fiction, frequently expresses the dual nature of African American life (Brown 139–140). Through this motif of duality, the theme of the quest for wholeness can be seen in not only this novel, but in many other literary works that depict African American life.[1] DuBois asserts:

[T]he negro is a sort of seventh son, born with a veil, and gifted with second-sight in this American world,—a world which yields him no true self-consciousness, but only lets him see himself through the revelation of the other world. It is a peculiar sensation, this double-consciousness, this sense of always looking at one's self through the eyes of others, of measuring one's soul by the tape of a world that looks on. (44)

Augie, ironically born with a caul,[2] is gifted with clairvoyance and is, as DuBois's quotation illustrates, unable to see himself for who he is. He measures his life by the image he cultivates, which is reflected by those who surround him, yet throughout the novel, he quests for wholeness—meaning and self worth.

God Sends Sunday, set in the late 1800s and early 1900s in the American South, depicts Augie's success as both a jockey and a gambler. He gains fame and fortune, yet with his achievements also come many temptations and pitfalls. Augie's life, like the profession upon which he embarks, involves a series of dualities: He is lucky, yet he is doomed to live a life of wandering and to die a tragic death (as his experience with the jack-ma-lantern foretells); he is highly sociable, yet his contact with people leaves him unfulfilled and anxious; he enjoys the solace and comfort of working with horses, yet his success with them leads to his downfall on more than one occasion. Throughout his life, Augie longs for that which can make him whole, yet he knows that ultimately he will be doomed to wander, unfulfilled and searching, for all his days, trapped in a limited world of dualities.

As a child, Augie is repeatedly told that he is lucky because he was born with a caul, and he also possesses the power of clairvoyance. However, he feels his later encounter with the jack-ma-lantern condemns him to a life of wandering and searching.[3] Thus, the dual notions of luck and failure shape his life, and the sporting life becomes a truly appropriate occupation for him since with horse racing and gambling, the dualities of profit and loss are inherent. While Augie feels he is lucky, he also has foreseen that he will ultimately run out of luck and that his life will end in a tragic manner:

[A]s a youngster, he had seen a "jack-ma-lantern" in the swampy woods, and that had also helped fix the course of his life. Augie believed that he was bound to wander all his natural days, that there would be no rest for him any place until he had exhausted his luck and met the final disaster that awaited him. He knew that it was because of the caul that he could see these things, but when the jack-ma-lantern suddenly appeared, he took that for a "sign." (10–11)

Bontemps, however, does not leave Augie's destiny as the driving force in the text; the author brings the issue of free will into the novel. In many ways, Augie's choices lead to a self-fulfilling prophecy, for his decisions are often motivated by his quest for wholeness. Because of his diminutive stature, his childhood stutter, and his race, he feels that he continually struggles to find a place where he feels comfortable within his culture. He longs for acceptance and adoration, thinking that these will fill the void that lies within him. Unfortunately, the lauds he receives from friends and acquaintances leave him unfulfilled, as do the vast amounts of money and material goods he accrues; and he continually wanders, not only because of his incident with the jack-ma-lantern but also because he lacks something essential within himself. The missing component to Augie's persona provides an example of the more general theme expressed by many writers in the African American literary tradition—the quest for self-respect and, in turn, wholeness.

While racial issues are at the forefront of Bontemps's consciousness, his work, unlike that of some of his contemporaries—Richard Wright, Ralph Ellison, and Nella Larsen—adopts a more subtle approach to addressing the quest for wholeness and other race-related themes. Bontemps's writing depicts those elements of culture with which he was familiar; he includes folk traditions and ethnographic information akin to that of Zora Neale Hurston and Charles Chesnutt in his work. Doubtless, horse racing and gambling were well-known pastimes to Bontemps, for he was born in Alexandria, Louisiana, in 1902 and was raised by an uncle and grandmother who maintained distinctive Louisiana ties even though they had relocated to California when Bontemps was quite young. Bontemps's Uncle Buddy, who served as the inspiration for Augie in the novel, likely enlightened the young Bontemps about the sporting life.[4] One result of these influences is that Bontemps's work provides readers with a tremendous amount of cultural information about this particular subcommunity.

The dualities about which Bontemps writes likely derive from his own conflicted upbringing. His father was very conservative and religious while his Uncle Buddy lived a wilder, less-structured life (Canaday 163–164). His mother, though she died when he was young, encouraged Arna Bontemps to read and to learn, while his father encouraged him to become a stonemason—an occupation that the elder Bontemps held. These dualities shape his literary work. Hence, the author makes few direct comments or judgments regarding horse racing and gambling. Bontemps fully understood the difficulties inherent in an African American man's ability to move out of poverty and into a life of wealth and ease, and his subtle commentary focuses on the character's decisions and the ways in which these illustrate the nature of Augie's free will. Bontemps makes the assertion that while luck and destiny may help one to succeed or lead to one's failure, the choices that a person makes, or is allowed to make, ultimately lead to success or failure. Within this framework, the quest emerges as a motivating force for decision making.

Augie's decision to stow away on a steamboat headed for New Orleans marks the character's quest for wholeness. He wanders throughout the city until he finds his way to the fair grounds and, inadvertently, to his future career. Once at the fair grounds, Augie asks to ride one of Mr. Horace Church-Woodbine's race horses; but instead of riding as a jockey, he becomes a stable hand who travels with the stable from New Orleans to San Antonio, Mobile, and Louisville. After a few seasons of traveling with the racing string, he finally gains a position as a jockey. His transformation from backwoods stable hand to admired and lauded jockey again involves his belief in his own luck. After he becomes a jockey, he fully enters the "sportin' life" and all this life entails—from fancy clothing to loose women to gambling with cards and dice.[5]

Part of Augie's decision to become a jockey is linked to the luck he believes surrounds him, and the other part of his decision is motivated by his need to be fulfilled by achievement, which derives from his feelings of inadequacy and need to be whole:

For example, he was able to see spirits, he could put curses on people and he could remove them, and above all, he was lucky—un-failingly lucky. . . . Becoming a jockey was significant to Augie's life primarily because of the curious transformation it promptly wrought in his character. With horses he gained a power and authority which, due to his inferior size and strength, he had never experienced with people. From the time of his birth, Augie had never been a participant in the life around him. . . . But after he became a full-fledged jockey he was a new person. (10–20)

After ascending to his position as jockey, Augie comes to define himself as a mack, which was a term used in the early half of the twentieth century for sporting men. In English, mack (short for *mackerel* according to the *Oxford English Dictionary*) means one who ministers to sexual debauchery—a bawd, a pimp, a procurer. It can also mean a person of considerable status in the street hierarchy, who by his lively and persuasive rapping has acquired a stable of girls to hustle for him and give him money.[6] Thus Bontemps's novel bridges past and present street culture. Using this term to indicate the sporting life, Bontemps depicts the macks as young men who dress in a flashy manner, gamble, drink, and engage in sexual exploits. Related to Augie, this image, furthermore, reflects the dualistic nature of his life—while on the one hand, Augie becomes a mack, on the other, he does not fully embrace the lifestyle since the motivation for the formulation of his newfound identity is to obtain the respect and adoration of Florence Dessau, his boss's biracial lover, whom he worships from afar. While Augie does not involve himself in prostitution as do other macks, he does lead the sporting life, discovering women and gambling almost simultaneously.

He quickly realizes that he must attain the trappings of wealth and higher social class by adorning himself in rich apparel, which he thinks will make him more appealing to Florence and hence fulfill his yearning for her. Upon returning to New Orleans after his victories in both racing and gambling at dice games, he begins to outfit himself as befits someone of his newly found fame:

Augie set about immediately to adorn himself for the big killings among the women folks along the line. . . . His high-roller [hat] had tiny naked women worked in eyelets in the crown. His shirts had two-inch candy-stripes of purple, pink, green, or orange, and the sleeves hung so low they covered his knuckles. The cuffs were fastened with links made of gold money, and just below them on Augie's third finger a rich diamond flashed opulently. His watch charm was a twenty-dollar gold piece, and his shoes had mirrors in the toes and dove-colored uppers with large pearl buttons. (25)

Augie's transformation becomes complete as he moves on to another social circle: "Augie quit passing time with the ordinary poor-mouthed blacks; he decided to identify himself exclusively with a fancier crowd—macks, pimps, gamblers, prize-fighters, and other jockeys like himself" (26). Augie's luck holds during the early part of his career, and both his friends and enemies repeatedly proclaim his luck. Bontemps describes St. Louis, another stop on Augie's riding schedule, as "capital of the Negro Sporting wheel" (52). Driving his departure for St. Louis is Augie's obsession with Florence Dessau.

While in St. Louis, he embarks upon an ill-fated affair with Della, a woman with whom he becomes involved simply because she resembles Florence and because he thinks this affair will fulfill that which is missing in his life. Augie struts pridefully around town, and his appearance at the cakewalk—a traditional African American dance—illustrates his longing for approval. Though Augie and Della win the contest, the victory remains a hollow one. Again, the dual nature of his existence becomes clear—he appears to have everything a person in his position could want or need, yet he remains unfulfilled, still questing for that which will make him whole:

With so many impressive pairs on the floor, it became apparent that selecting a winner was to be no simple task. . . . There was a hush, then a burset of cheers and furious applause.. . . Every head turned, every neck strained. Little Augie had taken the floor with Della Green.
He wore a full dress suit made of leaf-green satin, with a cape and top hat to match. His lapels were gold, as were also his pumps and the knob of his green cane, and his hair was oiled and pressed to his head like patent leather. Della's dress was plum-colored, her petticoats gold; she too wore gold slippers. Their walk was simply an elaborate strut, but it was effective enough. (79)

Nevertheless, this episode concludes with Augie in a vexed state: "But Augie was not interested in this, it was like an anticlimax to him; his success had already been complete" (79). The couple's success at the Cottonflower Ball and Cakewalk serves as an outward demonstration of his prosperity and luck, yet Augie is filled with discontent, for as lovely as Della is, she is not Florence, whom Augie has transformed into his obsession. While the sporting life has brought him fame and fortune, he remains restless and always wanting. His occupation and lifestyle become a double-edged sword, and ultimately he leaves Della in hopes of finding fulfillment with Florence.

Again, his quest ends badly, for once Florence's white neighbors realize that she is keeping company with Augie, she is evicted from her beautiful town house, and she and Augie are forced to live below the style to which she has become accustomed. Augie soon realizes that life with her is less pleasing than he dreamed it would be. In addition to the trouble with Florence, his luck begins to wane: "All that winter Augie fought off bad luck. He carried a good-luck 'hand' in his coat pocket and a money 'hand' in his pants—small wads of cloth containing loadstones [sic] and other magic ingredients mixed by a conjurer and sewed up tight" (105). These talismans, despite his belief in them, bring him no luck, and Florence leaves him because his luck and his money are gone. Augie's life as jockey and gambler bring him many riches, and his ultimate downward spiral is brought about by the ill-fated love match with Florence. Augie's social nature causes him pain and anxiety; he loves Florence, yet she gives him little in return for his efforts. He is willing to sacrifice all for Florence, yet the very act of sacrifice leads to the dissolution of their relationship. Once again, Augie remains unsatisfied.

Destitute and desolate, Augie leaves for California to find his sister Leah, armed only with his accordion, his memory for blues music, and the clothes on his back. He finds his postracing life difficult, yet he again returns to the solace of animals and nature to calm himself and attempts to quell his wandering nature. As a child, he enjoyed spending time with animals: "The odor of clean animals appealed to Augie. He had loved the old critters and mules up on the plantation—he worshiped the perfect creatures. He knew in his mind that this was the place for him" (15). Once in California, Augie again seeks comfort in nature—working on his sister's farm and caring for her animals: "He was standing beside the railroad embankment, pants drawn up under his arms and hat slipping over his ears, minding Leah's two young heifers. Once more he felt at peace with the whole world. The heifers were grazing in the wild alfalfa along the roadside. Meadow larks were singing on a dozen fence posts" (131). His contentment, however, is short lived. By the end of the novel, Augie flees California for Tijuana after inflicting a near-fatal stab wound on Lissus, who has begun an affair with Beulah, the woman for whom Augie has developed a longing. As he prepares to flee Leah's home, he laments his departure: "I thought I was fixed for life . . . but I ain't stayed heah no longer'n I stayed anywhere else" (193). He must wander yet again in search of the elusive wholeness he has sought for so many years. Down and out, he mutters to himself after losing his hat and a few more of his last possessions while running from villainous Tisha: "I ain't nobody. I ain't nothin'" (197). However, as he hitches a ride on a truck to Tijuana, he is once again revitalized as he continues his quest: "A strangely familiar feeling of exhilaration came to Augie" (199). Once again, however, the duality of his existence becomes apparent as the two parts of his life collide—the desolate and the invigorated.

Bontemps's faithful dedication to detail gives readers a glimpse into the world of the early half of the twentieth century of macks and sporting men. In addition to providing verisimilitude, references to gambling, dancing, music, and horse racing become central elements of this text and document the role of these traditions of this ethnic and cultural subgroup. Augie's life in *God Sends Sunday* becomes a series of dualities. He is lucky but doomed to wander; he is sociable yet cannot sustain human relationships well; he is successful with horses, yet his success leads to his downfall. These ironies lead him to a life of wandering and questing for wholeness that remains elusive throughout the text. Scholar Michael Awkward has written: "Afro-American double consciousness is not always resolved" (67), and *God Sends Sunday* clearly depicts this lack of resolution, for Augie lives outside mainstream society and ultimately, leaves his own African American community because of his inability to find the missing elements that form his complete sense of self. Bontemps's novel realistically portrays the sporting life of the late 1800s and early 1900s of America, and within this work, the author explores the important literary issues of duality and the quest for wholeness.

NOTES

1. Barbara Christian has specifically addressed this quest for wholeness in her critical volumes. In addition, see bell hooks's and Elizabeth Brown-Guillory's work for more information about this theme placed in terms of African American women writers.

2. A caul is a white, filmy covering that sometimes forms across the face of babies before birth. At birth, the caul has to be cleared away by the attendant or doctor in order for the child to breathe, and a child born with a caul is considered to be lucky and to have the ability to foretell the future. See Radford and Radford for more information.

3. The jack-ma-lantern motif is prominent in central and northwestern Louisiana and Southeast Texas. The figure is usually a ghost figure who carries his head under his arm. The head is sometimes lit like a jack o' lantern; the story circulates generally around the time of Halloween as one of the many scary stories told among groups of children. The figure is generally seen as malevolent. See Aarne and Thompson for more information.

4. The novel, though its ultimate intended function was to entertain, documents the many recreational and occupational cultural traditions of this group. Over the past three hundred years, Louisiana residents of all ethnic origins have indulged in the recreational practice of gambling on horse races, with dice, cards, or other games. Since the time of the French and Spanish Colonial periods, Louisianans have enjoyed placing wagers upon almost any contest. Gambling was present as early as 1785, when the Spanish governor of Louisiana, Estevan Miro, issued an edict that barred gambling and dueling among other activities of the colonial territory (Baudier 203). During the early French colonial period, soldiers frequently held shooting contests and horse races. In and around Marksville, Louisiana during the Easter season, French colonists and soldiers made wagers on eggs that were *pacqed* or knocked together. The participants would pair off, and winners of each round would knock eggs until an uncracked egg remained. The person possessing the victorious egg won money for his prowess in the contest. This tradition continues today in both official and informal contests. In 1826, gambling in New Orleans had become so pronounced and, in some people's eyes, problematic that Timothy Flint wrote the following in his memoir of travels to the west (which New Orleans was at the time): "It is a questionable point, and has excited discussion here, whether it is not disgraceful to the city, to license gambling, and other houses of ill fame. . . . Fatal duels frequently occur. They [the male residents] are profane and excessively addicted to gambling. This horrible vice, so intimately associated with so many others, prevails like an epidemic. Money gotten easily, and without labour is easily lost. Betting and horse-racing are amusements eagerly pursued, and often times to the ruin of the parties. A Louisianian will forego [*sic*] any pleasure, to witness and bet at a horse race. Even the ladies visit these amusements, and bet with the gentlemen" (309–337). These contests, however, involved relatively small amounts of money compared to the contemporary multimillion-dollar gambling industry in Louisiana. The best known wagering in the state has involved dice-based games, cards, and horse racing for many years. Donald W. Hatley, in his article about gambling in the Louisiana Delta, notes the change in this age-old folk tradition: "The proximity to New Orleans as the port of entry for such games as vingt-et-un (Twenty-One or Black Jack), roulette, faro, poker, and craps and, later, the availability of cash from commercial fishing and soybean farming contributed to a lively gambling tradition in the Louisiana Delta. Today, except for a few crap shooters in the 'quarters' and a periodic 'bar game,' gambling in the Delta has moved to the 'Boat' (Lady Luck docked at Natchez). However, before the 1970s, in hunting camps, crossroads grocery stores, and package liquor stores, games of every size and description could be found. In fact, for eight years in the 1970s, a 'Bean Game' was the largest poker game in Louisiana" (1). Today, Louisianans and neighboring states' residents spend millions of dollars yearly in casino gambling, which now has replaced many of the street-corner or small-town dice and poker games. "Playing the horses" now takes place at corporate facilities that are comfortably heated and air conditioned; yet during the time in which Arna Bontemps's

God Sends Sunday was set, race tracks were not as extravagant and were certainly less comfortable for patrons and employees. In Bontemps's realistic text, he depicts the life of a jockey, Augie, as he moves across the South riding horses and gambling professionally.

Horse racing has remained a significant cultural activity in Louisiana since the colonial period. Bontemps would have likely been familiar with the importance of this sport to residents. The town of Lecompte, just a few miles to the south of Alexandria, was, in fact, named for a famous race horse, Lecomte, in the 1850s. However, when the railroad depot was painted in 1882, the painter inadvertently added the letter p to the word; hence, the town today is spelled as Lecompte (Eakin and Barber 14). Lecomte, the horse, was highly acclaimed in the region; in February 1854, the *Spirit of the Times*, a well-known sporting paper of the era, called the horse "the most promising and finest colt in America." The achievements of this animal and his owners, the Wells family, have been documented in both the oral tradition and in newspaper articles of the time. Lecomte raced at tracks across the South, but his major battles took place in New Orleans and Natchez, Mississippi. Horse racing and breeding served as important economic boosts to many rural areas of the South, and even in the contemporary period, many continue the tradition. Creoles on the Cane River near Natchitoches continue to raise and train race horses, and horse clubs and horse culture still maintain an important place in African American and Anglo communities in Louisiana. Bontemps's character, Augie, likely because of the author's upbringing, reflects the culture and traditions of the region.

5. The bones or dice, as they are more often called, even today generate a series of dice calls that circulate widely in the South. Don Hatley asserts the following: "While most white gamblers around Jonesville prefer cards, there is a dice shooting tradition and region-specific folk poetry in the dice calls. . . . Charlie Keenan laments that nobody wants to work with the dice at the new Louisiana casinos. 'People just won't get down and talk to them. Everybody's either too uptight, or they just don't know that you're supposed to talk to the bones, you know "work" em'" (14). Gamblers still maintain dedication to the art and sport of wagering; and, indeed, these dice calls have circulated since the late 1800s throughout the South. Not unlike Augie, who becomes rich from his winnings and lives a flashy lifestyle, today's gamblers can often be found in casino gift shops, clothing boutiques, and jewelry shops spending their winnings in the same manner as Augie, Bontemps's fictional character from almost one hundred years ago.

6. Ironically, W.E.B. DuBois criticized the novel for its emphasis on this aspect of African American culture.

REFERENCES

Aarne, Antii, and Stith Thompson. *The Types of the Folktale.* Folklore Fellows Communications. Helsinki: Suomalainen Tiedeakatemia, 1961.

Awkward, Michael. *Inspiriting Influences: Tradition, Revision, and Afro-American Women's Novels.* New York: Columbia University Press, 1989.

Baudier, Roger. *The Catholic Church in Louisiana.* New Orleans: Louisiana Library, 1972.

Bontemps, Arna. *God Sends Sunday.* New York: Harcourt, 1931.

Brown, Lloyd W. "The Expatriate Consciousness in Black American Literature." *African American Literary Criticism, 1773 to 2000.* Ed. Hale Arnett Ervin. New York: Twayne, 1999. 135–140.

Brown-Guillory, Elizabeth. *Their Place on the Stage.* Westport, CT: Praeger, 1988.

―――. Lecture. Houston: University of Houston, 1990.

Canaday, Nicholas. "Arna Bontemps: the Louisiana Heritage." *Callaloo: A Journal of African-American and African Arts and Letters* 4.1–2 (1981): 163–169.

Christian, Barbara. *Black Women Novelists: The Development of a Tradition 1892–1976.* Westport, CT: Greenwood Press, 1980.

―――. *Black Feminist Criticism: Perspectives on Black Women Writers.* New York:· Pergamon, 1985.

DuBois, W.E.B. *The Souls of Black Folk.* New York: Signet, 1982.

Eakin, Sue, and Patsy Barber. *Lecompte, Plantation Town in Louisiana.* Baton Rouge: Venture Productions, 1982.

Flint, Timothy. *Recollections of the Last Ten Years, Passed in Occasional Residences and Journeyings in the Valley of the Mississippi.* New York: DaCapo Press, 1968.

Hatley, Donald W. "Gambling Money Don't Have No Home: Playing Poker and Shooting Dice in the Louisiana Delta." *Louisiana Folklife* 21–22 (1997–1998): 1–16.

hooks, bell. *Yearning: Race, Gender and Cultural Politics.* Boston: Southend Press, 1990.

Radford, E., and M. A. Radford. *The Encyclopedia of Superstitions.* Ed. Christina Hole. New York: Barnes and Noble, 1996.

Part III

Put a Body on 'Em: Gender and Sports in American Literature

The Female Voice in American Sports Literature and the Quest for a Female Sporting Identity

Susan J. Bandy

The female in mainstream American sports literature is the quintessential outsider, and her voice registers her condition as one of marginality: nonexistence, invisibility, muteness, blurredness, and deformity. She is nonexistent as an athlete, invisible in the arena, voiceless as a female character, imprisoned within an oppressive, phallocentric language of a male author, and reduced to stasis and immobility.[1] According to Luce Irigaray in her critique of Freud, this is the case for all women in literature and dominant discourse who are "off-stage, off-side, beyond representation, beyond selfhood" (*The Speculum* 22). Irigaray further argues that according to the "'logic of sameness' in this language, woman is always described in terms of deficiency or atrophy" (*This Sex* 69). There is masculinity, and there is its absence. In mainstream sport literature, the male voice affirms sport as his arena and asserts his place in it, made real and authentic by the absence or lack of the female, in both character and voice. A female character in this literature is not one of Christian Messenger's "frontier roarers, ritual hunters, school sports leaders, publicly acclaimed heroes, team members, and anti-heroes" who populate this literature. Rather she is Hemingway's Lady Brett Ashley in *The Sun Also Rises,* Margo Macomber in "The Short Happy Life of Francis Macomber," Fitzgerald's Jordan Baker in *The Great Gatsby*, and Malamud's Memo Paris or Iris in *The Natural*. In these and other classics of American sport literature, female characters embellish male athletic prowess and heroism and fulfill their traditional and archetypal roles as temptress, mother, or commodity. She is, according to Messenger, an adversary to "some aspect of male physical self-definition" because "women never truly belong in any male ritual sports narrative except as a problem, prey, or potential sacrifice" (154).

As the voiceless "other" in this literature, she is an outsider; and, as Colin Wilson proposed in his classic work, *The Outsider,* she lives in another world, another reality, which creates a divided and fragmented self. In the case of sport literature, she is outside the game as a spectator, a cheerleader, or the prize; she is present, but she is not a player. Such divisions, according to Wilson, compel the outsider to go in search of a genuine, harmonious, and undivided self. When female authors begin to write about sport, the female voice in this literature, as is the case with American literature in general, echoes "the quest for autonomous self-definition and self-determination . . . [the need] to define oneself as authentically as possible from within" (Ostriker 59) in order to overcome the authorized dualities of female existence, as Alicia Ostriker noted in her masterful account of women's poetry in America, *Stealing the Language: The Emergence of Women's Poetry in America*. Even if this female voice is only that of a spectator, it is nonetheless a voice that shuns the status of the outsider or the "other" by beginning to celebrate its subjective identity in connection to sport.

In this quest for a sporting identity, one can hear a voice that celebrates the ludic, the playful essence of sport, to a greater extent than one finds in "mainstream" sport literature, as Sharon Carson and Brooke Horvath have noted in their analysis of sports poetry ("Women's Sports Poetry"). When the agonistic, or competitive, element begins to surface in women's writings, it does so in such a way as to reflect another sense of the competitive—*competere,* to strive together—and thus to connect the ludic with the agonistic.

The female tendency to make connections between seemingly disparate entities (such as the ludic and the agonistic) has been examined in Ostriker's historical analysis of female poets. When defining a personal and female identity, poets attempt to make connections, the first of which is with their bodies, and then to interpret external reality through the medium of their body. From these connections with the body, there is further need for connections with others and with nature.[2]

The "contact imperative," as Ostriker explains, underlies a rejection of the linear and hierarchical "vertical grid" in women's poetry. Even in their seemingly linear and singular quest to know and define themselves, women seek unity in the form of mutuality, continuity, connections, identification, and touch, which allows them to escape this vertical grid of dominance and submission, a world all too familiar to the experience of women. This tendency toward connecting brings circularity or connectedness to this women's sport literature, one that is resistant to linear hierarchies. Framed within the context of a female desire for connections, the intertwining of and connection between the ludic and the agonistic in women's writings about sport become one of its defining features. As diverse and varied as these writings are, two seemingly contradictory human inclinations or desires resonate throughout, even at times direct, this literature, simultaneously reflecting both the ludic and the agonistic dimensions of sport. One finds a need for community, connections, continuity, and mutuality—the ludic motif—and a quest for autonomous self-definition and self-determination—the agonistic or competitive motif—at the same time. These desires reveal themselves in a number of prevalent, recurring, and connected motifs in this literature: the impact of exclusion, female reactions to exclusion, the centrality of the body, the female identification and merger with nature,[3] the crucial connections women seek with others, the discovery of self, and the very nature of sport.

A female sporting voice among accomplished and recognized female figures in American literature is heard for perhaps the first time in 1912 with the publication of Amy Lowell's "A Winter Ride," a poem about horseback riding.[4] In contrast to what one might expect from Lowell and the Victorian ideals of her time, the speaker seems to enjoy both a connection with her horse and with nature: "Strong with the strength of the horse as we run," she writes "[w]ith the vigorous earth I am one" (Haynes 16). Such freedom as Lowell expressed accompanied the increasing physical freedoms that women in American culture began to experience in the late nineteenth century as they entered the sporting arena as participants rather than spectators. Lowell's contemporaries and successors began to write about their experiences in sport and other physical activities and to incorporate these into their literary works.

Not surprisingly, as the quintessential outsiders in sport, for many women writers finding one's place and creating an identity for oneself in an unknown arena are central and unifying themes. Although this literature is diverse and varied, echoing through it can be heard a voice in search of an identity where the female previously had neither place nor voice. The response to women entering sport in increasing numbers is a literature that expresses an impulse to be free, for women to define themselves as something other than spectators or cheerleaders. The voice may merely be one of an outsider who observes and interprets sport, but often it is a voice that conveys a desire to understand sport as an experience, as a *known* phenomenon.

From an historical perspective, the notion of being the outsider in sport is the first perspective or motif that appears in women's writings about sport, both in American literature and in literature from other countries.[5] That literature, which has the theme of exclusion at its center, expresses acceptance of the role of outsider, spectator, and cheerleader.[6] These writings, which typically offer rather casual social commentary from the female perspective of observing men and boys participating in sport, are chronicles and observations that reflect the role of women as spectators in sports.[7] As females cross the boundaries of sport in greater numbers, however, the writing becomes more reflective and critical. Some of the first of these critiques of the outsider tend to involve male characters who are outsiders in sports that are marginal in the strictly defined sense of American sport (i.e., these characters do not participate in elite and school sports such as football, basketball, and baseball). Of particular importance in this regard is Carson McCullers's short story, "The Jockey." The central character is a jockey who lives a solitary and marginal existence that is contrasted with the lives of owners, trainers, and bookies while offering a critique of the relationship between social class and sport. One can also see a critique of race when "niggers" are outsiders in Sonia Sanchez's poem, "on watching a world series game," and in a "wite [*sic*] man's" game, with Carl Yastrzemski, "another wite hero" in American's most famous pastime, "and the name / of the game / ain't baseball" (Chapin 85).

While some authors accept the role of females as outsiders and spectators who can maintain connections to sport as such, other voices are more self-reflective as the impact and meaning of exclusion are recognized. The first reaction to exclusion seems to be one of acknowledgment. The recognition that sport is a male domain is often followed by an awareness of masculinity and the role of women as spectators in masculinity's celebration. In Lillian Morrison's poem "The Sprinters," female spectators watch male bodies "pummeling and pistoning" and shout and pound for victory in the stands, knowing that "[b]esides ourselves / (It is for us they run!)" (Bruce 107).[8] One has the same sense of observing bodies in motion in sport in May Swenson's "Watching the Jets Lose to Buffalo at Shea," in which the question of gender surfaces again when the football could not be nested or nursed long enough to put it in the "cradle of grass at the goalposts" (Knudson and Swenson 65). Similarly, one sees an awareness of these clearly defined roles in Muriel Rukeyser's poem "Boys of These Men Full Speed," in which the males are skating full speed towards middle-age, while the female stands and shakes, "woman of that girl" (Berg and Mezey 390).

Although very little direct critique of masculinity appears in most of this literature, a sure and confident voice speaks to the unfair exclusion of women, which is rightfully recognized as the consequence of the intimate association between masculinity and sport and the construction of a femininity that has precluded the involvement of women in sport. Such ideas are expressed in myriad ways from women's opposition to hunting, to the female constraints of beauty, to the female-expressed need for and celebration of community, continuity, and mutuality. Such a celebration of the ludic in sport, as central to sport's essence, can perhaps be regarded as a critique of the relation between masculinity and sport's purpose. It can be regarded also as the appearance of a female subjectivity in regard to sport literature; that is to say, it foreshadows and reveals an awareness of the "self" or the "I" within the sporting context.

In addition to this rather indirect critique of masculinity, there is also a direct reaction to exclusion in much of this literature. This reaction typically takes one of two forms: either resignation to and lamentation of women's prescribed role in sport or rebellion against it. Oddly enough, both reactions are expressed in relation to age through the view that sport is for young girls, not for mature women. When women accept their exclusion, they often do so when they are older, reflecting, as Laura Jensen does in her poem "Golf," on her inability to play golf, having no opportunity to do so as a child when "other worlds were possible / . . . likely" (65). Similarly, Barbara Smith writes in "Late Bloomers," a poem about an aging body, "long past reshaping / Thus coming late to your lifelong joy" (120). In stories and poems of rebellion against exclusion, the protagonists are often young girls who simply must grow up and become women, at which point they can no longer play sports. A striking similarity exists between Nancy Boutilier's character in her short story "Hotshot" and Ellen Gilchrist's "Revenge." Each protagonist is a young girl who wants either to play basketball or to compete with the boys in track and field. They are outsiders who choose to rebel against those who want them to grow up, wear appropriate clothes for young girls, and give up the idea of playing basketball or pole vaulting. To some extent these protagonists are successful in their rebellion—Rhoda in "Revenge" discards her bridesmaid dress and Mary Jane pumps to pole vault in the moonlight. However with no one there to see it, she laments: "Sometimes I think whatever has happened since has been of no real interest to me" (Schinto 191). Although this reflection can suggest the importance of her feelings of accomplishment, an underlying theme in the story is that this may be the last time she will ever be allowed to do such a thing. On rare occasions when older women rebel against their exclusion, they often do so by running, which somehow offers them a way to cast off or at least oppose the constraints of being female. In Leslie Ullmann's poem, "Running," the speaker runs to forget the pain of her husband's love affair, an illness she had "in another country," and in spite of her neighbor's remarks that when she was that age, "I wanted babies" (27–29). More obviously, Stephanie Plotin's "Marathoner" discards her restrictive clothing and rejects the admonitions of her partner who told her to "Dress Respectably" (60).

In this literature, the exclusion of women from sport is inextricably linked to the female body, to its relatively inferior status in terms of physical strength and endurance, to its procreative and societal role, and, perhaps most important, to the contemporary ideology of female psychological and biological frailty upon which the initial exclusion of women was based in the nineteenth century. As the body has been the source of women's confinement and exclusion from all public life—sport included—it is also, as will be shown, a source of women's liberation.

As is the case with women's literature in general, in the literature about sport a vast array of perceptions and attitudes concerning the body is expressed, ranging from a hatred of the body to a recognition of its vulnerability to a celebration of its power.[9] In writing about the body in particular, one notices the multiplicity that has been identified in French feminists' *l'ecriture feminine*. In some of the literature appears a hatred of the body, a rejection of the female body, and an internalization of cultural values regarding female beauty. In Deena Metzger's poem, "Little League Women," for example, an observer brutally rejects her own femininity as personified in the female spectators at a Little League baseball game. Described as "Jap cows," the observed women, who "sweat under their breasts," have flanks that "ripple with fat"—images of the rage of exclusion manifested in the female body (Chapin 83).

Closely associated with this rejection of the body are attempts to control the body, to make it conform to cultural notions of beauty. If the body is not rejected outright, then it must be controlled through exercise regimes and diet—at once an expression of rejection and an objective regard for the body. The body, more than any theme or motif, expresses the theme of the divided self that is rooted in the authorized dualities of female existence that are expressed in women's writings. Because sport has been considered a male arena, when a woman enters this arena such dualities must be confronted. This duality is the central motif in Lorna Crozier's poem, "The Swimmer," whose body "separates like milk / into what is heavy and what is not." The swimmer "wonders how she'll bring / these parts back together" and if she can become an ordinary woman with children. Or perhaps she will willingly drown, "as she becomes one / with her body" with her shadow and her drifting star (Brooks and Brooks 158). Such conflict over societal roles is also expressed eloquently and painfully by Cynthia Macdonald's "The Lady Pitcher," who attempts to reconcile her identity as a tough softball pitcher who dreams of victories as well as marriage, knowing that "she will have them and probably not it" (Janeczko 91–92).

These culturally authorized dualities provoke further doubt that explicitly concerns the female body, a "what if" I become strong and physically competent, or, as Tobey Kaplan expresses in her poem, "what if I become a body builder?" What will happen to a woman who has a well-defined and redefined body with dancing and rippling flesh or a woman who has a tape measure and barbells in the trunk of her car? Will she become a strong woman with a body that "curls up alone" and "carries the weight of dreams"? (Martz 19). The female body is, as Colette Guillaumin suggests, a "body for others," an idea that can be seen in Diane Ackerman's woman who is "Pumping Iron." There is little doubt that she does not want the "bunchy look / of male lifters"; rather she wants to be trim with a body that "two hands might grip / as a bouquet" (Knudson and Swenson 155). Dancers, in particular, seem especially bound to notions of bodily beauty, as form is so integral to the aesthetics of dance. The aging dancer in Nancy Boutilier's poem "The Dancer" has been a dancer for too long. No longer a beautiful legend, she starves herself, wanting to smooth away unwanted flesh, until finally "she explodes. / Vomiting anger. / Retching between hope and none." As she tries to rid herself of her imperfections, "her self," she unsuccessfully tries to disappear (25–27). Also in writings about dance, the dance is connected to bodily desire. Diane Wakoski's belly dancer realizes that "men simper and leer / glad for the vicarious experience and exercise," but they do not realize that she is dancing for "their frightened, / unawakened, sweet / women" (Gilbert and Gubar 2270).

Unlike dance and exercise, sport seems to provide females with different perceptions of the body and perhaps another identity in relation to the body. In recent literature, doubts about the body are replaced with affirmations of the body as a source of power, joy, and fulfillment. Bodily strength and physical skill challenge predominant notions of femininity, gender, and sexuality. In what Susan McMaster calls a "curious new world / of body direct" in "Learning to Ride," the horseback rider learns "a whole new language, / of heat and sweat." In addition, she learns how to control the body, whereas before that, the only muscle she could control was the tongue. She learns how to push the body, "till it trembles, groans." Then, at last, the mind flies and the heart soars "across the mind's divide" (Brooks and Brooks 205–206). As women are connected to sports as athletes, injury and then the aging body surface as themes in some of this literature, although it can be argued that these themes are not as prevalent in women's literature as they are in men's writings about sport. In some cases, as in Grace Butcher's "Runner Resumes Training After an Injury," injury is not always portrayed negatively; it is the joy when "[h]armonies reappear" and Butcher's speaker sings her own comeback (Hargitai 41). However, for Judith Hougen's softball player, who comes out of retirement, "[t]he nights are long" with hot baths and liniment for the knees which are like "two small sloshing buckets / of pain" (Hargitai 42)

Writings about the body in sport come closest to expressions of Hélène Cixous's *jouissance,* to a renunciation of the constraints of femininity and as a joyful means of connecting to the sport experience and to teammates. Ambivalence toward the body dissipates in Maxine Silverman's "Hard-Hitting Woman: Winning the Serve," in which the speaker finds a new use for her body—volleyball. She finds pleasure in using her body for something other than the practicality of conveying her through town or the passion of "lying down beside another one." Pleasure is sometimes as simple as standing at the baseline, blasting the ball over the net; it is the quivering of muscles, a glowing fatigue and so a welcomed expression of bodily power and shared competition with teammates (Martz 28).

As the literature concerning the body reflects a passion and need for connection, mutuality, and continuity, so too does the literature concerning human relationships. Perhaps because of this "contact imperative," this urgent need to connect, the ludic is celebrated to a greater extent than the agonistic motif in much of this literature. There are vicarious celebrations of great athletes, watching Hyacinthe Hill's great Olympians, for example, winning when they win (Martz 12). Even when athletes who are different and better become the subject, envy is tempered with a fascination and a greater emotional connection. In Adrienne Rich's "Transit," a poem about two skiers, one with a "strong impatient body" and the other who is the "cripple," the crippled skier wonders what "we have in common / where our minds converge" (Bandy and Darden 157–158). Similarly, Diane Wakoski's "Red Runner," who "burns / through the continuous rain," is intriguing and provides a means of connection for a nonrunning "middle-aged woman, / bundled in a coat" (304–305).

Although sport has been a means of connecting nonathletic females with significant males in their lives—fathers, grandfathers, and brothers—as sport has become a more acceptable activity for women, connections are made in sport between mothers and daughters and among teammates. Sexuality and sexual relationships with teammates have been explored in several works whereas homosexual relationships have been largely unexamined in mainstream sport literature. The work of Jenifer Levin has explored gender and sexuality in the sporting milieu and has addressed the issue of homosexuality more than other female authors. In addition to the better-known *Water Dancer,* Levin has also written a short story, "Her Marathon," and a novel, *Snow,* in which the protagonists are lesbian and athletes. With this blending of gender, sexuality, and competition, Levin also offers, as Carson and Horvath suggest in their analysis of *Water Dancer* (37), a new notion of competition and a "female" idea of power, not as power-over (power as dominance) but as power-to (power as competence). The notion of the agonistic, as a striving together, is placed in another light in Levin's work, when athletes who compete with and against each other are also partners or lovers. Such stories become a vortex of the agonistic and the ludic, given power and complexity by love and affection.

In some of the more recent writing, the perspective turns inward toward connections with the sporting experience itself rather than outward towards teammates and others.[10] As women enter competition seriously, as they run marathons, surf in dangerous waters and climb vertical mountains of snow and ice—rather than simply ride bicycles or dance in public—they come to terms with defeat and failure—and even confront death. A change in the voice occurs in these works; it becomes fearful, yet knowing and willing, sometimes even confident in the face of challenge. If we compare, for example, the feelings of Amy Lowell in her poem "Winter Ride," in which she expresses the joy of touching the wind and the sunlight and of her union with the earth, with the feelings of Janet Roddan in her prose memoir, "April Fools on Polar Circus," there are noticeable and extraordinary differences. For Roddan who climbed Polar Circus, a long alpine climb of 1,500 feet of vertical gain in the Canadian Rockies:

The dance with fear fascinates me. Learning to accept fear, to take it in without letting it take over is one of the challenges of climbing ice. Climbing leads me into myself, through my hidden doors, into corners and attics. The doorway through fear always appears ominous, locked shut, insurmountable, impossible. Fear talks to me, whispers my weakness: it speaks of conditions, of my own mortality – it whispers "hubris." Fear sharpens my senses. It dances through my body. It tunes me. It wraps its fingers around my heart and squeezes gently. I learn to welcome fear and the edge it brings me, the whispered warnings, the adrenaline. The tango with fear makes me wise. (Da Silva 109)

Even in the literature about women who are or who want to be elite athletes, this duality of purpose—the ludic and the agonistic—is lived by those who must by the very nature of competition and achievement differentiate themselves from others. In Stephanie Grant's story about a high school basketball player, the voice of a competitive athlete is also heard:

As we won more and more, I grew increasingly frustrated with my inability to score. I wanted to be part of the team in a way that I wasn't. I wanted to slap hands with everyone, triumphant, after an especially tough basket. Or, more truthfully, I wanted everyone to slap my hand, the way they slapped Kate's and Irene's. . . . I wanted the cool indifference of excellence. (Levy 25)

What one senses in these and other works is a simultaneous celebration of the ludic, the playful, and the agonistic, the competitive. Grant's basketball player wants to be a member of the team, yet she wants to be the best player, with "the cool indifference of excellence."

One can argue also that some female voices, as interpreters of the meaning or essence of sport, seem very different from the voices of Morrison and

Swenson, for example. As previously discussed, Morrison and Swenson observed sprinters and football players from the bleachers and spoke of the role of women in sport and gender respectively. In contrast, other voices explore more abstract, subjective, and universal meanings of sport as writers search beyond the boundaries of gender. In Diane Ackerman's "Golden Section, Giants Stadium," which also focuses on the performance of male athletes, the speaker asks Beckenbauer "about the rhythm / of the mind that searches for perfect order / in imperfect places," a mind that "can turn even ceremonial violence / to the mercy of a workable peace" (243–244). In Muriel Rukeyser's "A Game of Ball," the speaker wonders about "[t]his place where the gods play out the game of the sky / And bandy life and death across a summer ground" (232).

Although women's writings about sport attempt to enjoin the ludic and the agonistic dimensions of sport, it certainly can be argued that the ludic motif (the playful, the communal), fueled by the contact imperative, is perhaps a more predominant theme than the agonistic. However, as we examine these poems, stories, and memoirs, we may consider that the agonistic surfaces in subtle and important ways. It seems to reside in the confident, knowing voices of the female authors and their protagonists who yearn for and find a shared, tactile experience of a common desire in sport.

NOTES

1. Such tendencies in women's sport literature have been noted in women's literature generally, as Alicia Ostriker has suggested in *Stealing the Language: The Emergence of Women's Poetry in America*, 59–90.

2. As French feminists like Hélène Cixous and Luce Irigaray and American feminists like Adrienne Rich and Mary Daly have argued, bodily desire informs much of this poetry; and from such desire comes a writing that is fluid, tactile, multiple, and simultaneous. It can be argued, and should be further examined, that the centrality of the body in women's writings about sport in general, as well as poetry in particular, has brought forth literature that is also fluid, tactile, multiple, and simultaneous.

3. Although female identification and merger with nature is an important and recurring theme in this literature, discussions of it have been excluded because of length requirements. For discussions of this theme refer to Bandy and Darden, 113–152.

4. Most of the short stories, poems, and prose memoirs discussed in this essay are included in Bandy and Darden.

5. A treatment of women's writings about sport from an international perspectives is also given in Bandy and Darden.

6. For further discussion of the theme of the outsider, see Anne Darden's essay, "Outsiders: Women in Sport and Literature," *Aethlon: The Journal of Sport Literature* 16 (1997): 1–10.

7. Refer to Lady Muraski Shikubu's *Tales of Genji*, which chronicles the hunting expeditions, polo games, horse races, and football matches of the upper-class male of the 11th-century country life in Heian, Japan, and Margaret Cavendish's "The Hunting of the Hare," which offers a view of hunters and hunting in seventeenth-century England, as examples of such writing.

8. "The Sprinters" has also recently been published in Lillian Morrison. *Way to Go!: Sports Poems*. Honesdale, PA: Boyds Mill Press, 2001.

9. As Darden and I have suggested, it can be argued (and should be further examined) that there is a historical and evolutionary pattern concerning the attitudes about the female body as these have been expressed in literature. Moreover, a woman's view of her body is informed, even fashioned, by her experiences in sport, her level of competition, and the intensity of her engagement in sport.

10. Some of the most poignant writing of this sort is done in the form of prose memoirs and autobiographies. Of these, two are noteworthy: Jewelle L. Gomez, "A Swimming Lesson," in *Forty-Three Septembers* (Ithaca, NY: Firebrand Books, 1993) and Sara Hall, *Drawn to the Rhythm* (New York: W.W. Norton, 2002).

REFERENCES

Ackerman, Diane. *Jaguar of Sweet Laughter: New and Selected Poems*. New York: Random House, 1991.

Bandy, Susan J., and Anne S. Darden. *Crossing Boundaries: An International Anthology of Women's Experiences in Sport*. Champaign, IL: Human Kinetics, 1999.

Berg, Stephen, and Robert Mezey, eds. *The New Naked Poetry: Recent American Poetry in Open Forms*. Indianapolis: Bobbs-Merrill, 1976.

Boutilier, Nancy. *According to Her Contours*. Santa Rosa, CA: Black Sparrow Press, 1992.

Brooks, Kevin, and Sean Brooks, eds. *Thru the Smoky End Boards: Canadian Poetry about Sports and Games*. Vancouver, BC: Polestar, 1996.

Bruce, Emra. *Sports in Literature*. Lincolnwood, IL: National Textbook Co., 1991.

Carson, Sharon, and Brooke Horvath. "Sea Changes: Jenifer Levin's *Water Dancer* and the Sociobiology of Gender." *Aethlon: The Journal of Sport Literature* 9:1 (1991): 37–48.

———. "Women's Sports Poetry: Some Observations and Representative Texts." *The Achievement of American Sports Literature*. Ed. Wiley Lee Umphlett. Rutherford, NJ: Fairleigh Dickinson University Press, 1991: 116–131.

Chapin, Harry B., ed. *Sports in Literature*. New York: David McKay and Co., 1976.

Da Silva, Rachel, ed. *Leading Out: Women Climbers Reaching for the Top*. Seattle: Seal Press, 1992.

Dodge, Tom, ed. *A Literature of Sports*. Lexington, MA: D. C. Heath and Co., 1980.

Gilbert, Sandra, and Susan Gubar, eds. *The Norton Anthology of Literature by Women: The Tradition in English*. New York: W.W. Norton, 1985.

Guillaumin, Colette. "The Constructed Body." *Reading the Social Body*. Eds. Catherine B. Burroughs and Jeffrey David Ehrenreich. Iowa City: University of Iowa Press: 40–59.

Hargitai, Peter, and Lolette Kuby, eds. *Forum: Ten Poets of the Western Reserve*. Mentor, OH: Poetry Forum Program, 1978.

Haynes, Williams, and Joseph LeRoy Harrison, eds. *Winter Sports Verse*. New York: Duffield and Co., 1919.

Hougen, Judith. "'Muscles' Hougen Comes Out of Softball Retirement." *Tar River Poetry* 27.1 (1987): 42.

Irigaray, Luce. *The Speculum of the Other Woman*. Ithaca, NY: Cornell University Press, 1985.

— — . *This Sex Which Is Not One*. Ithaca, NY: Cornell University Press, 1985.

Janeczko, Paul B., ed. *Poetspeak: In Their Work, about Their Work*. Scarsdale, NY: Bradbury Press, 1983.

Jensen, Laura. "Golf." *Shelter*. Port Townsend, WA: Dragon Gate, 1985. 64–65.

Knudson, R. R., and May Swenson, eds. *American Sports Poems*. New York: Orchard Books, 1988.

Levy, E. J., ed. *Tasting Life Twice: Literary Lesbian Fiction by New American Writers*. New York: Avon Books, 1995.

Martz, Sandra, ed. *Atalanta*. Los Angeles: Papier-Mache Press, 1984.

McCullers, Carson. *The Ballad of the Sad Cafe and Collected Short Stories*. Boston: Houghton Mifflin Co., 1955.

Messenger, Christian K. *Sport and the Spirit of Play in Contemporary American Fiction*. New York: Columbia University Press, 1990.

Ostriker, Alicia Suskin. *Stealing the Language: The Emergence of Women's Poetry in America*. Boston: Beacon Press, 1986.

Plotin, Stephanie. "Marathoner." *Hanging Loose* 54 (1989): 59–60.

Rukeyser, Muriel. *The Collected Poems of Muriel Rukeyser*. London: McGraw-Hill Book Co., 1978.

Schinto, Jeanne, ed. *Show Me a Hero: Great Contemporary Stories about Sports*. New York: Persea Books, 1995.

Smith, Barbara. "Late Bloomers." *Aethlon: The Journal of Sport Literature*. 8.2 (1991): 120.

Ullman, Leslie. "Running." *Dreams by No One's Daughter*. Pittsburgh: University of Pittsburgh Press, 1987: 27–29.

Wakoski, Diane. *Emerald Ice: Selected Poems, 1962–1987*. Santa Rosa, CA: Black Sparrow Press, 1990. 304–306.

"Monsters" and "Face Queens" in Harry Crews's *Body*

Andrew J. Price

The sport of bodybuilding has always been fueled by fantasies of radical agency and self-creation. In the gym, the body is only so much material "stuff" to be fashioned by the imagination and will of the bodybuilder. As bodybuilding photographer Bill Dobbins puts it, bodybuilders "use muscles the way sculptors use clay, creating a muscle structure that is shapely, balanced, and well-proportioned" (10). Ideologically, the sport acknowledges no limits to the creative efforts of the body sculptor. The bodybuilder can take his body as far as his dedication and discipline will take him. Elaborating on the importance of freedom and self-determination noted by Dobbins, bodybuilder and literary critic Leslie Heywood observes that "the idea that hard work and the right supplements and/or drugs will allow you to make yourself into whatever shape you want is everywhere in bodybuilding rhetoric and advertisements" (96). In the world of bodybuilding, the bodybuilder is heroic because through pain and sacrifice he takes his body further than ordinary men, constructs a self of Olympian proportions, and transcends the corporeal limits that confine the rest of us. Bodybuilding revolves entirely around this heroic individual (there are no teams in this sport), making it a site in which deep-seated values of the individual, autonomy and masculinity converge.

Given these ideological commitments, one might ask: What happens when women become bodybuilders? Can women bodybuilders avail themselves of the same ideals of freedom and self-determination that motivate their male counterparts? Are female bodybuilders authorized to "make yourself into whatever shape you want?" What happens when women bodybuilders develop the heavily muscled and "ripped" physiques that have historically been seen only on men? How far, in fact, *can* women go in bodybuilding? These are questions with implications beyond the relatively small subculture of women's bodybuilding. Indeed, the scholarly works of Laurie Schulze, Anne Balsamo, Marcia Ian, and Maria R. Lowe have argued that the question of "how far" women can go in bodybuilding is so pressing because what is up for grabs is nothing less that the culture's enduring commitment to a system of two "intelligible genders."[1] The female bodybuilder who goes "too far" becomes dangerous to the dominant culture because her body destabilizes notions of the "natural" differences said to exist between male and female bodies, and threatens to expose "masculinity" and "femininity" as cultural constructs with deep ties to structures of power and privilege. The discomfort so often created by female bodybuilders—as well as the various strategies aimed at appropriating the transformative potential of their bodies—reveals much about how the culture responds to transgressive forms of embodiment of all kinds.

In this chapter, I examine Harry Crews's *Body*, a novel that provides insight into the anxieties and contradictions engendered by the sport of women's bodybuilding. Published in 1990, Crews's novel follows the Miss Cosmos contest, a thinly veiled reference to bodybuilding's Miss Olympia competition, the international event that sets the standard for the ideal female physique. Crews's fictional showdown between the muscular yet feminine Shereel Dupont and the hypermuscular Marvella Washington becomes his vehicle for joining the debate about "how far" women can go in developing their physiques in a sport that is putatively about the "[b]ody, and nothing else" (147). Crews constructs his narrative so as to elicit identification with women bodybuilders who wish to challenge prevailing gender norms by developing muscular bodies. Thus, *Body* assails the sport's use of traditional ideals of beauty to limit contestants who are trying to be the best in their sport. In women's bodybuilding, it is a commonplace, as Dupont's trainer Russell Morgan states, that "[n]o matter how spectacular the body, a woman needed a pretty face to win" (147). Such priorities deflect attention from what truly matters—the muscular body—and recast competitive athletes as beauty pageant "face queens" (147). Yet while Crews critiques the abuse of "femininity," he reserves the right to deploy it to censor women who build their bodies to the point where they absolve themselves of its conventions altogether. Such women become "monsters" whose muscular excesses leave them unsuitable for taking "home to mother" (75). Heterosexist ideals, it turns out, override all other concerns in *Body*. Put another way, for Crews, the female bodybuilder is always viewed through the appropriative lens of male desire. *Body*, at the very least, complicates Crews's claim to be a feminist ally and raises important questions about what it might mean for men to be "for" women's bodybuilding.

In a 1992 interview in *The Georgia Review*, Crews cites *Body* as a text that establishes his feminist credentials. Admitting that he had received "flak" from feminists after the publication of his first "three or five books," he goes on to claim, "I was the rankest kind of feminist before I ever heard that word or before it was abroad and everybody was talking about it" (548). Such commitments, Crews explains, derive from his respect for the resiliency and strength that have historically sustained American women in their struggles with patriarchy, a respect that can readily be seen in *Body*. Crews presents both Shereel Dupont and Marvella Washington as pioneering athletes who have endured much pain and sacrifice—and trained as hard as any man—to get to the top of their sport. Dupont and Washington stand as flesh-and-blood monuments of "discipline and deprivation and single-minded focus of will and, finally, of pain" (145). Indeed, the novel's opening chapter vividly showcases the enormous physical effort and tolerance for pain required to become an elite female bodybuilder. Lifting weights in the hotel gym before the start of the contest, Shereel works on bench presses with one hundred fifty pounds for multiple sets until her muscles "burned like fire" (11). Her physical strength is matched by an equally strong capacity for self-denial. So that she does not exceed the weight limit of her competitive class, she reduces her occasional water intake to a mere four ounces. Yet her discipline and deprivation have brought her significant personal rewards. Looking at herself in the mirror, "she could not believe the smooth sliding of muscle against muscle cleaving tautly to her fine bones" (12). It is through her prodigious physical labor and self-denial that she comes to realize "what it was to be special, special in her blood and flesh and sweat and most of all her pain" (12). Echoing Shereel's words, Marvella thinks of bodybuilding as a sport that "made me special" (187).

The sense of being "special" that derives from both women's physical labors, however, is about more than bodily perfection—about more, that is, than the narcissistic pursuit of some "ultimate shape" (11)—for the term speaks to the self's innermost yearnings for freedom and self-ownership. It is therefore a significant ideal for both Shereel and Marvella, but especially Shereel who has long been haunted by the specter of living as "just another Turnipseed in south Georgia" (21). Her former existence as Dorothy Turnipseed revolved entirely around the patriarchal ideals of service to family and others. To be "just another" woman from south Georgia is to submit to a formulaic life of diminished possibilities: education at a community college, work as a secretary, marriage and children. Opposed to the connection and rootedness indicated by Dorothy Turnipseed, "Shereeel Dupont" conveys the stand-alone strength and name recognition befitting an international corporate giant. Thus, when Shereel contemplates a possible future with her boyfriend Nail Head, she thinks of participating in the relationship not as "Dorothy Turnipseed, typist, from Waycross, Georgia" but as "Shereel Dupont, Miss Cosmos . . . somebody to reckon with" (228). The ideals of self-assurance and freedom embodied by Shereel Dupont are not sponsored by standardized notions of feminine beauty (with their emphasis on slimness and vulnerability) nor the cultural imperative that woman be for others. On the contrary, Shereel Dupont implies the kinds of connections between women's bodybuilding and values of individual autonomy spelled out by Heywood when she argues that "[w]omen's bodybuilding is an unequivocal self-expression, an indication of women's right to *be*, for themselves, not for children, partners, fellow activists, not for anyone else" (171).

What it means to be "special" as a female bodybuilder fully emerges when Shereel competes at the Miss Cosmos. As Scott Romine demonstrates, Crews presents this scene so as to emphasize Shereel's competitive need to free herself from all forms of connection and dependence—as daughter, sister, fiancée, as Russell's pupil (84). Here, in the world of competitive bodybuilding, even blood, the archetypal symbol of family, is "not a metaphor for kinship obligations" but a source of the "pump" that bodybuilders crave (81). Performing squats backstage, Shereel lifts until she feels "her quadriceps start to flush with blood, then her hamstrings, and finally as she moved steadily and easily under the weight, her calves" (219). Significantly, when she hears her father's voice, she "ignored it" (219). Referring explicitly to the bodybuilder's need for freedom and self-possession, Shereel tells her mother, just before she is about to take the stage, "Dorothy's dead. . . . It's *Shereel* time" (203). As Shereel Dupont, she competes as a sovereign athlete "locked within herself" (233). Preparing herself for the climactic showdown with Marvella, she "felt something move in her that was very nearly an audible *click*, a click that always felt like a bolt sliding shut, sliding shut and locking her in with herself and locking everyone else out" (218). On the competition stage, the sensation of being one with her perfected body is total.

And the raw nerve of the audience's love forced her so deep inside herself that she felt if she wanted to, if she *needed* to, she could isolate every cell of her body from every other cell of her body. . . . When her music ended as she hit the last pose and held it, she gave herself over to the thunderous applause that beat in her ears before finally beating with her heart in her blood. She was pure body, the bodiness of body, and in perfect control. (222–223)

For the female bodybuilder, to exist as "pure body" is to realize in a dramatically visible way the dream of self-ownership and individual freedom. It is to be nourished by that precious form of autonomy located "deep inside" (222). Alphonse Turnipseed seems to recognize that the transformation undergone by his daughter is not just a matter of the outer body but something deeper, more foundational: "She made herself into somethin' else" (219).

Therein lies the danger, of course: that the female bodybuilder will turn herself "into somethin' else," perhaps something unsettling, unrecognizable, no longer in keeping with the culture's sense of what it is to be a woman. To embrace the sovereign female bodybuilder is to risk opening up a Pandora's box. Commenting on the inherent subversiveness of the female bodybuilder, Schulze observes that "[t]he deliberately muscular woman disturbs dominant notions of sex, gender, and sexuality, and any discursive field that includes her risks opening up a site of contest and conflict, anxiety and ambiguity" (59). Crews is well aware of the "contest and conflict" brought about by the entrance of women into the sport. In fact, he presents bodybuilding as a sport ideologically conflicted by the growing size of its female competitors. "With men it was easy," Crews explains. "Men needed to be as big, as thick, and as defined . . . as could possibly be accomplished" (74). Masculinity is simple: One can never be masculine enough, the body can never be too large. The nicknames of the novel's male characters, significantly, attest to their monstrous size and space-consuming presence: "Russell Muscle" Morgan, Wallace "The Wall" Wilson, Billy "The Bat" Bateman. What kind of physique best exemplifies perfection for the female bodybuilder, though, is not nearly so simple: "Nobody knew or could agree on what women wanted or needed to be. Not even women themselves" (74). In head-to-head competition against Marvella, Shereel explains to Nail, "[s]ometimes it's her and sometimes it's me" (123). The element of added drama at this year's Miss Cosmos competition is that it will finally answer the question currently dividing the sport: "How big is the perfect woman?" (88). At what point, in other words, does the female bodybuilder's pursuit of her own vision of physical perfection—her wish to stand on stage and be "pure body"—violate the limits of male desire? At what point does the universally desired "perfect woman" become the undesirable "somethin' else?"

That the appropriately muscular body has aesthetic qualities capable of creating powerful desire is a given in *Body*. The physiques of bodybuilders are meant to be viewed, even lustily stared at. As Julian Lipschitz, desk clerk at the Blue Flamingo Hotel, notices early in the novel, one does "not have to worry about staring at them in an unseemly way. They liked it, unseemly staring, even loved it. It seemed to be the point of their lives" (28). Compared to athletes in other sports, bodybuilders do not really *do* anything in competition: the real work is done in the gym prior to the contest. On the stage, they merely *are*, Olympian bodies there to be taken in by the viewer's eye. The word most often used by Crews to describe bodybuilders, both male and female, is "monument," a word reinforcing the ideal that the body exists in order to elicit the audience's aesthetic appreciation, even its desirous gaze. In the case of male bodybuilders, the ability of the muscular body to compel such a desirous gaze is cultural capital. Bodybuilding's most famous competitor, and one of its largest, Arnold Schwarzenegger, was able to convert bodybuilding fame into a prolific film career because he could bank on this capital: "He could not act, but who the hell cared? All he had to do was take off his shirt to be worth ten million dollars because every man's dick in the audience got hard and every woman got wet to the knees" (74–75). In the darkened movie theatre, all viewers submit to the "magic, mystery, and fantasy" called into being by Schwarzenegger's body (75). However, if Schwarzenegger's body produces the kind of "fantasy" that can be marketed to the masses, the body of the female bodybuilder who goes "too far" creates very different, more disruptive, effects. Whereas Schwarzenegger's body makes him as "[g]ood as God" (74), Crews argues that the massive female bodybuilder's body looks "like something God had made suffering from a divine hangover and caught in delusional terrors beyond human imagination" (75). She stands on stage the deformed and excessive creation of God acting in a disturbingly ungodlike manner. She has no claim on male desire, for her body violates the strict codes governing the relations between sex, gender, the body and desire.

Russell Morgan has formulated an approach to the sport intended to prevent such disruptions from occurring in the first place (thus, *Body* does acknowledge crucial tensions between the female bodybuilder's desire for self-ownership and the goals of the male gatekeepers of the sport who promote bodybuilding to the larger culture). On the one hand, Morgan would purge the sport of any vestiges of the beauty contest. As it stands, a double standard cripples the sport, preventing it from attaining the same respectability enjoyed by male bodybuilding. As Morgan and Wilson know, a male bodybuilder can "win the world" and still "have a face as ugly as the ass of a baboon," yet the sport still requires its female contestants to be "face queens" answerable to conventional beauty norms (147). Though Russell deplores such double standards because the competitor who wins should be the bodybuilder whose body attests to the sacrifice and pain she put in at the gym, he knows he must comply with them or else. Thus, he insists, that Shereel lose her "Georgia accent" (11), effectively erasing any marker of her geographical and working-class origins. On the other hand, what he will not subject to erasure, on the grounds that it would relegate the sport to permanent status as an unprofitable subculture, is her femininity.[2] Therefore, Morgan trains Shereel "clean." However, the decision to do so is not justified on the grounds of the health risks associated with steroid use or any violation of fair play. Instead, it comes from Russell's conviction that if female competitors build bodies that too closely resemble the bodies of male athletes, the assault to our culture's system of gender values would be enough to kill the sport. The woman who goes "too far" in bodybuilding cannot be used to sell gym memberships or bodybuilding supplements, for, as Russell knows, her overly muscular physique does not yield the kind of visual pleasures men expect from a woman's body, nor does it inspire women committed to dominant notions of femininity to emulate her example. Referring to the monstrous size of competitors like Marvella, who are "downright scary," Russell asks, "[w]here is the mother in Peoria, Illinois, who would suggest to her teenaged daughter that she go down and join a weight gymnasium so that she could build herself a body like that?" (136).

That Crews, too, evokes mothers in order to make the case for limits on female bodybuilders can be taken as an indication that he shares Russell's commitments. Thus, when Crews interrupts the drama of the Miss Cosmos to supply readers with a concise history of women's bodybuilding, it is to censure women who go "too far" on the grounds that they "could not be taken home to mother" (75). According to Crews, women's bodybuilding enjoyed a period of ideological consensus coinciding with the reign of Rachel McLish. McLish was no mere "face queen," for she had ample muscle by 1980s standards, but she remained conventionally feminine, and her competitive posing routines were cleverly choreographed to capitalize on her sex appeal. (Like Schwarzenegger, she also went on to a career in films). The crisis now facing women's bodybuilding dates from the departure of McLish and the arrival of more heavily muscled competitors: "[F]ollowing Rachel McLish's reign as world champion, if you put a worldclass bodybuilder in a dress, she could not be taken home to mother or many other places because they looked like men tricked out in women's clothing. Out of posing briefs and off the stage, they were monsters to behold" (75). McLish emerges as Crews's model female bodybuilder because her own desire for sovereignty never ran afoul of heterosexist norms. Hence, McLish was a "new woman" who was not really all that "new" after all: In other words, her muscularity was never so excessive that it could be read as a sign of masculinity or a same-sex drive. Her muscularity merely represented a new kind of sex appeal that could be enjoyed without having one's own heterosexuality called into question. "Monsters," by contrast, represent the dangers of unconstrained sovereignty, of the reckless pursuit of muscularity without regard for the "natural" differences between men and women upon which heterosexual desire is founded. In *Body*, there can be no call for desiring such "monsters," for in the homophobic logic that governs the narrative, such a desire would put one in league with the "she-men" and "dirt-track specialists" who, along with the massive woman, have altered the landscape of bodybuilding (142). By calling on the cultural authority of the mother, Morgan and Crews seek to restore to bodybuilding all the ideological comforts of home.

As *Body* illustrates, the kind of control over disruptive women that Morgan (and, it is clear, Crews) desires is strengthened by the sport's traditional emphasis on the individual. Because bodybuilding is not a team sport, there is little opportunity for female athletes to converse with one another to discuss their vision of what the sport could be. It is significant that Shereel and Marvella do not engage in a single conversation in *Body*. They exchange glances; they feel each other's presence; but they do not talk. Because the female competitors are deprived of the opportunity to discuss their sport, they have relatively little ability to alter the content and direction of the sport's ideology. It comes as no surprise, therefore, that both women have adopted many of the values of their mentors. For Russell Morgan, bodybuilding revolves entirely around the individual bodybuilder who reaches the top through the figurative uses of violence. With testosterone-fueled rhetoric, he urges Shereel to adopt the view that bodybuilding is "fucking *war*" (42). Global domination is the goal of this war. Contestants come to the Miss Cosmos dreaming of becoming a "worldbeater," of "winning the world" (34). "It's those scumbags against us," he tells Shereel the day before the Miss Cosmos. "I want to see some hate cook in you" (20). Conceived wholly as war, bodybuilding is an enterprise that pits individuals against individuals. There can be no room for friendship, collegiality, or empathy between fellow competitors (any possibility for collective action by female bodybuilders is thus foreclosed). "You don't have any friends here," Russell instructs Shereel. Reflecting her mentor's philosophy of the sport, Shereel's posing routine at the Miss Cosmos is set to the Rolling Stones' classic rock single "Street Fighting Man." Under the tutelage of Wallace Wilson, Marvella has accepted a similar view of bodybuilding. Like her role model, heavyweight boxer Joe Frazier, "Marvella wanted her competitor's heart. Winning wasn't good enough. Only total destruction satisfied" (78).

That Shereel harbors inchoate, unformulated suspicions that this construction of the sport is neither natural nor inevitable is suggested though never pursued by Crews, for as the showdown with Marvella approaches, Shereel becomes more resistant to Russell's teachings. In fact, there are indications early in the novel that she wishes to distance herself from his views about bodybuilding. In Chapter 2, she critiques Russell's antagonistic attitude toward his nemesis,

Wallace Wilson. While Russell sees Wilson as an enemy to be destroyed, Shereel gently rebukes her mentor, arguing that he's "not a bad guy" (20). Perhaps, she subtly but effectively posits, opponents need not be thought of as enemies. Later, when Shereel encounters the Washington sisters in the elevator of the Blue Flamingo Hotel, she silently laments that under the value system of competitive bodybuilding they could never be friends. Thinking of Vanella Washington, the youngest of the five sisters, Shereel thinks she "had always wished she could get to know her. She thought they would be immediate and close friends. But even if it had been possible, Russell would never have allowed it" (119). What new ways of thinking about bodybuilding might emerge if Shereel and the Washington sisters had opportunity to talk about their experiences, about competition and the business of building bodies? What kinds of alternative values might then be allowed to emerge if a true "sisterhood" among competitors were established? Perhaps as sovereign competitors they could envision a future for the sport free of the masculinist logic that has colonized it. The tragedy in *Body*, ultimately, is that no countervailing system of values ever takes root. After her second-place finish, Shereel commits suicide—the final acknowledgment of and submission to the unforgiving winner-take-all logic of the game.

In *Body*, any questions of alternative constructions of the sport are effectively closed out. Crews's purpose is not to systematically critique the masculinist foundation of women's bodybuilding—an approach that would surely be the starting point of any "rank" feminist examination of the sport—but, instead, to lament the direction in which the sport is headed. When Marvella Washington wins the Miss Cosmos, readers are invited to share in the kind of loss Russell Morgan experiences earlier in the novel, a loss that is similar to "the way he might feel if he went home one night and instead of walking into his own house, he made a wrong turn and walked into the house of a neighbor where everything was strange and where he did not belong" (142). Like all the competitors gathered at the Cosmos, Marvella is a "monument," but her body does not cause in Russell the agreeable stirring of heterosexual desire that ought to be the true measure of a Miss Cosmos: "He would no more have thought of fucking her than he would have thought of fucking a statue of General Lee in a public park" (145). If the future belongs to monsters like Marvella, then the outlook for women's bodybuilding is indeed bleak. And this is certainly the future. Shereel is the last of her line; after her death, there are no more Duponts to take her place. Marvella, on the other hand, is one of five Washington sisters, insuring that a Washington will inevitably reign as a "worldbeater" for years to come. More disturbing than their numbers is the fact that they are literally sisters. While Shereel's inability to connect with her fellow competitors plays a part in her death, the Washington sisters thoroughly enjoy and benefit from their sisterhood. They travel together, work out together, even speak, quite hilariously, in unison. Theirs too is a sisterhood impervious to male control. As Wallace Wilson frets, "[t]hey trained hard enough, never missed a day in the gym, but they were unpredictable in every other way. They simply would not listen, or if they did listen, they paid no attention to what they heard" (182). Readers are left to ponder the future of a sport that rests on female athletes who incite homophobic nightmares, who defy the best appropriative efforts of their male mentors, and who could never be permitted to reside in mother's home.

Yet an approach to *Body* informed by feminist concerns might argue that it is not the "monstrous" size of more recent competitors like the Washington sisters that compromises the sport, but bodybuilding's own reactionary logic as expressed in such sexist formulations as "how big is the perfect woman?" As *Body* shows, though, the logic of what the bodybuilding world calls "flex appeal" has enormous purchase on the men who support the sport. Even a superficial examination of bodybuilding magazines, Web sites, and advertising reveals that no other way of constructing the female bodybuilder has gained significant traction in the culture. Relinquishing this logic, therefore, would be a major step for men who would be "for" women's bodybuilding, one requiring that they appreciate the difference muscularly large women present without then reinscribing that difference within dominant discourses of femininity. If women's bodybuilding is *not*, as Heywood argues it should be, "a crucial space of sovereignty or self-ownership, where . . . actions are performed for the purpose of claiming a space in their lives for themselves and their own development, independent of the desires of others" (95), are there really any compelling reasons for feminists and their male allies to support it? An additional step for men would be to take seriously the ways in which muscular women expose "femininity" as a regulatory fiction tied not to a state of nature but to social and political exigencies. This would open up the way, in turn, for interrogating "masculinity," for if the female bodybuilder unmasks "femininity" as a questionable cultural ideal, then it deprives "masculinity" of its "natural" standing as well. After all, gender relations are not only historic but relational. Accepting female bodybuilders, especially the "monsters," requires that men commit to ridding themselves of the homophobia upon which "masculinity" rests and learn to understand and appreciate women who build "masculine" bodies—perhaps making way, in the process, for accepting men with "feminine" bodies and other kinds of bodies currently written off as "unintelligible." Such a move would indeed be liberatory, for it would be to acknowledge and legitimize forms of desire that fail to comply with the norms governing sex, gender, and the body—desires that *Body* writes out of its discourse of masculinity and into a discourse of perversity.

Readers might learn much from Earline Turnipseed, who is the only actual mother in the novel. Baffled by her daughter's body, Earline still manages to urge her on at the Miss Cosmos, proclaiming, "I don't understand . . . but you my youngun and I love you" (203). Readers, not bound by ties of family to Shereel, cannot be expected to love Shereel, but there can be no real future for women's bodybuilding if men cannot learn to relinquish the claims of the heterosexist gaze and learn instead to understand women who choose to build.

NOTES

1. Key works include Laurie Schulze, "On the Muscle"; Anne Balsamo, "Feminist Bodybuilding," in *Women, Sport, and Culture*, eds. Susan Birrell and Cheryl L. Cole (Champaign, IL: Human Kinetics, 1994) 341–352; Marcia Ian, "From Abject to Object: "Women's Bodybuilding," *Postmodern Culture* 1.3 (1991): 17 pars., 28 Dec. 2002 <http://www.jefferson.village.virginia.edu/pmc/contents.allhtml>;. Maria R. Lowe, *Women of Steel: Female Bodybuilders and the Struggle for Self-Definition*. For a treatment of "intelligible genders," see Judith Butler, *Gender Trouble: Feminism and the Subversion of Identity* (New York: Routledge, 1990) 23 ff.

2. Russell's commitments to femininity are shared by the International Federation of Body Builders, the organization that runs the sport's major competitions. In 1991, it issued the following guidelines to female bodybuilding judges: "First and foremost, the judge must bear in mind that he/she is judging a woman's bodybuilding competition and is looking for an ideal feminine physique. Therefore, the most important aspect is shape, a muscular feminine shape. The other aspects are similar to those described for assessing men, but in regard to muscular development, it must not be carried to excess where it resembles the massive muscularity of the male physique" (qtd. in Lowe 133).

REFERENCES

Crews, Harry. *Body*. New York: Touchstone, 1990.

Dobbins, Bill. *The Women: Photographs of the Top Female Bodybuilders*. New York: Artisan, 1994.

Heywood, Leslie. *Bodymakers: A Cultural Anatomy of Women's Body Building*. New Brunswick, NJ: Rutgers University Press, 1998.

Lowe, Maria R. *Women of Steel: Female Bodybuilders and the Struggle for Self-Definition*. New York: New York University Press, 1998.

Lytal, Tammy, and Richard R. Russell. "Some of Us Do It Anyway: An Interview with Harry Crews." *Georgia Review* 48 (1994): 537–553.

Romine, Scott. "Harry Crews's Away Games: Home and Sport in *A Feast of Snakes* and *Body*." *Southern Quarterly* 37 (1998): 74–87.

Schulze, Laurie. "On the Muscle." *Fabrications: Costume and the Female Body*. Eds. Jane Gaines and Charlotte Herzog. New York: Routledge, 1990. 59–78.

Hypermasculinity and Sport in James Dickey's *Deliverance*

Mark S. Graybill

Rarely is James Dickey's most famous novel discussed as sport fiction. This is surprising, given the story's focus on four suburbanites from Atlanta who are forced to become amateur athletes *in extremis* when a weekend of canoeing and hunting in rural Georgia turns into a high-stakes contest with two ruthless local men. After killing with an arrow the "red-neck" who has sodomized his companion Bobby Trippe, outdoor sport enthusiast Lewis Medlock underscores for the rest of the group, including Drew Ballinger and the narrator-protagonist Ed Gentry, the competitive context in which these events have unfolded:

> "Lewis," Drew said. . . . "This is not one of your fucking games. You killed somebody. There he is."
> "I did kill him," Lewis said. "But you're wrong when you say that there's nothing like a game connected with the position we're in now. It may be the most serious kind of game there is, but if you don't see it as a game, you're missing an important point." (126)

While assuming that a character speaks for his author is always a dubious interpretive strategy, the way Dickey frames the theme of competition in the rest of the novel lends this passage considerable importance.[1] Why, then, has there been little attention to the novel as sport fiction? Critics with an interest in the genre, of course, tend to be preoccupied with works featuring the so-called core American sports, football and baseball. I suspect, however, that *Deliverance* has largely been ignored because it fits too uncomfortably within existing paradigms of sport fiction in other, more telling, ways.

Consider, for example, Jacob Rivers's recently published *Cultural Values in the Southern Sporting Narrative*, which omits any discussion of *Deliverance*. Since Dickey was an indisputably major southern writer, his best-known work should merit at least passing mention. Moreover, because Rivers concentrates on hunting stories, the book would seem a natural choice for inclusion. But *Deliverance* offers a dark, unromantic perception of sport that Rivers probably cannot abide. The writers who do receive attention in his study, including Alexander Hunter, Archibald Rutledge, and Caroline Gordon, produce fiction "that celebrates the cultural values of their society in innocuous and inoffensive terms"; they use sport to return to "the past for models of order, harmony, and virtue with which to confront their sense of widespread moral chaos" (Rivers 59). In contrast, Dickey graphically depicts the violent potentialities of sport that have characterized it since ancient times and continue to color it today. For Rivers, hunting supplies writers a way to explore the civilized (and civilizing) capabilities of sport. Norbert Elias has written about the psychosocial dynamics of fox hunting in eighteenth- and nineteenth-century England, observing that the "hunters imposed on themselves and their hounds a number of highly specific restraints" such that the exercise "was governed by an extremely elaborate code" (161). Dickey subverts the hunting narrative so beloved by his fellow southerners, however, substituting human prey for animal game and transforming the hunt into an extreme form of combat sport with few rules to keep the most deleterious human impulses in check.

Christian Messenger, unlike Rivers, does at least address *Deliverance* in *Sport and the Spirit of Play in Contemporary American Fiction*. But while his reading grows out of a more sophisticated theoretical approach than Rivers's, it implies a similar nostalgia that ultimately leads to a rejection of Dickey's novel. According to Messenger, *Deliverance* demonstrates the erosion of the Ritual Sports Hero, "a solitary figure coming to learn what he [is] capable of in a primal arena" (30). In contrast to earlier figures in sport fiction, Ed Gentry and his fellow "heroes" are unable to "comment on the ills of the larger society" (30), to return from their travails in the wilderness and share ritualistically knowledge that might effect a personal and communal disavowal of evil. Messenger writes disapprovingly that the object of the game becomes the successful "concealment" of the murders the men commit in order to survive: "The inability to ritualize hangs over *Deliverance* like a pall and best shows the decline of the contemporary Ritual Sports Hero. Ultimately, getting out alive and 'innocent' is the highest goal of the suburban men and at odds with their initiation. The 'good kill' and the 'proper burial,' the tracking of the wounded animal in courage: these large motions of the rite are impossible" (40). The book apparently suffers from its inability—or, I would argue, its unwillingness—to represent sport as a vehicle for transcendence of a corrupt world filled with injustice and violence.

The novel's skepticism toward the notion of sport as deliverance, however, should be lauded rather than reproved. An old but dubious attitude persists in American culture that sport is beyond rebuke because it provides both participants and spectators an escape from personal and social problems and because it always builds character and instills a respect for rules and fair play, countering the basest, most problematic aspects of our nature. Study across the disciplines, however, shows that sport reflects, rather than deflects, those aspects. D. Stanley Eitzen observes that "[s]ociologists, in particular, find the study of sport fascinating because [they] find there the basic elements and expressions of bureaucratization, commercialization, racism, sexism, homophobia, greed, exploitation of the powerless, alienation, and the ethnocentrism found in the larger society" (4). While the pecuniary nature of modern sport, which yields the bureaucratization, commercialization, and greed Eitzen mentions, is largely absent in *Deliverance*, the novel exposes and magnifies the way in which sport too often breeds the intolerance and injustice that go hand in hand with the other items on his list, to which one might add classism. On that subject, Messenger complains that "Dickey . . . muddle[s] the lessons of the nightmare weekend and cancel[s] the class antagonisms [between the city men and the mountain men] that he creates and then leaves unresolved," bristling at how "[t]he sacrificed backwoodsmen are completely expendable 'others' in every sense" to the very end (40–41). Yet as numerous researchers and scholars have argued, sport does not always diminish such class hostilities, but in fact often exacerbates them.[2]

In my view, Messenger focuses on the wrong "other" in *Deliverance* anyway. The most important other in this novel is woman or, more precisely, the feminine. Several critics have grappled with the marginalized position of the female in *Deliverance*, but no one has done so in the context of sport.[3] Meanwhile, the amount of writing on issues of gender and sexuality in sport generally has grown dramatically during the last two decades. Even as women's athletics have gained prominence in recent years, research indicates that sport remains the domain of males and maleness. Varda Burstyn's *The Rites of Men: Manhood, Politics, and the Culture of Sport* is the most comprehensive and provocative study to draw this conclusion. It also provides the best framework within which to read *Deliverance* as sport fiction.

Masculinist ideology, contends Burstyn, drives sport and the capitalist system in which it thrives. "Masculine dominance is constructed, embodied, and promoted in the associations, economies, and culture of the modern sport nexus [and] masculinism, through sport, encourages and promotes other ideologies and other forms of inequality—notably economic, racial, and biotic hierarchies" (4). Central to Burstyn's argument is the concept of hypermasculinity, the "exaggerated ideal of manhood linked mythically and practically to the role of the warrior" (4). Hypermasculinity characterized the oldest significant institutionalized sporting event, the Olympic Games, which, Burstyn observes, "were rehearsals for military action" from which Greek women were banned as athletes or spectators on pain of death (29). Though modern sport culture uses more sophisticated strategies to marginalize women than did the ancient Greeks, hypermasculinity remains the core component. It yields "surplus aggressivity," a state defined by "more than the necessary aggressivity required to maintain relations of personal and social viability [which] is produced through the creation of a feminine-phobic, overcompensating masculinity that tends to domination and violence" (23).

Deliverance explores the exhilarating but destructive power of hyper-masculinity and surplus aggressivity through a series of "games" that take place on the playing field of the wilderness (the river, the forest) but have serious implications for the competition that occurs within American society at large. Though generally interpreted as a celebration of manhood, *Deliverance* actually raises troubling questions about hypermasculine sport culture that it never answers with the certitude required of a celebration. The novel does not so much glorify the way men partition themselves from women via sport as it reveals the devastating violence and emotional impoverishment that such an arrangement may generate among men themselves. Though Dickey cultivated a macho public image—an image too readily accepted as "the real Dickey" by the author's detractors—he has written a book that actually interrogates the machismo of sport, illustrating Burstyn's point that a "gender culture that requires men to disavow the feminine is dangerous not only for women but for men themselves" (173).[4]

While Dickey, unlike Burstyn, seems uninterested in matters of bureaucracy, business, and politics in sport, preferring to remove his male characters from city life and confront them with survival in a primitive environment, in an important way, the social system that houses contemporary American sport culture creates the occasion for, if not the scene of, Ed Gentry's participation in the expedition. Many men value sport, with its emphasis on the absolutes of individual skill, strength, and performance, because it counters those aspects of late capitalist society that stress meaningful collectivity over individuality, nurturing over domination, femininity over masculinity: As Burstyn puts it, "health, education, and welfare are seen as 'feminine' and 'soft' apparatus of government, wasteful and of dubious value in [the] hypermasculine ideological frame" (23). Though Ed, the vice president of an advertising agency, is not obviously part of any such apparatus, he feels himself too much with a world that is overwhelmingly feminine. He may engage Lewis in friendly debate about the wisdom of rejecting that world completely, but ultimately Ed admits the seductiveness of Lewis's sport "fantasy life": "I'm so tanked up with your river-mystique that I'm sure I'll go through some fantastic change as soon as I dig the paddle in the first time" (52). Though uttered in the semi-ironic voice of the urban sophisticate, Ed's statement confirms the notion that pulls at him through the first thirty pages of the novel—that sport might offer deliverance from an ambiguous, complex, feminized world. This is what leads him to accept Lewis's invitation. Though more conflicted than Lewis, Ed largely shares Lewis's disdain for "the system" and yearns to escape it by entering the male preserve of sport.

Before embarking on the trip, Ed negotiates uncomfortably a world overflowing with women. On his way to work, he notices he is surrounded by "secretaries and file secretaries and file clerks, young and semi-young and middle-aged, and their hair styles, piled and shellacked and swirled and horned, and almost everyone stiff." The scene "fill[s him] with desolation." To assert some modicum of masculine control over the situation, Ed attempts to turn the women into sexual objects, searching the throng "for a decent ass" (15). He boards the elevator in his building, again enclosed by women, and after arriving in his office supervises a photography session for an advertisement promoting women's underwear. Dickey has the young model hold a cat, a well-worn symbol of femininity, for the shoot. Ed recalls the young female model as he has intercourse with his wife prior to his excursion with Lewis. It is his wife Martha who best connotes the feminized world that Ed inhabits before his trip. When she asks if it is her fault that he wants to get away for the weekend, he answers no but thinks to himself, "it partly was, just as it's any woman's fault who represents normalcy" (27). She is "a good wife and a good companion" who possesses a "toughness that [gets] things done" (26), but those things are stifling, even frightening, to Ed. Martha's toughness—as a wife, a mother, and, most tellingly, as a nurse—is that of the caregiver, of the nurturer, of those who represent the "soft" social apparatus that Burstyn mentions. Ed longs for the physical robustness of the male athlete, to embody it and be in its presence.

Lewis Medlock exudes such hypermasculine strength. Though as a strategist he is mentally agile in a way universally sanctioned by sport culture, Lewis stands out largely because of his body. "The ideal of big masculinity, embodied in bulk and muscularity, draws on the historical legacy of men's culture and the warrior cult" (Burstyn 151), but it holds greater sway in contemporary sport culture than it has in the past, as each generation of athlete seems exponentially to get bigger and stronger—in football, boxing, Olympic strength sports, and even in basketball and baseball, where muscularity used to be relatively unimportant. Though Ed compares him to "Johnny Weismuller in the old Tarzan movies," Lewis's body fits more comfortably the post-Schwarzenegger mold, even if his method of physical conditioning, involving "sit-ups and leg-raises," seems a little quaint by today's standards. "I had never seen such a male body in my life, even in the pictures in the weight-lifting magazines," says Ed, transfixed by the veins that appear when Lewis moves. He looks as if he is "made out of well-matched red-brown chunks wrapped in blue wire" (102–103). The power contained in those muscles allows Lewis to hold, until just the right moment, the arrow shot that later kills Bobby's rapist. But Ed intuits even earlier that in a contest with the rural inhabitants of the area Lewis's body will set him apart from the other players.

Among those competitors, "there [are] none like Lewis" (56). Indeed, the first two mountain men Ed and Lewis meet, as Lewis tries to hire someone to deliver their cars downriver by the trip's end, look "like two pro football linemen in their first season after retirement when they are beginning to soften up" (66). Although Ed becomes nervous as Lewis haggles with the one named Griner about his price (a game that foreshadows the much more dangerous one to follow), as the trip proceeds, he relies upon, even fantasizes about, Lewis's physical dominance. That quality stems from Lewis's superior body, which looms large in Ed's imagination even after Lewis becomes incapacitated by a leg fracture sustained during the key sequence on the river rapids where Drew dies. Ed tenderly observes his idol lying "quietly on the floor [of the canoe] with his pants unbuttoned and belt undone; he look[s] like some great broken thing." He admires that Lewis, even in this state, has devised a "new system" to protect his body that consists of using his hand to brace his maimed leg, and focuses once again on Lewis's primordial strength: "[H]is bracing arm was rigid; the tricep muscle quivered continually with the river, and in it you could see every rock" (215). The ambiguity of the pronoun "it," which could refer either to the powerful river or Lewis's arm, is telling.

Ed's attitude toward Lewis bespeaks a homoerotic attraction, glimpsed in Ed's mention of Lewis's unbuttoned pants but even more obvious elsewhere. Beginning with the novel's first scene, when he stares at Lewis's hand moving over the map of the area they will explore, Ed is fascinated by his companion's appendages. His almost fetishistic obsession reveals itself most fully after Lewis kills Bobby's rapist and saves Ed himself from an impending sexual assault: "I would have liked nothing better than to touch that big relaxed forearm as he stood there," Ed reports. The attraction, however, extends beyond Lewis's arms to his hips and his "graceful" legs (128). Interestingly, while Ed admits embarrassment at the thought of the Kitt'n Britches model's body being too exposed, he is comfortable gazing at and touching Lewis's body:

His bare legs were luminous, and the right leg of his drawers was lifted up to the groin. I could tell by its outline that his thigh was broken; I reached down and felt of it very softly. Against the back of my hand his penis stirred with pain. . . . It was not a compound fracture . . . but there was a great profound human swelling under my hand. It felt like a thing that was trying to open, to split, to let something out. (149–50)

The way Ed regards Lewis's "stirring penis" and the massive "swelling" of his wound indicates again that, though Lewis is hurt—perhaps *because* he is hurt, and suffers the trauma quietly, the way an injured athlete–warrior is supposed to do—Ed remains a thrall to Lewis's sexual power. As he "softly" touches the damaged but "hard" Lewis, Ed becomes, if temporarily, the feminized male he elsewhere ridicules Bobby for being. Daniel Schwarz, one of the few commentators to mention the homoerotic overtones of the Ed–Lewis relationship, remarks that these overtones emerge as a result of "male bonding without cultural sanctions" (13). Yet Varda Burstyn observes that homoeroticism—which she distinguishes from homosexuality, a "conscious and positive" rather than an unconscious and destructive orientation (293)—grows out of the homosocial structure of American sport culture, inherited from the ancient Greeks and embraced enthusiastically beginning in the late nineteenth century. Society has unfortunately deemed this arrangement not merely acceptable, but necessary.

Like Michael Messner and others, Burstyn discusses the Victorian theory of "spermatic economy" that "promulgated [sport] as a way to divert the sexual energy of males from deviant ends" (78)—namely, masturbation, illicit heterosexual activity, and homosexuality.[5] As Messner explains, "the key to maintaining the male bond was the denial of the erotic [because] . . . it was believed that homosocial institutions such as sport would masculinize young males in an otherwise feminized culture, thus preventing homosexuality." But Messner focuses on how this idea evolved in such a way that today, "the erotic bond between men [who play, shower, and live together] is neutralized through overt homophobia and through the displacement of the erotic toward women as objects of sexual talk and practice" (95–96). Burstyn highlights the way male athletes in the Victorian era unwittingly cathected male teammates and even opponents, usually unwittingly, making *them* objects of sexual desire:

[T]he sexual cleavage between men and women—their 'separate spheres' and cultures, the need to resist the internalized 'overwhelming' mother, and the need to achieve male bonding outside the family—could not have been maintained without some successful redirection of eroticism away from highly constrained heterosexual relations into homosocial ones. The shift of energy and eroticism to the homosocial men's terrain via sport involved the linkage of eroticism to the violently instrumental (hyper-masculinist) values of men's culture. (100)

This transfer of energy likely continues in contemporary American society, where sport is just as powerful a ritual for men as it was in the nineteenth century—arguably even more powerful. While concerned about the way that male sport culture victimizes women through off-the-field sexual exploitation and violence, Burstyn also recognizes the potentially destructive effect that the homosocial and homoerotic foundations of sport can have on men themselves.

So does Dickey. The violence that always exists as possibility in any contest becomes actuality with Bobby's rape and the murders that follow. Implicit homoeroticism transforms before Ed's and our eyes into an explicit, degrading form of homosexual domination. In the context of sport culture, the assault can be seen as an especially grotesque version of the violence men perpetrate on one another in the competitive environment, including subtle acts of domination such as taunting and trash-talking and the overt brutality displayed by Mike Tyson, Dennis Rodman, and any number of professional football players over the last thirty years. For anyone who has ever been subjected to the humiliation that the locker room can breed—Dickey himself evidently experienced hazing as a cadet and football player at Clemson College (Hart 54)—Ed's comparison of Bobby, as he helplessly removes his pants in preparation for buggery, to "a boy undressing for the first time in a gym . . . [with] his hairless thighs shaking, his legs close together" resonates with stark, frightening clarity (113).

The hypermasculinity and surplus aggressivity that Ed has admired mostly as potential in Lewis take a perverted shape in the rapist's act, which spawns further acts of violence. Earlier in the novel, Lewis speaks approvingly about the superior instincts and decisiveness of mountain people ("we're lesser men," he says [47]). Bobby's rape allows Lewis to unleash violently those attributes in himself. The way he kills the assailant figuratively repeats the rape, as he splits the man open with his phallic arrow. Later, Ed kills another man the same way. A particularly chilling kind of homoeroticism inflects that act; as his enemy comes "closer," Ed feels "a peculiar kind of intimacy" with him

(191). Later, tracking his prey, trying to think as the mountain man thinks, Ed feels his consciousness interface momentarily with the other man's, as if in a psychological embrace. When it ends, he says, "in a way I was sorry to see it go" (199).[6] If Ed's trip into the woods is prefaced by a desultory sexual encounter with his wife that indicates not so much love as the desire to escape the feminized world of his home and his job, this portion of his ordeal concludes with a strange, figurative homosexual intercourse that demonstrates the dangerousness of the alternative realm, where hypermasculinity, homo-sociality, and, in the most extreme circumstances, perverted homosexuality reign.

More than one critic of *Deliverance* has argued that far from questioning masculine values the novel exalts them. After all, by emerging victorious from the most perilous game of his life, Ed lives out a fantasy that many men have entertained. He returns home to a nurturing wife, but remains closer to Lewis, bound to him by their secret shared experience. Hypermasculine values seem to have been exposed not as destructive but as life affirming. And they constitute a silent legacy that can be passed on to Ed's son Dean, who sees Lewis as "something of an idol" and emulates him by "lifting weights" (276). A disgusted Daniel Schwarz surveys Dickey's novel and indicts it for espousing an "ideology . . . that longs for a frontier spirit when men were *men*; [Dickey] belongs to a tradition that includes Forrest Gump, Rush Limbaugh, and Ayn Rand" (18). Christian Messenger maintains that Lewis's repugnant values ultimately win the day, that with this character, Dickey "presents an authoritative, ocular voice in utter seriousness" (41). If such assertions about *Deliverance* were on point, it would be difficult to read the novel as a complex work of sport fiction.

These interpretations fail, however, to take into account the various ways Dickey undermines the hypermasculine value system to which Lewis and Ed adhere. In response to an interviewer's charge regarding his novel's machismo, Dickey observed that "[t]he character who professes to possess this mysterious quality, Lewis, is put out of action, and the self-effacing Ed Gentry must perform all the tasks that Lewis has spent hours and months and years in preparing himself to do" (Hart 451). Going a step further, Peter G. Beidler articulates with great attention to detail the techniques of narrative distortion and irony that Dickey uses to subvert the idea that Gentry himself ascends to the status of hypermasculine hero. In Beidler's reading, which unearths evidence that Ed attacks not his would-be sodomizer but an innocent hunter, the killing is not an act of heroism but a serious mistake. The man's teeth, eyes, his honorary sheriff's card, his general disposition before Ed kills him—that of "a hunter enjoying a good view [rather] than a vengeful ambusher" (Beidler 31)—all mark him as someone other than Ed's intended victim. Ed fights through his strong doubts about whether he has the right man because to do anything else would paralyze him with guilt.

Though Beidler does not comment on Gentry as a kind of athlete *in extremis*, his thesis has important implications for my reading of the novel as a sport fiction. As Beidler asks rhetorically, "[h]ow can a novel be said to be an attempt to celebrate manliness and masculinity when its most manly character is put out of commission half-way through the novel, and his replacement bungles his one important manly assignment by murdering an innocent man?" (38). The identity of Ed's victim is just one of several significant ambiguities that Dickey never resolves. Is Drew actually shot by the second red-neck, or is there a less sinister explanation for his falling out of the canoe to his death? Could Lewis have saved Bobby from at least part of his assault, or does he delay because, as Dickey biographer Henry Hart suggests, "he take[s] voyeuristic pleasure in seeing his friend buggered"? (450). If one of the gratifications of sport is its governance by rules, for Dickey's characters, the game they play—a game with few rules and, most significantly, an ambiguous result—must be less than satisfying.

While Ed, who ultimately convinces himself of the positive effects of his trip, would dismiss such disturbing and unresolved questions, there are hints that they still haunt him unconsciously, as when he imagines that Dean sometimes looks at him differently, almost suspiciously, "from the sides of his eyes" (276). Perhaps this detail means more to the reader than it does to Ed, for even if he has suppressed the memory of his own savage potential—of how he considers castrating his victim, of decapitating him even while staring into his eyes (200), and, more shockingly, how he considers shooting Bobby with the dead man's rifle—the reader has not necessarily forgotten. In the end, I believe, the game in which Ed has been a player means something different to us than it does to him, and thankfully so.

NOTES

1. This passage is one of many to draw upon the "game" metaphor. At times, Ed uses the term to mean "charade" or "role-playing." But from early on, when Lewis mentions that the trip might conclude in time to see "the last half of the pro game on TV" (7), as well as when Ed considers playing golf instead of joining his friends (36), Dickey establishes the importance of athletic competition to his characters. Their experience in the woods—which pits them against the river, against the hillbillies, and against one another—clearly constitutes a more harrowing kind of athletic contest. In some ways, the popular film adaptation of *Deliverance*, for which Dickey wrote the screenplay, treats the sport theme more overtly. It also, however, mostly ignores the homoeroticism that I discuss later in this essay—possibly on the assumption that the average moviegoer might find such material offensive.

2. In addition to the works by Eitzen, Varda Burstyn, Norbert Elias and Eric Dunning, and Michael Messner cited here, see George H. Sage, *Power and Ideology in American Sport*.

3. See, for example, Donald Greiner's *Women Enter the Wilderness* and Carolyn Heilbrun's "The Masculine Wilderness of the American Novel," which Greiner cites significantly. Robert Barshay and Sally Robinson have each written useful analyses of gender issues in the film version of *Deliverance*.

4. Henry Hart's biography, *James Dickey: The World as a Lie*, reveals an ambiguous figure whose public masks usually represented only part of the truth behind them.

Dickey "often played up his role as sexist, racist, and militarist to bait and enrage his critics," including, most famously, fellow poet Robert Bly (346).

5. Lewis Medlock, insofar as he is uninterested in "talk about sex" (8), might embody this theory, though his admission that his first "wet dream [occurred] in a sleeping bag" suggests differently (86).

6. Henry Hart has also noted the homosexual dynamics of this scene (254). Throughout his biography, Hart alludes to Dickey's own homosexual tendencies, though it is never entirely clear how much these were real and how much they belonged to the artful "lies" Dickey loved to tell.

REFERENCES

Barshay, Robert. "Machismo in *Deliverance*." *Teaching English in the Two-Year College* 1.3 (1975): 169–173.

Beidler, Peter G. "'The Pride of Thine Heart Hath Deceived Thee': Narrative Distortion in Dickey's *Deliverance*." *South Carolina Review* 5 (1972): 29–40.

Burstyn, Varda. *The Rites of Men: Manhood, Politics, and the Culture of Sport.* Toronto: University of Toronto Press, 1999.

Dickey, James. *Deliverance*. New York: Delta, 1970.

Eitzen, D. Stanley. "American Sport at Century's End." *Sport in Contemporary Society: An Anthology.* Ed. Stanley D. Eitzen. 6th ed. New York: Worth Publishers, 2001.

Elias, Norbert, and Eric Dunning. *Quest for Excitement: Sport and Leisure in the Civilizing Process.* New York: Basil Blackwell, 1986.

Greiner, Donald J. *Women Enter the Wilderness: Male Bonding and the American Novel of the 1980s.* Columbia: University of South Carolina Press, 1991.

Hart, Henry. *James Dickey: The World as a Lie.* New York: Picador USA, 2000.

Heilbrun, Carolyn. "The Masculine Wilderness of the American Novel." *Saturday Review* 29 Jan. 1972: 41–44.

Messenger, Christian. *Sport and the Spirit of Play in Contemporary American Fiction.* New York: Columbia University Press, 1990.

Messner, Michael A. *Power at Play: Sports and the Problem of Masculinity.* Boston: Beacon Press, 1992.

Rivers, Jacob F., III. *Cultural Values in the Southern Sporting Narrative.* Columbia: University of South Carolina Press, 2002.

Robinson, Sally. "'Emotional Constipation' and the Power of Dammed Masculinity: *Deliverance* and the Paradoxes of Male Liberation." *Masculinity, Bodies, Movies, Culture.* Ed. Peter Lehman. New York: Routledge, 2001. 133–147.

Sage, George H. *Power and Ideology in American Sport: A Critical Perspective.* Champaign, IL: Human Kinetics Books, 1990.

Schwarz, Daniel R. "Reconfiguring *Deliverance*: James Dickey, the Modern Tradition and the Resistant Reader." *Weber Studies* 13.2 (1996): 5–19.

The Football Elegies of James Dickey and Randall Jarrell: Hegemonic Masculinity versus the 'Semifeminine Mind'

Diederik Oostdijk

In 1966, *Life* magazine featured a lengthy article on the poet James Dickey (1923–1997) called "The Unlikeliest Poet," which gave Dickey's reputation "its most substantial boost" of the decade, according to his biographer Henry Hart (350).[1] It was unusual that a popular general-interest magazine such as *Life* would devote such a prominent story to a contemporary poet, but as the article's title suggested, Dickey was no ordinary poet. Physically he measured over six feet and was a broad-shouldered man with an attractive smile. His vita was also untypical for a poet. The article noted that Dickey had been an outstanding athlete whose college football career at Clemson was cut short by the outbreak of World War II. Dickey reportedly went on to become a decorated combat pilot during that war. After his honorable discharge from the Air Corps, he transferred to Vanderbilt, but he "found himself banned from the game [of football] by a conference rule designed to keep coaches from stealing each others' returning service athletes" (O'Neill 66). Dickey subsequently embarked on a career in the advertising industry, inventing jingles for Coca-Cola and Lay's potato chips, among others. He wrote his poems in his spare time. A few years after the interview, Dickey would become a national celebrity when his novel *Deliverance* (1970) became a bestseller and its movie adaptation (1972) a box-office success. From all signs, Dickey indeed looked like "The Unlikeliest Poet."

What the journalist from *Life* and many other people at that time did not know was that Dickey was an inveterate liar. Throughout his life, Dickey concocted stories that embellished or distorted actual events, especially regarding his youth. Paul O'Neill took Dickey at his word without checking his sources, for he gullibly wrote that "in his college freshman year at Clemson [Dickey] was a football star with pro potential" (67). However, in his detailed biography of the late poet, Henry Hart argues that professional football "was never a possibility for Dickey" (51). The cold facts of Dickey's college career were that he barely made the freshman team at Clemson and did not make the varsity team at all, let alone star on it, as O'Neill alleges. His suggestion that eligibility rules prevented Dickey from playing football at Vanderbilt was also simply not true. The competition was too stiff, and when Dickey "realized that he would never play in a game, he quit" (Hart 129). He earned a reputation as a 120-yard hurdler, but he was never a college football star.

There is a pattern of lies in Dickey's life, many of which were only recently debunked. Dickey had never been a fighter pilot during World War II, but a radar observer in night fighters, which, in his eyes, was less prestigious. During his Air Corps training, Dickey tried one solo flight, which ended almost disastrously, and he was washed out. As a child, Dickey had dreamed of becoming a pilot, and he was bitterly disappointed that he had failed. As Ernest Hemingway and William Faulkner had done before him, "Dickey transformed his military experience into a tantalizing myth" (Hart 65). He, for instance, claimed in interviews that he had crashed down in the Pacific Ocean and had flown over Nagasaki when the second nuclear bomb was dropped, neither of which was true.

The mere facts of Dickey's prevarication are less interesting than the reasons behind his lies and what they tell us about his poetry and prose. What motivated Dickey to tell such blatant lies? The answer is inevitably complex, but Hart believes that Dickey's "penchant for tall tales and cavalier behavior" can be partly attributed to the South's tradition of storytelling. It may also have a root in his fascination for French existentialism. Dickey once cited Albert Camus who had said, "man is essentially what he has made of himself" (qtd. in Hart xv). By implication, this means that you are the person that you want to be. Dickey expounded this theory elsewhere by saying that he did not believe there was one true self but that every person consists of "a saint, a murderer, a pervert, a monster, a good husband, a scoutmaster, a provider, a businessman, a shrewd horse trader, a hopeless aesthete" (qtd. in Hart xvii). Dickey was the sum of all these and other personalities wrapped up in one person. Yet the person he wanted to be the most, "the Platonic conception of himself," to borrow a phrase from F. Scott Fitzgerald's *The Great Gatsby*, was a fighter pilot and a football star. Like James Gatz, who one day woke up and decided he would be Jay Gatsby, Dickey, at an early age, concocted the persona of what Hart calls "an all-American heterosexual superman" (41) and "to this conception he was faithful to the end" (Fitzgerald 104).

Dickey's demeanor as "an all-American heterosexual superman" can be linked to a theoretical concept known as hegemonic masculinity. Hegemony is a sociological term that describes how dominant groups maintain their power by ensuring that less powerful groups endorse or tolerate the existing state of affairs. Hegemonic masculinity, then, is the prevalent form of masculinity within a specific culture at a particular time. Hegemonic masculinity in contemporary American culture privileges physical strength and bravery, heterosexuality, suppression of vulnerable emotions, economic independence, control over women and other men, and intense interest in sexual conquest. Sport, especially football, is believed to be "a training ground for hegemonic masculinity" as it emphasizes "distinctions between boys and men, physical size and strength, avoidance of feminine activities and values, toughness, aggressiveness, and emotional self-control" (Sabo and Panepinto 125, 124).

Without exception, James Dickey fit all these criteria of hegemonic masculinity. The notorious *Life* article even zeroed in on Dickey's manly physique, saying that he "stands 6' 3", weighs 205 pounds," and has "huge biceps," which is particularly odd in a portrait of a poet (O'Neill 66). Similarly, the article also details how much money Dickey made, emphasizing his economic independence. Moreover, Dickey's womanizing was legendary, and he was intensely competitive with other men. *Life* presented Dickey as the kind of person he wanted to be but, as I will argue, not necessarily the person he was. It presented him as "The Unlikeliest Poet" because he looked like "an all-American heterosexual superman." The poet's history as an alleged football star is "unlikely" because generally we do not associate poetry with football, or with masculinity for that matter. They seem—at least in contemporary American society—antithetical. To put it more crudely, poetry is for girls or nerds and football is for jocks, and never the twain shall meet. Poetry requires sensitivity and vulnerability, which seem anathema to football and hegemonic masculinity.

His self-aggrandizing storytelling aside, James Dickey had much in common with another Middle Generation poet, Randall Jarrell (1914–1965), even though Jarrell was about nine years older and was sometimes characterized as somehow effeminate. Both poets were born in the South, both were involved in the Air Corps during World War II, and both became celebrated war poets. Dickey and Jarrell also both attended Vanderbilt University, became known for their biting criticism, and wrote children's books. Both poets, moreover, adored football. Jarrell wrote one poem about football, "Say Goodbye to Big Daddy," a borderline sentimental elegy about the unconventional and genteel African American linebacker Eugene Lipscomb. Dickey composed four poems about football, including one elegy "For the Death of Lombardi," on the tough-minded Green Bay Packers coach.[2] Focusing on these two poems, I will explore the relationship between these poets, their shared interest in football, and the ways their attitudes towards sports intersect with gendered conceptions of their own lives and work. Of particular interest in this respect is that for Dickey masculinity is a central theme, while Jarrell once claimed that he had a "semifeminine mind" (*Letters* 19).

As James Longenbach has noted in his article "Randall Jarrell's Semifeminine Mind," critics, friends, and colleagues often stressed "Jarrell's lack of manly qualities" (49). Robert Fitzgerald, for instance, remembered Jarrell as "one of the few men I have known who chortled. He really did. 'Baby doll,' he would cry, and his voice simply rose and broke in joy" (71). Eileen Simpson confirmed that Jarrell frequently used out-of-date, girlish expressions, such as "Gol-ly, "Gee whiz!" and, again, "Ba-by doll!" "all delivered in a high-pitched twang." In her memoir *Poets in Their Youth*, Simpson also remarked how Jarrell did not "drink or smoke" and disapproved of "sexual innuendoes in conversation," which are typically associated with male behavior (110–111). Jarrell even challenged Simpson to measure whose waist was smaller and was proud that his was half an inch smaller. Even Robert Lowell's more neutral qualifications of Jarrell as "very tender and gracious" and "incapable of vulgarity, self-seeking, or meanness" render Jarrell in feminine rather than masculine terms (92).

Jarrell's poetry is often considered somehow feminine as well. Not only did he write numerous poems from the perspective of women, his style "also seemed feminine to many readers," as Longenbach claimed (50). Stephen Burt has suggested that this may be caused by Jarrell's frequent use of tags, rhetorical questions, and a certain indirectness, which, according to sociolinguists, are often used by women (39–40). Jarrell's worst detractors frequently lashed out against his poetry, using words such as "corny, cute, folksy, infantile, pathetic, self-indulgent, sentimental, and tear-jerking" (Longenbach 50). In 1951, after reading Jarrell's volume *The Seven-League Crutches*, James Dickey sided with these critics when he wrote in a letter to his wife Maxine: "It is like nothing so much as listening to a garrulous, self-pitying, thoroughly untalented . . . old woman tell the same tiresome, sentimental story of her tiresome, sentimental life over and over" (qtd. in Hart 159).

It is dangerous to put too much importance on this offhand comment uttered in the privacy of a letter. As we will see, these insulting remarks are not indicative of Dickey's overall judgment of Jarrell's worth. It is my contention that part of this critique can be attributed to the fierce sense of competition he felt towards other poets, not in the least towards Jarrell, whose fame exceeded his own at the time. In 1951, Dickey was only twenty-five, and in that year he was just beginning to get published in the esteemed magazines of his day. Almost ten years his senior and from Dickey's neck of the woods, Jarrell was an easy and convenient target. Vilifying Jarrell as an old bag was a matter of course for the poet who was aiming to become the number-one American poet. Dickey's attack on Jarrell was by no means a youthful whim, for as Hart explains: "As a writer, Dickey exposed his competitiveness by attacking most of his peers and claiming that he alone was completely original" (20).

However, Dickey was much more ambivalent about Jarrell than the quip in the letter to his wife suggests. As if to emphasize his ambivalence, Dickey wrote a review of Jarrell's *Selected Poems* in two voices, one appreciative of Jarrell and the other disparaging him. Published in 1956, this article is still one of the most original and thought-provoking essays on Jarrell, exposing his weaknesses but also expressing his brilliance. The article's opening shows why Dickey composed his essay in this unusual way:

A. Why are we Two?
B. I find my opinions of Randall Jarrell's poetry are so violent that I have summoned you, or created you, out of niggling and Opposing Winds, to furnish me with arguments against which my own will stand forth even stronger, which I should like them to do.
A. I am glad you have created me. I think it good for writers to have the most violent

possible arguments brought into play against them. Even unfair arguments. If the work is strong enough, all these will be overcome. (*Babel to Byzantium* 13)

Dickey's letters around this time show his hesitance about lashing out against Jarrell. Using a metaphor derived from warfare (or bowling), he told a friend that he was "undecided whether to strike or spare" (*Crux* 92). In a letter to Ezra Pound, Dickey sounded more openly belligerent, saying that his review got in "some good licks against a man by the name of Jarrell, whose work has been to some extent influential, in a bad and sentimental way, here for the last few years. He should read [Basil] Bunting, and either change or kill himself" (*Crux* 94).

This aggressive, adverse, and spiteful tone returns in the guise of the B voice in Dickey's review. It is "dull beyond all dullness of stupefaction or petrifaction," he claims. "[W]hen I read it from end to end I know more of boredom than the dead do." The poems "are the most untalentedly sentimental, self-indulgent, and insensitive writing that I can remember" (*Babel to Byzantium* 13). B feels that Jarrell often states the obvious and that taking his subject matter from ordinary life and reflecting "reality" does not do the trick. A, on the contrary, posits that Jarrell's *Selected Poems* is "a Triumph," that Jarrell "writes about the things we know," that it "takes *courage* to be sentimental nowadays," and, to sum up, that Jarrell is "a serious, important poet, with a great deal to say, a style of his own, and all the rest" (34, 36, 46, 45). It is A who has the last word, which suggests that Dickey's kinder, more compassionate side has won. Still, B seems more passionate and eloquent throughout, and his words reverberate the longest.

In 1960, Dickey clashed again with Jarrell, not in print but in person, when the two met at Hollins College for a poetry reading. Dickey related the events to fellow-poet James Wright, which again shows that Dickey saw poetry as a sporting contest and that his sense of competition with Jarrell still flourished:

After the readings, which were received with an enthusiasm which actually frightened me, Jarrell and I sat for two and a half hours arguing in front of the several hundred students and guests, and let me tell you it was exhausting! We agreed on almost nothing (and I mean nothing!) and we cut and slashed and parried with deliberate and desperate urgency. The audience was violently partisan, and seemed to me more or less equally divided; there was wild applause after each bit of repartee (by Jarrell) and each bit of raving (by me), and at one point I thought I actually detected the wonderful sound of "Go! Go! Go!" as we went at it hotly: the sound of a crowd cheering for the home team to score in the last quarter, or the sound of a good, knowledgeable and enthusiastic crowd at a jazz festival, when one of the musicians (for some reason I think of tenor sax players) goes from technical virtuosity into inspiration, or art. It was a great experience for me. God knows what I said, but I certainly said it, I am sure. After it was over we fell into each other's arms (literally!) and there was more applause and we then went out and got drunk and promised each other we wouldn't be influenced by the other's work, swore undying fealty to poetry, and so back home! (*Crux* 259)

Considering his history of lying, Dickey's narration of events is questionable, especially since Jarrell hardly drank at all. It is nevertheless a revealing letter that underlines his competitive edge and shows that he saw Jarrell as a worthy opponent despite their differences. The male bonding that supposedly goes on in the end—embracing each other, drinking, and making promises—is essentially the camaraderie of the locker-room, which Dickey probably hankered after, but it also has homoerotic overtones. Despite his heterosexual image, Dickey craved male companionship and was fascinated by homosexuality, as Hart has detailed. Dickey's passionate description and word choice—"went at it hotly" and "falling into each other's arms (literally!)"—emits more excitement than seems requisite.

Jarrell had not been a collegiate football player and considering his small waist this was probably a wise decision, but he enjoyed playing touch football, that less aggressive alternative to regular football. Jarrell's favorite game was tennis, however; he made the varsity team at Vanderbilt and even became a college tennis instructor at Kenyon College where he pursued a master's degree. Still, watching the game of football gave him inordinate pleasure. As Lowell has pointed out, Jarrell was especially fond of Sundays' "long afternoons of professional football" when he could not be pulled from his television (Lowell 98). Whereas Dickey described football in "In the Pocket" and "Breaking the Field" as a rite of passage that separates the boys from the men or a survival-of-the-fittest struggle that is a metaphor for life, Jarrell was more intrigued by the game's playful elements or the entertainment it offered. He was either intrigued by the way the fans dressed or by the mascot, Tiger, who tried to eat one of the cheerleaders, as much as by the game itself. A letter to his wife-to-be Mary von Schrader is indicative of the humorous way in which he described the actual game:

Do you like Football? One cute thing happened when a pass-receiver had been knocked down in the end-zone, he protested indignantly though not very hopefully to the referee; and when pass interference was allowed the boy was so delighted he actually jumped up and down and clapped his hands. The best thing there was a tiger: I don't think he was a real tiger, since he did the Charleston, led cheers, and walked upright half the time (*Randall Jarrell's Letters* 274).

"Say Goodbye to Big Daddy" is the only poem that grew out of Jarrell's fascination with football. In the 1960s, it was still unusual for a respected poet to write a poem about sports, which may explain why Jarrell wrote only one such poem and why it was not published during his lifetime. The occasion for writing "Say Goodbye to Big Daddy" was the untimely death of Eugene Lipscomb, a defensive tackle for the championship-winning Baltimore Colts and one of the liveliest players in the league. After a troubled childhood but successful football career, Lipscomb, who was nicknamed Big Daddy, had died at the age of thirty-one in 1963, according to the autopsy, because of a heroin overdose.

Jarrell's elegy reflects on the death of this public figure whom he knew only through the media. "Say Goodbye to Big Daddy" owes much to an interview article in *The Saturday Evening Post* in which Lipscomb sketched his unsettling life. Being orphaned at eleven when his mother was stabbed to death left Lipscomb "scared most of [his] life." In a surprisingly candid moment, especially for a formidable and seemingly intrepid football player, Lipscomb admitted: "Every once in a while it gets so bad I cry myself to sleep" (36). By quoting these lines and relating how Lipscomb was "hurt by smaller men" and used gallantly to help his opponents get up after tackling them, "so that 'the children / Won't think Big Daddy's mean,'" Jarrell emphasizes the mellow and vulnerable character of this gentle giant in a hostile or uncaring world (*Complete Poems* 344). In his devastating conclusion, Jarrell argues that the millions of viewers who admired, identified with, or vicariously were Eugene Lipscomb while looking at the little screen, will soon have forgotten about him in a culture that quickly forgets its dead heroes:

The big black man in the television set
Whom the viewers stared at—sometimes, almost were—
Is a blur now; when we get up to adjust the set,
It's not the set, but a NETWORK DIFFICULTY.
The world won't be the same without Big Daddy.
Or else it will be. (*Complete Poems* 344)

Compassionate, friendly, kind, and vulnerable, Lipscomb seemed the antithesis of a stereotypical football star or of hegemonic masculinity. While mourning Lipscomb's death, Jarrell seems to celebrate Lipscomb's "semifeminine" qualities. It is this semifeminine approach toward the typically masculine topic of football that makes the poem so effective and touching. Jarrell upsets or subverts the reader's expectations all around—in terms of what poetry should be concerned with, what an elegy is, what a football player should be like, and how a man should or should not behave. Richard Flynn has found drafts for an essay that Jarrell wrote in the 1950s that contained a rhetorical question from the "mainstream" society that echoes these sentiments and also perfectly sums up Jarrell's objections to American culture: "Why don't you stop being neurotic, and subversive, and effeminate, and aesthetic, and Un-American, and be like us?" (qtd. in Flynn 93). Jarrell felt that American society in the postwar era expected its citizens to conform to certain standards of behavior, many of which he disagreed with, and in which he felt himself to be an "effeminate" outcast.

Six years after Jarrell wrote his poem, in 1971, Dickey was commissioned to write his football elegy by the National Football League. The legendary Green Bay Packers coach Vince Lombardi had died the previous year of intestinal cancer, and the NFL was honoring him with a book. Looking for someone who could write a poem about Lombardi, the NFL turned to Dickey, perhaps because after the notorious *Life* interview he was known as the formerly football-playing poet. Dickey was initially hesitant because he could not make up his mind about Lombardi as a person: "He seems to have so many contradictory properties as a human being, some of them good—or at least as we Americans think of good—and some of them quite plainly reprehensible, and even pathological" (Letter to Dave Boss, 1 February 1971). Lombardi's work ethic and ability to inspire his players was legendary and helped small-town also-rans from Wisconsin, the Green Bay Packers, win four national championships in the 1960s. Yet he was also extremely conservative and rode his players hard in intense training sessions that were likened to military camps. The subject soon inspired Dickey, but his ambivalence about the Packers' coach is evident in "For the Death of Lombardi."

Dickey's final product was thus "no whitewash, no sweet-scented throwaway elegy," as he assured the NFL when sending the poem (Letter to Dave Boss, undated). Indeed, Dickey is surprisingly critical, not only of Lombardi but also of the aggressiveness that football promotes and the increasing commercialism that has infiltrated the game. "[D]runk / On much-advertised beer," the fans root for players to inflict pain on other players, while the players' bodies are patched up with tape or anesthetized with painkillers (*Whole Motion* 390). Neither the fans nor the players seem particularly conscious of how exploitative professional football is as they follow the mantras of their favorite coach. Towards the end of the poem, Dickey's speaker seems disgusted with the sport's violence and excessive emphasis on profit, which is conveyed by juxtaposing images that connote combativeness or commerce:

> We stand here among
> Discarded TV commercials:
> Among beer-cans and razor-blades and hair-tonic bottles,
> Stinking with male deodorants: we stand here
> Among teeth and filthy miles
> Of unwound tapes, novocaine needles, contracts, champagne
> Mixed with shower-water, unraveling elastic, bloody faceguards
> (*Whole Motion* 391–392).

Elegies tend to be hagiographic, but "For the Death of Lombardi" is an exception because Dickey's speaker is remarkably censorious of Lombardi, who is pictured on his deathbed when he is spoken to. Lombardi is likened to General Patton, the hard-driving, manic field commander from World War II who slapped his own soldiers for alleged cowardice. "For the Death of Lombardi" pivots on a saying attributed to the late football coach: "Winning is not the most important thing: it is the only thing!" The poem's middle-aged speaker comes to question this belief and wonders whether Lombardi has exploited his players' meanest character traits in order to win meaningless victories. As the crab—a metaphor for the cancer that spreads through Lombardi's body—proceeds to attack yet another vital organ, like a defensive lineman in pursuit of the quarterback, Lombardi and Dickey's speaker realize that in the game of life there are only losers, as everyone eventually succumbs to death:

> When the surgeons got themselves
> Together and cut loose
> Two feet of your large intestine, the Crab whirled up whirled out
> Of the lost gut and caught you again
> Higher up.   Everyone's helpless
> But cancer. (*Whole Motion* 391)

Like Dickey at the time, the speaker is a middle-aged man who wistfully dreams of a career in football but was not, the initial lines suggest, good enough to make the grade: "I never played for you. You'd thrown / Me off the team on my best day" (*Whole Motion* 391). It is ironic that Dickey seemed more honest in his poetry than in his public persona. Here, as elsewhere in his poetry, Dickey did not feel compelled to present himself as "an all-American heterosexual superman" but exhibited his insecurities more openly.

In tone, style, and content, "For the Death of Lombardi" is an almost Jarrellian poem. The drawn-out thoughts and lines, the insecurity of diction, the many rhetorical questions, and the lack of formal control are all stylistic elements that Jarrell frequently used. The middle-aged speaker, who is preoccupied with aging and gains a sudden and rare yet disillusioning insight into life while delivering his narrative, is another typical trademark of Jarrell's poetry. Dickey's elegy is also tonally diverse, in the sense that Dickey's speaker addresses Lombardi in different ways throughout the poem, ranging from angry indignation to loyal care. Lombardi's demanding nature almost drives the speaker mad, but the poem ends with a promise of unconditional devotion: "[W]e're with you / We're with you all the way / You're going forever, Vince" (*Whole Motion* 392). Jarrell had already used such varieties of tone of voice, for instance in "A Girl in a Library" (1951). Still another, more important, similarity between the two poets is that Jarrell sought to insert concrete images into his poetry and looked for accessible subject matter drawn from real life. In fact, in a letter to Dickey mailed on April 23, 1965, Jarrell congratulated Dickey on this particular aspect of his poetry: "[Y]ou seem to me a real poet, your poems come out of life and not literature, and the best are a wonderful surprise, both natural and strange." Dickey must have been delighted reading this since Jarrell's opinion of his work mattered to him the most, as he subsequently admitted in an interview (*Voiced Connections* 191).

In spite of his sense of competition and his earlier attacks on Jarrell, Dickey felt a deep kinship with him. When reviewing Jarrell's final volume of poetry, *The Lost World* (1965), Dickey wrote sympathetically and respectfully of Jarrell. After Jarrell's death, Dickey praised him more wholeheartedly, and in *Self-Interviews* even admitted that he identified with Jarrell:

Randall Jarrell seemed so much like me. He had sort of the same background. He was more intelligent and well-read than I, but there seemed to be something in the temperament of the writer—I hadn't met him at the time—very much like the part of myself I wanted most to set down on paper. There was a humanistic feeling of compassion and gentleness about him. (34)

There is something amusing about Dickey's admission that Jarrell's sweet-tempered nature is similar to his, as it is the total opposite of the hyper-masculine man he sought to portray in the *Life* interview. Apparently, Jarrell's poetry awakened Dickey's vulnerability and sensitivity. An anecdote told by Dickey's daughter Bronwen seems to underline this point. In 1997, she published a eulogy about her deceased father in which she explained what sort of parent and teacher Dickey had been, perhaps in order to negate the image of the hard-drinking, womanizing, and philandering poet that the press represented in obituaries. Illustrating his popularity as a teacher, she relates this anecdote:

> There was one time when my father was reading his [*sic*] poem "Goodbye to Big Daddy" about the death of football player Big Daddy Lipscomb to his class, and this big ox-headed football player in the class started bawling in the middle of the reading. The class was dismissed, and my dad just went over to this guy and held him while he wept like a child, saying, "It's all right, Big Boy; it's gonna be okay." (19)

The irony is, of course, that it was Jarrell and not Dickey who wrote "Say Goodbye to Big Daddy," which Bronwen mistakenly claims as "his." Like Eugene Lipscomb, both James Dickey and this "big ox-headed football player" are tough on the outside, but much softer on the inside. Jarrell's semifeminine elegy, however, can be seen to break through their hegemonic masculine defense.

Both Dickey and Jarrell lived and wrote "in an age in which the most natural feeling of tenderness, happiness, or sorrow was likely to be called sentimental," as Jarrell once remarked in a different context (*Poetry and the Age* 99). Whereas Dickey responded to this *Zeitgeist* by concocting a hypermasculine public persona and revealing his true feelings only in some of his poems, Jarrell's life and work form a courageous contrast to Dickey's prevarications. Unlike Dickey, Jarrell did not brag or invent stories about his college years or army life. Jarrell also seemed much more comfortable with his feminine side, and he was not overly competitive. In his criticism, for instance, Jarrell could be harsh, but never in order to settle a score. Moreover, he "could make other writers feel that their work was more important to him than his own," something Dickey was clearly incapable of (Lowell 93).

In his poetry, Jarrell genuinely sought to capture real emotions and feelings. Occasionally Jarrell's poetry can sound inelegant or sentimental; his lines "Big Daddy Lipscomb / Has helped to his feet the last ball carrier, Death," for instance, are indeed awkward. Other lines in Jarrell's elegy, however, are both clever and functional. In the opening stanza, Jarrell refers to a Prudential Insurance Company advertisement as a simile for the way Lipscomb blocked his opponents, "like the Rock / Of Gibraltar in a life insurance ad" (*The Complete Poems* 344). For years, Prudential's advertisement depicted the familiar image of the rock, with the accompanying claim: "The Prudential has the strength of Gibraltar." Referring to a life insurance ad in an elegy is amusingly ironic, undermining the association of solidity between Lipscomb and Prudential with the suggestion of their shared vulnerability.

Moreover, when read out loud—which is what Jarrell intended for his poetry—few listeners can resist being moved by Jarrell's affectionate portrait of this doomed football player, a poetic expression of that "most natural feeling" of "sorrow." Deep down Dickey knew how emotionally effective Jarrell's poetry could be, and it is even plausible that he imitated Jarrell. "For the Death of Lombardi" contains so many features that are typically Jarrellian—the long-drawn-out lines, the rhetorical questions, the middle-aged speaker's epiphany, among others—that it seems likely that Dickey learned from "Say Goodbye to Big Daddy" and Jarrell's other poems. However, this can never be proven, as Dickey probably was not man enough to admit it.

NOTES

1. The author wishes to express his gratitude to Alan Cienki, Ian Copestake, and Suzanne Ferguson for their comments and suggestions on earlier drafts of this chapter.

2. Besides "For the Death of Lombardi," Dickey's football poems are "The Bee," "In the Pocket," and "Breaking the Field." Like "For the Death of Lombardi" and "In the Pocket," "Breaking the Field," was solicited by the NFL, but it is not included in *The Whole Motion*. Dickey also wrote on football in two of his novels, *The Casting* (unpublished) and *Entrance to the Honeycomb*.

REFERENCES

Burt, Stephen. *Randall Jarrell and His Age*. New York: Columbia University Press, 2002.

Dickey, Bronwen. "He Caught My Dream." *Newsweek* 17 Mar. 1997: 19.

Dickey, James. *Babel to Byzantium: Poets and Poetry Now*. New York: Farrar, 1968.

———. *Crux: The Letters of James Dickey*. Eds. Matthew J. Bruccoli and Judith S. Baughman. New York: Knopf, 1999.

———. Letter to Dave Boss. 1 Feb. 1971. James Dickey Papers. Robert W. Woodruff Lib. Emory University. Atlanta.

———. Letter to Dave Boss. Undated. James Dickey Papers. Robert W. Woodruff Lib. Emory University. Atlanta.

———. *Self Interviews*. New York: Doubleday, 1970.

———. *The Voiced Connections of James Dickey: Interviews and Conversations*. Ed. Ronald Baughman. Columbia: University of South Carolina Press, 1989.

———. *The Whole Motion: Collected Poems, 1945–1992*. Hanover, NH: Wesleyan University Press, 1992.

Fitzgerald, F. Scott. *The Great Gatsby*. New York: Scribner, 2003.

Fitzgerald, Robert. "A Place of Refreshment." *Randall Jarrell: 1914–1965*. Eds. Robert Lowell, Peter Taylor, and Robert Penn Warren. New York: Farrar, 1967. 70–75.

Hart, Henry. *James Dickey: The World as a Lie*. New York: Picador, 2000.

Jarrell, Randall. *The Complete Poems*. New York: Farrar, 1969.

————. Letter to James Dickey. Undated. James Dickey Papers. Washington University Lib. St. Louis.

————. *Poetry and the Age*. New York: Knopf, 1953.

————. *Randall Jarrell's Letters*. Ed. Mary Jarrell. Boston: Houghton Mifflin, 1985.

Lipscomb, Eugene (as told to Robert G. Deindorfer). "I'm Still Scared." *The Saturday Evening Post* 12 Nov. 1960: 91–94.

Longenbach, James. *Modern Poetry after Modernism*. New York: Oxford University Press, 1997.

Lowell, Robert. *Collected Prose*. New York: Farrar, 1987.

O'Neil, Paul. "The Unlikeliest Poet." *Life International* 22 Aug. 1966: 66–71.

Sabo, Donald F., and Joe Panepinto. "Football Ritual and the Social Reproduction of Masculinity." *Sport, Men, and the Gender Order: Critical Feminist Perspectives*. Eds. Michael A. Messner and Donald F. Sabo. Champaign, IL: Human Kinetics, 1990. 115–126.

Simpson, Eileen. *Poets in Their Youth*. London: Faber and Faber, 1982.

Dancing with the Bulls: Engendering Competition in Hemingway's *The Sun Also Rises* and Silko's *Ceremony*

Ron Picard

Ernest Hemingway and Leslie Marmon Silko would seem to have little in common. A major innovator of modern, literary aesthetics, "Papa" Hemingway is often held up as the exemplar of white male misogyny in high modernism. He is repeatedly regarded as epitomizing white patriarchal power and stoic control. In contrast, Silko's investment in her traditionally matriarchal Laguna heritage and her depiction of strong female characters have led scholars to embrace her as a powerful voice for feminist goals and values. Nevertheless, reading Hemingway's *The Sun Also Rises* and Silko's *Ceremony* "head to head," we discover intertextual points of contact that allow us to reconstruct these divergent voices as a kind of tandem that critiques and reimagines gender in competitive contexts.

While both novels explore cultural modes of competition such as bullfighting, hunting, and dance, they foreground the global collapse of cultures under the weight of military conflict. World wars psychologically and emotionally paralyze the male characters in these texts. As a fighter pilot in World War I, Hemingway's Jake Barnes epitomizes military definitions of aggressive masculinity. Yet his performance as hypermasculine pilot, operating a phallic joystick between his legs, emasculates him, and his reference to other victimized pilots in the Italian hospital demonstrates the common nature of this "occupational hazard." Jake elegiacally recalls his fellow patients and their plans to form a society (31). However, he follows Western conventions that require victims "to play it along and just not make trouble for people," thereby purchasing social acceptance through silent, "manly" but also submissive, stoicism (31). While Jake's narrative repeatedly breaks this code of silence, his inability to join his voice with those of others prevents him from combating the continued glorification of the fighter pilot. Postwar Jake, then, understands the duplicity that underlies the pilot's image; however, his conflicted voice provides no match for the powerful forces that lead others to pursue his path and to participate in such brutally wasteful conflicts.

Ceremony's World War II veterans represent many of these others who follow in Jake's wake. Rocky, Tayo, and the other Laguna enlistees carry their community's desire to escape their abjection and to compete within the white-dominated world of the U.S. military. Silko's text demonstrates how World War II military propaganda represses the suffering of veterans like Hemingway's Jake. Her army recruiter replaces the experiences of such World War I pilots with posters and color pamphlets depicting "a man in a khaki uniform and gold braid" standing in front of "a gold eagle with its wings spread across an American flag" (64). While the eagle and male figure symbolize victorious U.S. military power, the former also marks an appropriation of Indian religious tradition by the Euro-American state. With its gold eagle and gold-braided figure, the pamphlet gilds over the alienating, enervating losses of World War I veterans and the genocidal history of colonized Indians. The U.S. army thus builds a sense of masculine power by commodifying its past, separating its current recruits and future victims from those it has already consumed.

Both novels, then, represent the impotence that stems from violent military contests. Yet *Ceremony* locates the source of such destruction not simply in Euro-American institutions but in its own Laguna tradition of witchery. Subjects under the influence of witchery compete by controlling knowledge and dominating others. These competitive practices are fueled when subjects feel isolated and impotent, forgetting their participation within the intricate world around them. *Ceremony*'s witchery narrative envisions a "complete" world with only the seed of "white people" that is planted through a rivalry among witches from "all directions / witches from all the Pueblos / and all the tribes" including representatives with "slanty eyes" and "black skin" (133). These racial and geographic distinctions indicate difference as always already at the core of Laguna cosmology. Witches express these differences through competitive revelation and division. Like merchants displaying their wares, they present objects to prove their "superior" knowledge of unspeakable victimization:

dead babies simmering in blood
.   .   .
Whorls of skin
cut from fingertips
sliced from the penis end and clitoris tip. (134)

This list suggests the kind of sexual mutilation suffered by Hemingway's Jake, and the winner of the competition calls forth the genocidal history of Euro-American colonization, foretelling its culmination in nuclear apocalypse. Through this witch's invocation, white colonists conquer and destroy, having forgotten their place within the world. Without such knowledge, they imagine themselves as exclusive islands of subjectivity, isolated and threatened by external Others: "[T]hey see only objects / The world is a dead thing for them" and "They fear the world / They destroy what they fear / They fear themselves" (135). This last line reveals the denial at the heart of competition based on exclusion: Subjects are intrinsically tied to the opponents, the Others, with whom they compete.

Searching for such an interdependent model of competition, *The Sun Also Rises* and *Ceremony* turn toward ecological images and ancient traditions. The former text's vision of the Basque countryside resonates with the latter's exploration of Laguna's agricultural roots and its vital connection to the earth. Both novels look to the local landscape to regenerate their impotent subjects and to reconstruct communal, symbiotic forms of struggle while also noting the difficulty of functioning within such a context.

Ceremony's traditional medicine man, Ku'oosh, explains the delicate, complex nature of interdependence when he tells Tayo, "this world is fragile" and "the word he chose to express 'fragile' was filled with the intricacies of a continuing process, and with a strength inherent in spider webs woven across paths through sand hills where early in the morning the sun becomes entangled in each filament of web" (35). The shifting sand, rising sun, and glimmering web demonstrate the world's intricate and ever-changing struggle. The world is inherently unstable because it recapitulates the interactions of its living, moving parts. The loss of one worldly member threatens all the others. Without the rising sun, neither the sand nor the spider web can be seen. Sunlight is invisible without the glittering sand and glistening web. Furthermore, this visual image implies a seeing subject who also affects and is affected by this moving scene. The strength of this fragility, like that of the spider web, is its flexibility, its power to remake itself. Just as the web bends to accommodate a desert wind, the global system of interrelations adjusts with the moves of its members. But too much stress on the webbing/world can tear it apart. The world's fragility is therefore a cause for both concern and hope. Like the spider whose living body re/generates the web, subjects can coordinate their movements with the worlds around and within them to maintain a system that is mutually empowering, or they can neglect points of contact and, like insects in the web, blindly thrash around, damaging the network that sustains them.[1] Within this traditional Laguna view, then, Tayo's impotence does not represent individual failure but reflects the physical and spiritual competition, the play, among nurturing forces and destructive witchery within the global webbing.

Tracing Laguna's matriarchal understanding of the earth as a struggling body of interrelations upon Jake's narrative in *The Sun Also Rises*, we can look for moments that suggest a similar kind of intimacy between alienated subjects and their surroundings. For instance, the Basque peasants Jake meets on his way to Pamplona share much in common with *Ceremony*'s Laguna community. The Basques are an indigenous, marginalized group that resists dominant definitions and objectifying codes. Caught between France and Spain and denied national autonomy, these aboriginal "Europeans" resemble Silko's Southwest Indian populations bordering the United States and Mexico. Both groups defy border restrictions and officially sanctioned nationalities in favor of ancient, physical participation in the local landscape. When Jake sees an old man turned away on the Spanish side of the border, he asks the guard what the man will do. The guard responds, "[o]h, he'll just wade across the stream" separating the two countries (92). The guard's nonchalant admission to the existence of smuggling illustrates the local success of Basque subversion. The guard recognizes his inability to contain the local commerce that historically precedes the prohibitive national laws and static practices he is bound to uphold. The customs officer and Spanish law merely present an inconvenient detour for the Basque natives rather than impregnable opposition. By occupying the borderlands, the Basque peasants reveal the role their improvisational practices play in confronting the kinds of nationalism that alienate subjects from one another and the environments that sustain them. Like the ancient, seamless land they inhabit, the peasants compete against national borders and possessive trade restrictions.

While *The Sun Also Rises* documents the indigenous relationship between Basque peasants and the earth, its narrator, nevertheless, maintains a tourist's or reporter's stance toward his subject. For Jake, the Basque community seems to represent not lived experience but local color for his aesthetic appreciation of Pamplona's fiesta and its staged competition, the bullfight. In contrast, *Ceremony* foregrounds such "color commentary" by emphasizing Laguna's flexible struggle with the mutable earth. As a rancher who depends upon the land for his existence, Tayo's Uncle Josiah must accommodate drought. He understands that surviving involves negotiating environmental changes, not repressing or directly opposing them. For Josiah and other traditional figures in *Ceremony*, accommodation is not a sign of weakness but a competitive practice that combats paralyzing impotence. His alliance with Night Swan leads him to place his faith in Ulibarri's mongrel cattle descended from a "fine Hereford bull" (80) and "generations of desert cattle, born in dry sand and scrubby mesquite, where they hunted water the way desert antelope did" (74). His purchase of the cattle shows that he recognizes his limited power over his environment. Rather than restricting his behavior to fixed Euro-American values, Josiah adapts his strategies to his material circumstances. These special cattle can survive the drought on the Laguna reservation, whereas the European-bred and favored Herefords cannot. Josiah knows that divisive, unconditional responses lead only to failure, nihilistic hopelessness, impotence, and destruction. Reconciling his local needs with those of the land, Josiah strengthens his ties to the earth's fragile webbing.

Tayo follows in his uncle Josiah's footsteps as he battles white ranchers to rescue the stolen cattle. Understanding their steadfast urge to return home, Tayo reclaims the cattle not by imprisoning them but by accommodating this need. He encourages their instinctual drive southward by opening a gap in the white rancher's southern fence and joins the herd in their run through barbed wire. Like the Basque smuggler in *The Sun Also Rises*, *Ceremony*'s Tayo undercuts the legal restrictions upheld by Euro-American (anti)competitive practices. In the process, he saves his family's cattle from their commodification as fodder for Texas Roping, "the sport of aging cowboys" (212).

Unlike Laguna practices that accommodate and honor all participants in a global struggle for survival, this rodeo event injures and kills animals in order to uphold masculine metanarrative and repress white, male vulnerabilities. *Ceremony* emphasizes the waste involved in such Euro-American "sport" in its description of a rodeo bull that Tayo's cousin Romero rehabilitates. While whites reject the bull as a casualty of their games, Romero sees the animal's potential. Healing the bull's leg, Romero provides a male addition to Tayo's predominantly female herd, lending "bone and muscle" to Josiah's unconventional venture (226).

Ceremony's Romero and his rehabilitated bull call on us to reexamine the sport of bullfighting that lies at the core of Hemingway's novel. This sport serves as the centerpiece for the San Fermin fiesta, an event that Jake initially describes as a ritualized extension of Basque community. The peasants work their way into the city via "out-lying wine-shops" (152). They attend Catholic mass en masse. Their "riau-riau" dancers and musicians fill the streets, surrounding and obscuring the official procession of civil and religious authorities (155). Jake's rendering of the revelry resembles Mikhail Bakhtin's analysis of medieval carnival. According to Bakhtin, "[c]arnival is not a spectacle seen by the people; they live in it, and everyone participates because its very idea embraces all the people. While carnival lasts there is no other life outside it" (7). It celebrates "temporary liberation from the prevailing truth and from the established order" and suspends "all hierarchical rank, privileges, norms, and prohibitions" in favor of "becoming, change and renewal" (Bakhtin 10).

With its all-male dancing and bullfighting spectacles, the fiesta suggests an alternative reading of the relationship between competition and masculinity. The sporting event offers an approved cultural context for expressing otherwise prohibited desire; in fact, Jake describes the entire celebration of traditional manhood in queer terms.[2] The bullfighter not only epitomizes traditional machismo; he also unites the exclusive, all-male club of bull-fighting aficionados. Jake defines an "aficionado" as "one who is passionate about the bull-fights" (131), but he associates such passion with Montoya's secret smile: "He always smiled as though bull-fighting were a very special secret between the two of us; a rather shocking but very deep secret that we knew about. He always smiled as though there was something lewd about the secret to outsiders" (131). In addition to this secret display of unspeakable passion, aficionados recognize each other with an "embarrassed putting the hand on the shoulder, or a 'Buen hombre.' But nearly always there was the actual touching" (132). These men require physical intimacy to establish and maintain their unified worship of masculinity, but their embarrassment stems from the prohibition on such intimacy found in their masculine code. The violent sacrifice of the bull washes away the guilt associated with transgressing this taboo and authenticates their masculinity; it allows these men to express their homosocial or homosexual feelings for one another. The bull's commodification, then, provides a closet for queer community.[3]

Repressing their unspeakable desires, the aficionados embrace the same Euro-American masculine metanarrative that underlies *Ceremony*'s depiction of rodeo events. Unlike Silko's Romero, who heals a rodeo bull, Hemingway's Romero confidently defies death, wielding a phallic sword with which he defeats a brute natural force. A model of masculine control and artistic-athletic mastery, Romero courageously challenges death by working close to the bulls. Since the bulls are themselves common symbols of male virility, Romero's control over them demonstrates his absolute possession of masculinity. While Jake anxiously occupies the position of the dead and castrated bull, he identifies with Romero in order to regain a sense of potent masculinity. Jake's sexual infirmity seems to stand in the way of his relationship with Brett Ashley, so he markets Romero to her as a viable surrogate. Pimping for Brett allows Jake to substitute his model male for himself. If Brett rejects Jake's body, he can at least participate vicariously in her sexual exploits, choosing a body for her that he deems exceptionally male.

Yet hidden beneath this metanarrative of masculinity lies the commodification of the bull and bullfighter. As Hemingway's *Death in the Afternoon* illustrates, the bull's tragic performance ultimately relies on strictly controlling its breeding, testing its "bravery," and limiting its knowledge of bullfighting ritual. The bullfighter is as much a carefully controlled commodity as the animal he fights. The high priest of the bullfight, Romero plays a key role in its economy of desire; but his position as male icon also results in his commodification. Since aficionados define themselves according to their inside knowledge, or consumption, of this "best-looking boy" (163), they can maintain their sense of masculine privilege only by restricting Romero's ties to those they view as outside their circle. Nevertheless, as *Death in the Afternoon* reports, this custodial relationship does nothing to protect the prized possession. Like the bulls they fight, bullfighters traditionally end their careers in death or disgrace.[4]

The Basque peasants who flock to this ceremony of masculinity also suffer from its commodification. They flee complex, difficult lives to share in the feeling of potency and queer desire generated by bullfighting ritual. The running of the bulls provides an opportunity for them to display machismo, to demonstrate that they possess the bullfighter's *cojones*. Emboldened by their purchase and consumption of alcohol, these men risk their lives and the livelihoods of their families in order to pursue this masculine ideal. Jake's account of Girones's death illustrates the extent of this risk. Gored during the running of the bulls, the twenty-eight-year-old peasant leaves his wife and two children to struggle alone with the family farm. The full effects of the fiesta lie in the uncertain future of this fractured family. They are left to depend on one another and their community for survival. As Girones's widow and children ride off in their open-air "third-class railway-carriage" (198), their open-ended story disappears from Jake's text. Yet in glimpsing their presence, the novel hints at gender relations that transcend the commercialized bullfighting ritual and Jake's highly limited viewpoint. Like the cattle Jake hears in the Basque woods but cannot see (116–117), the brief appearance of Girones's family implies domestic narratives potentially built on nurturing support that are lost in the drunken excesses of the San Fermin fiesta and its hypermasculine competitions.

While the ancient, daily rituals of Basque life that foster community and ensure survival disappear from Jake's narrative along with the Girones family, *Ceremony* places such practices at the core of its narrative and suggests matriarchal revisions to bullfighting's commercially constructed "do and die" performance. Laguna ceremonies remind subjects to cultivate interdependence. Laguna hunters sprinkle cornmeal on the nose of a fallen deer in order to feed its spirit. They must "show their . . . appreciation; otherwise, the deer . . . would not come to die for them the following year" (51). From the matriarchal Laguna vantage point, physical survival depends on honoring a relationship bound by ongoing sacrifice, not on dominating and commodifying prey. All relationships are reciprocal, not mortally and unequivocally opposed. Laguna rituals, such as that performed by deer hunters, remind subjects of their limited place within an interdependent, competitive system that stretches infinitely through time and space. Subjects must choose to act carefully while recognizing that total control is an illusion.

The bullfight in *The Sun Also Rises* fails Jake as a healing form of competition because, unlike *Ceremony*'s deer ritual, it allows no space for openly recognizing and validating all participants. However, Jake's discussion of the bullfight goes beyond the narrow circle of aficionados who repress queer desire while reveling in masculine metanarrative. Jake hears of Girones's death from a waiter, the urban counterpart to the Basque peasant class. The waiter condemns the waste involved in this patriarchal ritual: "You hear?" he tells Jake, "Muerto. Dead. He's dead. With a horn through him. All for morning fun. Es muy flamenco" (198). His rejection of the event as "muy flamenco" involves a dismissal of southern Spanish culture and one of its most commodified elements, flamenco, but it also invokes the ethnic stereotype concerning the stingy, mercantile Dutch, for "flamenco" translates as "Flemish." Through his description of the ritual as "muy flamenco," or "quite Flemish," the waiter places responsibility for this waste on the romanticized Spanish occupation of Basque land and the financial interests that benefit from the exploitation and physical dissipation at the heart of the fiesta. His statement, then, indirectly indicts Jake's "masculine" performance as tourist-aficion. Assuming this subject position, Jake disregards and represses the local histories of Basque oppression.

Nevertheless, the terms "Flamands" and "Flamenco" in *The Sun Also Rises* also hint at complex, multicultural histories behind nationalistic and commercial exhibitions. "Flamenco" signifies both Spanish and Flemish culture. Furthermore, the similar construction of the three terms, "Flemish," "Flamenco," and "Flamands," testifies to the history shared by the speakers of these languages. As a competitive art form, flamenco represents more than a commercial product of an imperial and monolithic Spanish culture. Its artistic evolution exemplifies the diverse, intertwining racial and cultural struggles that make and remake the subjects who occupy the Iberian Peninsula. As a living artifact of repeated colonizations and cultural conflicts, it reveals "Spaniards" as continuously in process of becoming.

Although flamenco dancing is often accused of serving no political purpose, William Washabaugh demonstrates that in addition to "housing the worm of regressive politics, the core of flamenco also encourages progressive inclinations and, during the late-Franco period, was associated with resistance to Franco's dictatorship" (xiii). Flamenco's transformative politics may be found not in its highly traditional lyrics but in its performance. Like the witch's invocation in *Ceremony*, flamenco does not simply state but enacts its political process. One way that it operates is through what Washabaugh calls "synchronization . . . the coordination of behaviors of improvising artists" (17). Like highly trained athletic teams, flamenco singers, guitarists, and dancers play off of one another's improvisations. Their performance is a work in process as they continuously call and respond to each other. While Washabaugh notes that this shared invention may be harnessed to serve both "regressive" and "progressive" ideologies, it nevertheless may be used to promote a sense of community that would enable Jake and the other characters in *The Sun Also Rises* to overcome their tragically paralyzing alienation. However, Jake buries any exploration of flamenco beneath his frustrated desire to participate in the bullfighting sacrament of idealized masculinity and its illusion of power. Like the story of the Girones family, the tale of flamenco's political potential lies beyond the scope of Jake's patriarchal vision.

As if in response to the critique of flamenco in Hemingway's text, *Ceremony* presents flamenco performer and spiritual guide Night Swan. A major feminine force within the novel, Night Swan shares her dancing and her story with those she loves. Her narrative expresses not only the pain of rejection and betrayal but also confident, competitive defiance. As a professional flamenco dancer, she rejects the art form's association with the kinds of patriarchal competition that haunt and emasculate Hemingway's Jake. She brings her performance into the cafés that flamenco tradition reserves for men and gains the reputation for promiscuity imposed upon women who pursue this career. Her passionate, athletic moves threaten female as well as male composure, exposing cracks in complacent marriages characterized by fear and denial. She refuses to participate in the objectifying masquerade of masculine exhibitions. When a married lover denies responsibility for his desire and, instead, shifts the burden onto her with labels of "Whore" and "Witch," Night Swan pointedly responds, "[y]ou came breathlessly . . . but you will always prefer the lie. You will repeat it to your wife; you will repeat it at confession. You damn your own soul better than I ever could" (85). Her statement condemns the kind of fearful and irresponsible repression and objectification that characterizes competition in Hemingway's text. Failing to acknowledge his choice in their relationship, Night Swan's lover denies his role in her performance, sealing his fate as "a living dead man who sucked life from the living, desiring and hating it even as he took it" (85).

In contrast to her former lover, Night Swan does not retreat from her desire but explores it through her dance. In so doing, she assumes the "natural" power of "the bull and at the same time the killer, holding out her full skirts like a cape" (86). If Hemingway's Pedro Romero and his bovine victim become one in the instant of the bull's death, Night Swan embodies this union in her performance. Her movement rejects the traditional binary equation that calls for masculine victory at the expense of animals' or women's lives. Rather than claiming the false triumph of masculinity, her whirling female body asserts the artistic and athletic power of all subjects, blurring the lines defining "natural" killer and "cultured," "male" artist-athlete. Her performance is more than an artistic act or a cultural masquerade; it expresses the otherwise inexplicable, powerful aspirations that "had always been inside her, growing, pushing to the surface" (84). These feelings define her being in infinite terms. She shares them with her lover in a futile attempt to discover their "boundary" but eventually sees that their "horizon was an illusion and the plains extended infinitely" (85). Night Swan's performance, then, has no end. From her matriarchal perspective, performance is not about winning and losing but about challenging and adapting. It displays the growing and changing involved in living.

Night Swan's articulation of desire has clear ramifications for our reading of *The Sun Also Rises*. Her choreography invites us to revisit Jake's observations of the gay men who dance with Brett at the bal musette. Like Night Swan, these men reject patriarchal codes of competition which insist on denying "illicit" desires. As Wolfgang Rudat explains, Jake's angry reaction to their "composure" demonstrates his envy of such sexual poise (174). Their confidence allows these men to mock heterosexual norms by courting a woman—Brett or the prostitute Georgette—while simultaneously signaling their lack of sexual desire for her (Rudat 173). Rudat notes that such ironic performance only conceals and ridicules Jake's own unfulfilled desire for Brett, but I would add that Jake's observation of the queer display also reveals our narrator's vicarious participation in it. Jake's descriptions of Brett in this scene are always mediated by his observations of the other men. They filter Jake's view of Brett, and like the effect of Night Swan's flamenco performance upon her audience, their dancing draws Jake into their story, an intimate movement from which he fearfully retreats.

While Jake flees his queer rivals, Brett acknowledges their communal potential. Her habit of collecting and disposing of men may be read as an inversion of traditional gender roles; yet her attraction to mainly queer "male" figures may indicate a desire to form nurturing and complex coalitions. Although she eventually turns on Robert Cohn and his naïve romanticism, she dismisses the anti-Semitism of her intended husband Mike and accompanies Cohn to San Sebastian. Jake senses the possibility that she has had intimate relations with an African American musician whom she calls "a great friend of mine" (62). These affairs, like her association with gay men, allow her a sense of safety in queer alliance. Victims of anti-Semitism, racism, homophobia, and physical impotence, neither Jake, Cohn, the musician, nor Brett's gay dance partners occupy social positions secure enough to allow them to thoroughly dominate or objectify her. Significantly, Brett's arrival at the bal musette with these queer subjects marks one of the few times she is represented as sober throughout Jake's entire narrative. Since her drinking, like Jake's, acts as a repressive response to her victimization—she is most drunk when accompanied by possessive Mike Campbell—her sobriety demonstrates that she gains more from these men than freedom to drink; they also empower her to resist alcohol, replacing it with communal dance. Her association with marginal men allows her a sense of healing power. As a nurse, she tends to Jake's wounds. She tells Jake that she took Robert to San Sebastian because she "thought it would be good for him" (83), and according to Mike, Brett "loves looking after people. That's how we came to go off together. She was looking after me" (203). Even her relationship with Pedro Romero may be read as an attempted rescue, for it offers him a reprieve from his commodification within Montoya's bullfighting industry.

Ultimately, Brett's class consciousness and her accommodation to the divisive ideologies of her marriage partners make these moments of coalition brief. Nevertheless, her attempts at healing mark a movement in *The Sun Also Rises* toward the kind of revitalizing feminine force and community found in *Ceremony*'s Laguna tradition. Recuperating the kind of collective desire expressed and repressed in Brett's pursuit of dance partners as well as in Jake's vision of the bullfighting fiesta, Silko's novel invites us to revisit Hemingway's text, searching for fleeting moments of flexible, negotiable responses to competition. Together, these two works cooperatively struggle to engender strategies for surviving in dangerously competitive worlds.

NOTES

1. Illustrating the earth's fragility by way of the spider web, Ku'oosh invokes the traditional figure of Spider Woman, whom Paula Gunn Allen describes as "a spirit that pervades everything, that is capable of powerful song and radiant movement, and that moves in and out of the mind" (13–14).

2. Judith Butler defines "queer" as "a site of collective contestation, the point of departure for a set of historical reflections and futural imaginings . . . that which is, in the present, never fully owned, but always and only redeployed, twisted, queered from a prior usage and in the direction of urgent and expanding political purposes" (228).

3. Jake and Bill's fishing trip presents a similar opportunity. The fishing trip's designation as a homosocial male-bonding experience appears to offer Jake a culturally sanctioned context for accepting and even responding to Bill's coquettish invitation to homoerotic play on their hotel room bed (116).

4. For example, see Hemingway's description of Manuel Granero's and Chaves's careers (*Death* 45–46).

REFERENCES

Allen, Paula Gunn. *The Sacred Hoop: Recovering the Feminine in American Indian Traditions*. Boston: Beacon Press, 1986.

Bakhtin, Mikhail. Introduction. *Rabelais and His World*. Trans. Helene Iswolsky. Cambridge, MA: MIT Press, 1968. 1–58.

Butler, Judith. *Bodies That Matter*. New York: Routledge, 1993.

Hemingway, Ernest. *Death in the Afternoon*. New York: Scribner's, 1932.

——. *The Sun Also Rises*. New York: Scribner's, 1926.

Rudat, Wolfgang E. H. "Hemingway on Sexual Otherness: What's Really Funny in *The Sun Also Rises*." *Hemingway Repossessed*. Ed. Kenneth Rosen. Westport, CT: Praeger, 1994. 169–179.

Silko, Leslie Marmon. *Ceremony*. New York: Penguin, 1977.

Washabaugh, William. *Flamenco: Passion, Politics and Popular Culture*. Oxford, UK: Berg, 1996.

Part IV

**What a Beautiful Play!
Language, Aesthetics, and
Sports in American Literature**

Fouling Out the American Pastoral: Rereading Philip Roth's *The Great American Novel*

Derek Parker Royal

> It would seem rather that they were transfixed, perhaps for the first time in their lives, by the strangeness of things, the wondrous strangeness of things, by all that is beyond the pale and just does not seem to belong in this otherwise cozy and familiar world of ours.—Philip Roth, *The Great American Novel*

It has been roughly thirty years since the publication of *The Great American Novel*, Philip Roth's comically outrageous send-up of America's favorite pastime; and in light of recent developments in Roth's fiction, perhaps it is time for a reevaluation of the novel. At the time of its publication in 1973, reviews of the book were mixed. Many critics pointed out the novelist's excessiveness and lack of discipline, his misuses of satire, his problematic narrator, and his overall inability to follow up on the promise of *Portnoy's Complaint*.[1] Subsequent assessments of the novel have also been diverse, with most scholars pointing out the book's curious but nonetheless mediocre place within Roth's oeuvre. Yet while many of these studies have proved insightful, most are at least two decades old, written well before Roth's most recent critically acclaimed work.[2] His American Trilogy, including the novels *American Pastoral*, *I Married a Communist*, and *The Human Stain*, has garnered him increased recognition, and it is to these novels that one can turn to reassess his literary excursion into baseball. Much like the latest trilogy, *The Great American Novel* has at its core the demythologizing of American "truths," the most significant of these being the pastoral ideal.

As several critics have noted, baseball is one of our most prominent cultural manifestations of the pastoral. Roger Angell, for instance, emphasizes the timeless element of the game and, at its most ideal, the suspension of worldly concerns. In its refusal to be played against the clock, the game becomes "a bubble within which players move at exactly the same pace and rhythms as all their predecessors," allowing its participants to "remain forever young" (319–320). Similarly, Deeanne Westbrook notes the Edenic quality that has been historically placed on the game, where the ball field becomes an archetypal "walled garden . . . a metaphor for human society and culture expressed as a form of unfallen nature" (77). And Murray Ross, in his contrasts between baseball and football, sees the former as suggestive of a nostalgic ideal where peace, serenity, open space, and ritualized action can be found: "Baseball evokes for us a past which may never have been ours, but which we believe was, and certainly that is enough" (718).[3]

Even Philip Roth has acknowledged the pastoral tinges of the game. In fact, sports references can be found throughout his fiction: the athletic Potemkin family and its "sports tree" in "Goodbye, Columbus"; Trick E. Dixon's locker room "skull sessions" with his advisers in *Our Gang*; Jimmy "the Luftyid" Ben-Joseph and his desires to bring baseball to the Promised Land in *The Counterlife*; recollections of high school football games and their ethnic significance in *The Facts*; the all-around athlete, Seymore "Swede" Levov, in *American Pastoral*; and the empowering nature of boxing that Coleman Silk experiences in *The Human Stain*. But perhaps nowhere in his novels does he better articulate the romance of baseball than he does in *Portnoy's Complaint*. "Thank God for center field!" Alexander Portnoy tells Dr. Spielvogel in an effort to describe the baseball field as an escape from his neurotic home life:

Doctor, you can't imagine how truly glorious it is out there, so alone in all that space . . . just standing nice and calm—nothing trembling, everything serene—standing there in the sunshine . . . standing without a care in the world in the sunshine, like my king of kings, the Lord my God, The Duke Himself (Snider, Doctor, the name may come up again), standing there as loose and as easy, as happy as I will ever be, just waiting by myself under a high fly ball . . . just waiting there for the ball to fall into the glove I raise to it, and yup, there it is, *plock*, the third out of the inning. (68–69)

Such moments had given the young Portnoy a feeling of connectedness and a sense of purpose he found elusive at home. "For in center field," he waxes nostalgically, "if you can get to it, it *is* yours. Oh, how unlike my home it is to be in center field, where no one will appropriate unto himself anything that I say is *mine*!" (68). Roth articulates similar sentiments in "My Baseball Years," an essay that originally appeared as an Op-Ed piece in the *New York Times* on the opening day of the 1973 baseball season. He recalls in evocative rhetoric that his "feel for the American landscape came less from what I learned in the classroom about Lewis and Clark than from following the major-league clubs on their road trips and reading about the minor leagues in the back pages of *The Sporting News*" (237–238). He goes on to reveal that "baseball—with its lore and legends, its cultural power, its seasonal associations, its native authenticity, its simple rules and transparent strategies, its longueurs and thrills, its spaciousness, its suspensefulness, its heroics, its nuances, its lingo, its 'characters,' its peculiarly hypnotic tedium, its mythic transformation of the immediate—was the literature of my boyhood" (238).

Such grandiose language and its links to literature should not be taken lightly, especially as it comes from a novelist who once saw his writing as a "religious calling" and "a kind of sacrament" ("On *The Great American Novel*" 77). What is even more curious is that Roth's opening day reveries were published in the same year as *The Great American Novel*, a text that is anything but reverential toward the game. It is the story of the Ruppert Mundys, the hapless and homeless baseball team made up of misfits who, much like the biblical nation of Israel, wander from one field to another in search of communal definition. Along their way, Roth exposes the political hypocrisies, the social prejudices, and the ethnic- and gender-based stereotyping that unfortunately make up much of American history. And he does so through a narrative of excess, a wild series of comedic scenarios, at times outlandish and at times tasteless, in which the author doesn't hesitate to go "too far." In his baseball novel, Roth satirically confronts the pastoral ideal, but he does so not in order to demythologize or deconstruct the game. On the contrary, his targets are the American ideals and institutions for which baseball has come to stand. As Roth states in an interview that he playfully conducted with himself, he acknowledges that he never set out to satirize baseball but merely wanted to use the game to "dramatize the *struggle* between the benign national myth of itself that a great power prefers to perpetuate, and the relentlessly insidious, very nearly demonic reality . . . that will not give an inch in behalf of that idealized mythology" ("On *GAN*" 89–90). In creating an outrageous countermythology of the great American sport, Roth deconstructs the myth of the American pastoral (much as he does in his novel of the same name) and exposes its many gaps and fissures.

Reviewers of the three novels in Roth's American Trilogy have rightly noted that his most recent work is an attempt to represent the social, political, and psychological conflicts that define America in the latter half of the twentieth-century. What few critics have acknowledged, however, is that this serious narrative impulse predates even the first Zuckerman novels. As Maria tells her husband Nathan Zuckerman in *The Counterlife*, "[t]he pastoral is not your genre" (317). And this is what Roth has been telling his readers even earlier. The transgressive nature of *The Great American Novel* is perhaps Roth's first sustained critique of postwar America, and by reexamining the text through the narratological lens of his most recent fiction, the reader can gain a deeper appreciation of what many have considered to be a slight, and even highly problematic, novel.

It is without question that *The Great American Novel*, regardless of what one might think of its novelistic merits, is an antipastoral tour de force—or, as Jay L. Halio cleverly puts it, "tour de farce" (111)—but the question remains, in what manner does Roth perpetrate and sustain this critique?[4] Certainly, the contents lend themselves to the debunking of many of America's cherished myths. And, as I will continue to argue, these are many of the same issues that Roth foregrounds so dramatically in his American Trilogy. As in *American Pastoral*, with his baseball novel he explores the disastrously false assumptions of the melting pot myth; as in *I Married a Communist*, he exposes the economic and politically reactionary foundations upon which much of contemporary American politics rests; and as in *The Human Stain* he does not hesitate to represent the ambiguous and decentered nature of American (ethnic) experience. All of these issues could have been recognized years earlier in Roth's baseball novel. In addition to the wildly ridiculous makeup of the Ruppert Mundys, most members of which could be cast as "the Other," the team is made homeless due to their owners' greed. Frank Mazuma, exploitive owner of the Kakoola Reepers, is motivated only by showmanship and revenue. Angela Whittling Trust's winning Tri-City Tycoons (in many ways the most "apple pie Americans" in the Patriot League) function in nothing more than a heartless, almost robotic, manner of professional efficiency. The game's greatest pitcher, Gil Gamesh, is not only an arrogant gamesman but eventually becomes a Soviet spy bent on the destruction of the American way of life. The president of the Patriot League, with the blessings of baseball Commissioner Judge Landis, conducts an anti-Communist witch hunt and suspends or sends to prison many league players, a pursuit that eventually leads to the demise of the Patriot League. And, in what could be read as a passage that could apply to all three protagonists in the American Trilogy—Swede Levov, Ira Ringold, and Coleman Silk—the insouciant John Baal tells his team that they are always/already alienated in the world they inhabit. "You damn fools . . . *you* ain't from Rupe-it! You never was and you never would be," he screams. "[Y]ou were visitors [in Mundy Park] just like you are visitors here. You are makin' there be a difference where there ain't" (142).

In addition to noting these large-scale transgressions against America's favorite pastime, it is revealing to examine the ways in which Roth handles the individual manifestations of the pastoral. Although he appears as an analeptic recollection, Luke "the Loner" Gofannon casts a shadow over the text in that he stands as an ideal ballplayer against whom all others are judged. Scoring close to fifteen hundred runs for the Mundys and with a batting average of .372, Gofannon outshone all, including both Ty Cobb and Babe Ruth, in his abilities to run and steal, as well as to hit. In his prime, the fans would "give him a hand just for striking out, that's how beautiful he was, and how revered," and "he loved the game so much, he'd have played without pay" (84–85). There is also the league president, General Douglas D. Oakhart, with his Rules and Regulations that underscore the perfection of baseball. He believes in tradition and the purity of the game, as is demonstrated by his crusade against radio broadcast games: "[A]ll radio would do would be to reduce the game to what the gamblers cared about: who scored, how much, and when" (90). In a similar fashion, Mundys manager Ulysses S. Fairsmith gives an eloquent speech against the introduction of nighttime baseball, the written text of which is "laid out on a [Sunday newspaper] page of its own to resemble the Declaration of Independence." His argument in many ways captures the pastoral ideal of the game that many have come to hold:

Daytime baseball is nothing less than a reminder of Eden in the time of innocence and joy. . . . For what is a ball park, but that place wherein Americans may gather to worship the beauty of God's earth, the skill and strength of His children, and the holiness of His commandment to order and obedience. For such are the twin rocks upon which all sport is founded. And woe unto him, I say, who would assemble our players and our fans beneath the feeble, artificial light of godless science! (88–89)

And finally there is Roland Agni, center fielder and batting eighth for the Mundys. He, even more than Luke Gofannon, is the ideal specimen of a player, and in almost any sport: "[T]apering like the V for Victory from his broad shoulders and well-muscled arms down to ankles as elegantly turned as Betty Grable's," he is the perfect batter, runner, and catcher, "the most spectacular rookie since Joltin' Joe" (125).

It is significant to note that Roth eliminates every one of these pastoral embodiments, and he does so in a grotesque fashion. Luke the Loner dies in a car accident when he takes his hands off the steering wheel to tip his hat to his adoring fans. While campaigning for the presidency of the United States, General Oakhart, along with running mate, midget Bob Yamm, disappears without a trace in what is purported to be Communist sabotage to his plane. The religiously inspired Fairsmith dies in a dugout—"my God, why hast thou forsaken me?" (330)—as a result of Nickname Damur trying unsuccessfully to turn a double into a triple when his team was thirty-one runs behind the Tri-City Tycoons. And Roland Agni is accidentally shot by former umpire Mike "the Mouth" Masterson as he is attempting to wrestle from new Mundy manager and Soviet spy Gil Gamesh a hollowed-out baseball bat containing microfilm. By killing off each of these figures, and doing so in such a farcical manner, Roth is with flourish putting the fine touches on the broad antipastoral strokes of his text.

However, Roth's demythologizing becomes even more significant through the use of his narrative frame, the octogenarian and former sports writer Word Smith, or Smitty, as he is known. This use of the first-person narrative not only contextualizes the novel's plot (who better to chronicle the details surrounding the Mundys' ignoble 1943 and 1944 seasons than a sports writer with a keen eye for baseball's history and legends?) but, perhaps more importantly, it also underscores the complex nature of Roth's critique. As I have argued elsewhere, a careful reading of the narrative structure in Roth's recent fiction, particularly in *American Pastoral*, reveals much about the author's sometimes ambiguous attitudes toward his subject matter.[5] The same can be said of *The Great American Novel*. The novel is made up of nine sections, reflecting the nine innings of a typical baseball game, with Smitty as our sole source of information. Of the nine sections, he appears in the first person only in the Prologue and the Epilogue (making only a few brief third person appearances during the course of the story), framing the narrative proper with his conspiratorial theories behind the elimination of the Patriot League. The events that unfold in the seven regular chapters make up the tale of the Ruppert Mundys, the details of which we have to assume were gathered by a sports writer with behind-the-scenes savvy. And, as previously mentioned, these events, which are narrated by the former sportswriter, demythologize the sacredness of the sport in a variety of ways.

As with almost any first-person account, issues of narrator reliability are important here, and indeed, several critics have questioned Roth's distance from the opinions of his literary mouthpiece. Both Ben Siegel and Janis B. Stout have argued that Roth does not erect any ironic space between himself and Smitty, and if readers restrict themselves to just the seven central chapters, then such an argument would tend to make sense.[6] When the narrator does not thrust his opinions or his personal reminisces directly into his tale, there seems to be little difference between Roth the actual author and Smitty his narrative device. But the Epilogue and especially the Prologue make up a considerable amount of the novel, so much, in fact, that without them the story of the Mundys would appear as a straightforward (albeit farcical) account of a misfit team in a league that no longer exists.

Moreover, such readings of Smitty as a nonironic narrative device fail to take into account the context of the author's entire body of work. Throughout his career Roth has displayed an ambiguous style of narrative that makes it difficult to pinpoint any definitive ideological stance. This ambiguous play, or mischievousness (as Roth likes to call it), is all the more pronounced in his more experimental or postmodern novels, and *The Great American Novel* would certainly fall into that category. As Jerry Klinkowitz points out in his study of the novel, "[b]y integrating a putative author, his subject, and the tradition in which he writes, Roth establishes an immensely more serious context for his play than had been possible in [previous works], where bold-faced statement about patently ludicrous states of affairs was the only rhetorical mode necessary to make his point" (33). What is more, in an interview given soon after the publication of his baseball novel, Roth underscores this method of writing in what has since become his oft-quoted assertion: "Sheer Playfulness and Deadly Seriousness are my closest friends" ("After" 111). Read within the context of Roth's long history of playfully serious narrators—the neurotically unhinged Peter Tarnopol in *My Life as a Man*; the not-quite-dead, not-quite-alive Nathan Zuckerman in *The Counterlife*; the "real" Philip Roth in *The Facts* and *Operation Shylock*; the fantasy-prone Zuckerman in *The Ghost Writer* and *American Pastoral*—Smitty's relationship to his author would appear to be more complicated than some suggest.

Smitty sets the stage for the novel's antipastoral critique in that he is keenly aware of the fictions upon which the game, as it is presently played, is based. He more than anyone else understands that baseball is not the all-American sport that it professes to be—a temporary escape from the cutthroat, violent, and hectic world of commercial concerns where the timeless and tranquil nature of the game allows both players and spectators to connect in a shared community of fair play—but a business enterprise based solely upon economic and political interests. This is demonstrated early in the novel when Smitty, along with his fellow geriatrics, make a Chaucer-like pilgrimage to

Cooperstown for the Hall of Fame elections. When Commissioner Bowie Kuhn comes out to announce the results of the elections, he does not admit that "the BWAA was a cheat and a fraud and disgrace for having failed to announce [Smitty's] vote submitted for Luke Gofannon of the extinguished Patriot League." Instead, ironically enough, he states that nobody received enough votes to be elected and that this was an indication of the integrity of the institution of baseball. "*The integrity of the institution*," Smitty incredulously repeats. "Next they will be talking about the magnanimity of the Mafia and the blessing of the Bomb. They will use alliteration for anything these days, but most of all for *lies*" (24).

This emphasis on language as a masking device is central to Smitty's role as a narrator. As his name suggests, he goes to great lengths to define himself through words and possesses an almost maniacal affinity for alliteration. The significance of language is also inextricably linked to the game of baseball. Through his words, Smitty creates an alternative or counter-history of baseball that does not coincide with the one readers believe to be true. Through his narrative conduit, Roth intermingles the fictitious elements of his story—the existence of the Patriot League and its ultimate demise—along with actual historical figures and events. In this way, *The Great American Novel* anticipates such experimental works as *Operation Shylock*, a novel in which its narrator, "Philip Roth" (to be distinguished from the text's author of the same name), weaves fiction into fact and creates a counter-history that challenges readers' credulity. This rhetorical move, in many ways, brings to mind the debate between Roland Agni and Isaac Ellis over the Jewish Wheaties. Having scientifically formulated a version of the cereal that ensures athletic success, Isaac quarrels with Roland over which brand of Wheaties is "real." The ballplayer argues that eating the enhanced cereal and being assured of winning would be like throwing a game, to which Isaac counters that winning is what Wheaties is all about. Roland replies,

"But that's *real* Wheaties! And they don't make you do it anyway!"
"Then how can they be 'real' Wheaties, if they don't do what they're supposed to do?"
"That's what *makes* them 'real'!" (302)

This comic inversion of the real is what defines much of Smitty's (deconstructed) history of baseball. More to the point, the slippery usage of language calls into question the narrator's ability to capture the "true" essence of the sport. Such problems recall General Oakhart's suspicions of radio broadcast ballgames: "[Y]ou could not begin to communicate through *words*, either printed or spoken, what this game was all about" (90).

Philip Roth not only presents this ambiguity in the body of his tale but also invests it in the narration itself. In the scholarship, questions about Smitty's reliability have usually been an either/or game: He is either believable or he is not. But such strictly binary readings do not allow for the possibility that Roth may be holding out for both. Smitty seems caught between nostalgia and madness (Blues 80), and there are elements in his narrative that suggest both. On the one hand, he longs for the glory days of the Patriot League. His description of Luke Gofannon, his recollection of the Mundys' previous owner, the legendary Glorious Mundy, as well as his general obsession with the league's recognition in the Hall of Fame, all bring to mind a wistfulness for bygone days. This is rather unusual, coming from a narrative voice through which Roth demythologizes the game's pastoral tinges.[7] On the other hand, the aging sports writer is generally seen as nothing more than a curmudgeonly and delusional kook. In his insistence on pursuing "the truth," Smitty has more or less exiled himself from the baseball community and is no longer able to write its history. As such, he becomes disengaged from the "reality" of the sport and is left with no alternative except to ask Chairman Mao to publish his book.

Of course, Roth is having it both ways here. When Smitty writes to the Communist Chinese leader, he bemoans the fact that American publishers refuse to handle his mad text, curiously enough entitled *The Great American Novel* (*GAN* 400). But a book by the same name is what sits in the reader's hands, and seen in this way the novel both is and isn't there.[8] Such mischievousness helps to explain the many references to those Smitty calls "my precursors, my kinsmen" (37). Throughout the Prologue and Epilogue, the narrator summons the literary spirits of Mark Twain, Nathaniel Hawthorne, and especially Herman Melville. Such allusions make sense, given the fact that all three writers, at one time or another, are believed to have authored "the great American novel." But their invocation in Roth's text has a further significance. Both Hawthorne and Melville, and even Twain in many ways, have been read as practitioners of romantic irony. Through their narrators, these nineteenth-century writers were able to maintain apparently disparate ideas, wanting to be taken seriously while at the same time fully conscious of the comic implications of their own seriousness. This attitude is further demonstrated by a self-conscious recognition of the composition, or the constructedness, of the text.[9] Through Smitty, Roth playfully foregrounds the constructed nature of his own novel, and he does so by borrowing from a variety of rhetorical conventions: realistic reportage, brief chapter summarizations reminiscent of the nineteenth-century Victorian novel, collections of letters, newspaper editorials, official committee transcripts, government reports, and timelines that speed the reader through the action (indeed, almost all of chapter 7 is nothing more than a pastiche of styles). What Roth is suggesting here is that, just like the history created by his precarious narrator, the pastoral myths of baseball are nothing more than constructed fictions. And, by association, so are the ideals of America.

In the mischievous interview he conducts with himself—another example of an ambiguous two-sidedness—Philip Roth comments on his narrator and his self-ironizing critique of America:

By attributing the book to Smitty, I intended, among other things, to call into question the novel's "truthfulness"—to mock any claim the book might appear to make to be delivering up *the* answer—though in no way is this meant to discredit the book itself. The idea is simply to move off the question "What is America really like?" and on to the kind of fantasy (or rewriting of history) that a question so troublesome and difficult has tended of late to inspire. ("On *GAN*" 91)

The emphasis here is not on discovering the essence of America (or baseball, for that matter) but on the "fantasy" of the ideal, an alternative reimagining that underscores the manner in which narratives, or histories, are created. Roth goes on to reveal in his self-conducted interview that his novel was an attempt "to establish a passageway from the imaginary that comes to seem real to the real that comes to seem imaginary, a continuum between the credible incredible and the incredible credible" (91). This novelistic impulse anticipates almost exactly the narrative structure of *American Pastoral*. In that book, the narrator Nathan Zuckerman reimagines the tragic life of the all-around athlete Swede Levov and in the process reveals the fictions, however unlikely, upon which American identity is based. In his baseball novel, Roth never claims to know what America is "really like." Instead, he invests his narrative energies into "not knowing," a phrase that in its negative signification suggests a complete opening up of fictional possibility and becomes the basis for much of his writing. "*Not* knowing, or no longer knowing for sure, is just what perplexes many," he asserts during his self-conducted interview. "That, if I may say so, is why I invented that paranoid fantasist Word Smith . . . to be (purportedly) the author of *The Great American Novel*. What he describes is what America is really like to one like *him*" ("On *GAN*" 90).

Here is another way in which *The Great American Novel* can be reread in light of his more recent fiction. Most of *The Human Stain* revolves around the fallacious claim that "everybody knows" about the secrets of Colman Silk. However, as Roth makes abundantly clear, such an assumption is not only precarious but downright inimical to the creation of narrative. The idea itself is nothing but a fiction masquerading as a certainty: "'Everyone knows' is the invocation of the cliché and the beginning of the banalization of experience. . . . What we know is that, in an unclichéd way, nobody knows anything. You *can't* know anything. The things you *know* you don't know. . . . All that we don't know is astonishing. Even more astonishing is what passes for knowing" (209). Playing upon what is not known about Silk, the narrator Zuckerman creates a fiction that opens up his subject matter in ways that "really knowing" would not allow. This in many ways recalls Keats's famous notion of "negative capability." As he writes in an 1817 letter to his brothers George and Thomas, the phrase refers to the moment "when a man is capable of being in uncertainties, Mysteries, doubts, without any irritable reaching after fact & reason." For Keats, such an uncertainty leads not to pessimism and skepticism but to the belief that "with a great poet the sense of Beauty overcomes every other consideration, or rather obliterates all consideration" (1: 193). The "not knowing" about what America (or baseball, for that matter) is really about allows the novelist to freely articulate alternative narratives that can tell us volumes about the ways we delineate our national experiences.

Herein lies the power of Roth's ambiguity as inscribed through Smitty. This unlikely narrator, with his insider status, as well as his conspiratorial assertions, creates a countermyth that exposes the fiction of the pastoral ideal. In the process, his efforts underscore a *joie de vivre* that refuses to be frozen by any metanarrative. By reimagining the history of baseball, Word Smith suggests that the meaning of sport—indeed, the meaning of America itself—is an always ongoing process, constantly in flux and never static. The play of writing, then, becomes the play of baseball with its free-flowing actions, its emphasis on the importance of minute gestures, and its opening or freeing up of both space and time. This may be what Philip Roth was getting at, a return to the kind of joy Portnoy experienced out in center field or the feelings the novelist reveals in "My Baseball Years." In exposing the fiction of the pastoral, Roth was not completely dismissive of the sport, especially as a stand-in for America itself. Baseball, for him, still held out a defining quality worth holding on to. As he writes in his reflective essay, published immediately after the subversive baseball novel, "[b]aseball made me understand what patriotism was about, *at its best* [emphasis mine]" ("Baseball Years" 236). In *The Great American Novel*, Roth attempts to demythologize the game of baseball not only to expose constructively its (and America's) many inconsistencies and hypocrisies but perhaps more importantly to draw attention to the sheer gratification of creative play and its meaning for national identity, mischievous or otherwise.

NOTES

1. For a brief listing of reviews at the time of the novel's publication, see Ben Siegel (1975).

2. Such earlier critics include Ben Siegel (1975), David Monaghan (1975), Thomas Blues (1981), Walter L. Harrison (1981), Richard C. Crepeau (1983), Frank R. Ardolino (1985), Janis P. Stout (1986), Jay L. Halio (1992), Jerry Klinkowitz (1993), and Kerry Ahearn (1993). Roth's career has taken a marked shift since the early 1990s, with both the quantity and the quality of his output growing almost exponentially. During the 1990s his books won every major American literary award, including the National Book Critics Circle Award, two National Book Awards, two PEN/Faulkner Awards, and the Pulitzer Prize. Interestingly enough, scholarly attention to *The Great American Novel* became all but extinct at about this time.

3. These are just a few of the many references to the pastoral that can be found in sports literary criticism. See also Peter Heinegg (1985), Michael Novak (1985), and Donald Hall (1981).

4. In addition to Halio, other critics who highlight the antipastoral thrust of the novel include Siegel, Blues, and Ahearn. See also Roth's own comments in "On *The Great American Novel*."

5. See, for instance, my essay, "Fictional Realms of Possibility."

6. Stout goes as far as to accuse Roth of voicing blatant "prejudical clichés" and engaging in nothing less than "the senselessness of misogyny" (74). Such an egregiously myopic reading simplifies the novelist's creative intentions, not to mention leaving no room for ambiguous narrative play.

7. In his essay, Ahearn astutely demonstrates how an attachment to the pastoral can easily turn into kitsch.

8. Roth will create the same narratological condundrum twenty years later in *Operation Shylock*, just another example of how *The Great American Novel* can be best read through the lens of his later fiction.

9. For an insightful discussion on the tradition of romantic irony in nineteenth-century American literature, see G. R. Thompson (1988). He describes the tendency as a deliberate and often absurd breaking of dramatic illusion, an interplay between humorous and serious narrative, a blurring of the boundaries between reality and fiction, and a tendency to simultaneously sustain and undercut various cultural and metaphysical presumptions (267). One could easily apply such characterizations to Roth's fiction, especially *The Great American Novel*.

REFERENCES

Ahearn, Kerry. "'Et in Arcadia Excrementum': Pastoral, Kitsch, and Philip Roth's *The Great American Novel*." *Aethlon* 11.1 (1993): 1–14.

Angell, Roger. *The Summer Game*. New York: Popular Library, 1972.

Ardolino, Frank R. "The Americanization of the Gods: Onomastics, Myth, and History in Philip Roth's *The Great American Novel*." *Arete* 3.1 (1985): 37–60.

Blues, Thomas. "Is There Life after Baseball?: Philip Roth's *The Great American Novel*." *American Studies* 22.1 (1981): 71–80.

Crepeau, Richard C. "Not the Cincinnati Reds: Anti-Communism in Recent Baseball Literature." *Arete* 1.1 (1983): 87–97.

Halio, Jay L. *Philip Roth Revisited*. New York: Twayne, 1992.

Hall, Donald. "Baseball and the Meaning of Life." *National Review* 4 Sept. 1981: 1033–1034.

Harrison, Walter L. "Six-Pointed Diamond: Baseball and American Jews." *Journal of Popular Culture* 15.3 (1981): 112–118.

Heinegg, Peter. "Philosopher in the Playground: Notes on the Meaning of Sport." Vanderwerken and Wertz 455–458.

Keats, John. *The Letters of John Keats*. Ed. Hyder Rollins. 2 vols. Cambridge: Cambridge University Press, 1958.

Klinkowitz, Jerry. "Philip Roth's Anti-Baseball Novel." *Western Humanities Review* 47 (1993): 30–40.

Monaghan, David. "*The Great American Novel* and *My Life as a Man*: An Assessment of Roth's Achievement." *International Fiction Review* 2 (1975): 113–120.

Novak, Michael. "Sacred Space, Sacred Time." Vanderwerken and Wertz 725–732.

Ross, Murray. "Football Red and Baseball Green." Vanderwerken and Wertz 716–725.

Roth, Philip. "After Eight Books." *Reading Myself and Others*. Rev. ed. New York: Penguin, 1985. 99–113.

———. *The Counterlife*. New York: Farrar, 1987.

———. *The Great American Novel*. New York: Vintage-Random, 1995.

———. *The Human Stain*. Boston: Houghton Mifflin, 2000.

———. "My Baseball Years." *Reading Myself and Others*. Rev. ed. New York: Penguin, 1985. 235–240.

———. "On *The Great American Novel*." *Reading Myself and Others*. Rev. ed. New York: Penguin, 1985. 75–92.

———. *Portnoy's Complaint*. New York: Random House, 1969.

Royal, Derek Parker. "Fictional Realms of Possibility: Reimagining the Ethnic Subject in Philip Roth's *American Pastoral.*" *Studies in American Jewish Literature* 20 (2001): 1–16.

Siegel, Ben. "The Myths of Summer: Philip Roth's *The Great American Novel.*" *Contemporary Literature* 17 (1975): 171–190.

Stout, Janis P. "The Misogyny of Roth's *The Great American Novel.*" *Ball State University Forum* 27.1 (1986): 72–75.

Thompson, G. R. "The Development of Romantic Irony in the United States." *Romantic Irony.* Ed. Frederick Garber. Budapest: Akadémiai Kiadó, 1988. 267–289.

Vanderwerken, David L. and Spencer K. Wertz, eds. *Sport Inside Out: Readings in Literature and Philosophy.* Fort Worth: Texas Christian University Press, 1985.

Westbrook, Deeanne. *Ground Rules: Baseball and Myth.* Urbana: University of Illinois Press, 1996.

"And Drive Them from the Temple": Baseball and the Prophet in Eric Rolfe Greenberg's *The Celebrant*

Roxanne Harde

In the acclaimed novel *The Celebrant*, Eric Rolfe Greenberg chronicles the career of the first national baseball hero, Christy Mathewson, and the early decades of major league baseball, intertwining this history with the fictional story of a Jewish immigrant family of jewelers, the Kapp brothers: salesman Eli, designer Jackie, and manager Arthur. The final chapter of the novel closes with the fiery suicide of Eli, a chronic gambler about to lose everything in the Black Sox scandal, as he drives off Coogan's Bluff crashing explosively against the Polo Grounds, home of the New York Giants.

In the epilogue, Jackie, who is both Eli's betrayer and the narrator and title character, discusses the 1925 death of Mathewson. Jackie then describes Major League baseball between the 1919 Black Sox scandal—which Mathewson helped bring to light—and the first All-Star game in 1933. Jackie ruminates on early legends of baseball and on the perfection they achieved on the field, particularly on Mathewson. He pauses over the first time he saw Mathewson pitch, the no-hitter of 1901, and his own joy in celebrating Mathewson's artistry with his own, in the form of a ring inspired by the pitcher's perfection, the first of several rings he crafted to honor the pitcher and his works. After this straightforward accounting of personal and baseball history, Jackie offers an ambiguous summary of his relationship with Mathewson for the novel's final words: "[I]n his age and suffering he would accept that vision of my youth, entwine it with his own hard faith, and end in madness. Eli! Eli!" (269). Jackie's closing lament for Eli calls into question his decision to follow Mathewson's command that he not offset Eli's wagers by betting on Cincinnati, a command that meant sacrificing his brother for the greater good of baseball. However, Eli's name also begins both the twenty-second Psalm and Christ's last words: "*Eli, Eli, lema sabachthani?*" (My God, my God, why have you forsaken me?) (Psalm 22.1, Matt. 27.46, Mark 15.33). "Eli, Eli!" might lament a brother, albeit one representative of the corruption that nearly destroyed baseball in its early years, but the phrase also invokes both the Old Testament prophet and the New Testament savior, whose signs are vision and faith, and often madness. *The Celebrant*'s closing words reestablish its allegorization of Christ(y) Mathewson as a prophet-messiah and Jackie as his celebrant priest, but they also ring with the deep ambiguity that reverberates through the novel. Eli might be a representative sacrifice, a good thief suffering alongside Mathewson's Christ figure and finding faith in death, or he might be seen as a blasphemer justly punished according to Old Testament law. In either case, baseball is the thing revered, the faith upheld, and the moral code reaffirmed.

Representative figures are key to this historical novel, which works allegorically with several sources, chief among them the Hebrew and Christian sacred texts. However, in accord with Deborah Madsen's general contentions about postmodern allegories, *The Celebrant* turns away from any determinate referent, including the Bible, to register the type of disjunction and displacement that gives way to "an unregulated proliferation of signs" (9). In so doing, *The Celebrant* destabilizes its own points of cultural reference in order to both offer and interrogate baseball as a sacred text. As Paul Smith points out, whether postmodern or not, allegory imposes upon the reader a specific directive that resides "in some privileged moral sphere such as politics or religion" (107–108). Grounded in the early history of baseball and the biography of Mathewson, *The Celebrant* offers the pitcher as a New Testament messiah of baseball, sent to remove the corrupting influences that threaten the sport.[1] Richard Peterson correlates Mathewson's reputation as one of "baseball's purest players" to Greenberg's Jackie, who has "the imaginative sensibility to recognize greatness of form on the playing field and the moral intelligence to understand the value of integrity in baseball's performers" (108). However, the novel complicates the Christ(y)an message with the figure of Jackie, a devout Jew. In the resulting proliferation of signs, Mathewson is New Testament messiah and Old Testament prophet; Jackie plays out complimentary roles as an Aaron to Mathewson's Moses, a Christian priest to his savior, and a pagan artist worshiping him with his craft.

I am not the first critic to see *The Celebrant* as an allegory. Allen Hye posits many approaches to the novel, including as a messianic allegory (41). Eric Solomon also sees allegorical strains in the novel and goes so far as to consider the corrupted Hal Chase as a "nearly allegorical figure" (87).[2] Solomon locates pagan and idolatrous impulses in the celebratory rings-fetishes, and he traces the Christian and Jewish narratives as offered by Greenberg, including indicators of the fall, the Christian ethos of sacrifice translated to the playing field, and the Jewish ethos of justice. He also traces the postmodern impulses in the novel's deep ambiguities: the fundamental irony of Mathewson's self-sacrifice and the contradictions inherent in the Jewish Jackie's Christ(y)an adoration. I agree with Solomon that the novel "strengthens and questions parallels between baseball and religion" (98) but want to take his argument further with the contention that *The Celebrant* ultimately escapes both the

Jewish and Christian narratives in order to put forth baseball as a separate temple, a sacred space that invites reverence and insists on justice.

The diamond as sacred space is an underlying theme, one that relies on baseball history as its source. For example, Jackie, who at one point leaves the synagogue in as hurried a fashion as possible for the Polo Grounds, "that secular house of worship" (95), shows reverence for the sport by considering it a sacrilege to walk on the playing field at the close of the game. In the first place, Jackie calls into question his own judgment about baseball's secularity during an eschatological rumination on its legends, where the players go and how they abide (268). In the second place, when his brother Arthur comments on the remarkable experience of stepping onto a major league field, Jackie responds that he has never been on one, not having earned his place (152). A former sandlot pitcher, Jackie chooses to worship the sport as one does *torah*, at a "proper distance" (42). His profound knowledge of baseball enables him to see Mathewson's greatness and become his chief celebrant, but his reverence keeps him from transgression, unlike the "wave upon wave of celebrants" who converge on the field (99). Jackie's reverence for the game and for Mathewson's perfection leads to his creation of rings that duplicate the playing field, incorporating diamonds into a diamond, exchanging athletic brilliance for the glitter of precious stones. Jackie will not walk on the diamond, but he will set it in stone and metal, and his artistry seems an allegorical reference to the golden calf as much as to the ark of the covenant. The ball diamond and the diamond ring draw on sacred texts for their meaning, but the undecideability of their commentary only adds to the novel's religious indeterminacy.

Key to the indeterminacy of the novel's allegorical commentary is the indeterminacy of its main characters. The narrative places these men of many names—Yakov-Jacob-Jack-Jackie Kapinski-Kapp and Christopher-Christy-Big Six-Matty Mathewson—in continually shifting positions. The immigrant Yakov becomes the American Jackie pitching on inner-city ball diamonds. Uneducated, he nevertheless becomes the artistic foundation of the Kapp family's growing jewelry empire. His developing talent finds initial inspiration on the pitcher's mound in the form of Mathewson's first no-hitter, but Jackie seems as inspired by an accidental encounter with the nude and freshly showered Mathewson, an encounter that might be the cause of his quest for artistic inspiration in the galleries and museums of New York and then Europe. His infatuation with the pitcher's physical perfection casts a note of homoeroticism in a character otherwise defined by his happy marriage, which produces a son named Mathias, another Matty. Mathewson, the college-educated son Christopher of wealthy parents, moves in elite social circles but seems equally at home amidst the rough crowd that comprised the ranks of early professional baseball players.[3] Both men show remarkable finesse in a variety of situations, exhibiting intellectual and moral control in their dealings with everyone from difficult family members to sinister high-stakes gamblers.

The control demonstrated by Mathewson and Jackie is thoroughly tied to their identity as pitchers. Mathewson, one of the first five players inducted into the Hall of Fame, remains a model of the quintessential pitcher, a combination

of physical prowess and intelligence. Greenberg counters the historical pitcher
with Jackie, who blew out his arm throwing the curveball in his youth.
However, Jackie never lets go of his identity as a pitcher, a point made by
Hugh Fullerton, the sportswriter who uncovered the Black Sox scandal.
Fullerton describes Mathewson and Jackie as engaged in a similar pursuit of
perfection, Jackie in metal and gem and Mathewson on the diamond (196).
This diamond-for-diamond connection reverberates throughout the novel.
When he takes part in a pickup game, Jackie's pleasure in pitching, and
pitching fairly well after he recovers the "lovely thing" that is his curve ball, is
heightened by his son seeing him pitch and therefore knowing him as a pitcher
(176). Greenberg underscores the connection between these men as Jackie
narrates Mathewson's first no-hitter in the first person, placing himself in the
midst of the magic of teamwork when the Giants' defense rises to support their
pitcher: "I reach it; it is past me—but Strang is there" (27). Jackie's assumption
of Mathewson's perspective makes more of their relationship than simply that
of hero and fan or godhead and priest. Jackie hints at his ability to become
more than the observer of the pitcher's perfection. As he takes the active role,
if only in his imagination, Jackie suggests that whatever role is being played
out—historical, allegorical, imaginative—that role operates on levels other
than the narrative present of the no-hitter. His play-by-play commentary of the
last inning of the first World Series (1905) makes clearer the anagogical
intentions at play. In his description of the first game, Jackie notes, "[o]nce
more my focus narrowed until I seemed to live within him" (94), and he holds
that focus until he describes Mathewson pausing over what will be the final
pitch of the last game: "I thought that if he could he would order time to stand
still . . . but only gods and artists can stop time" (99). Where the novel
allegorizes Mathewson as a god and Jackie as his celebrant artist, Jackie
ostensibly denies them those roles.

As Greenberg connects Jackie to Mathewson through the course of the novel,
he positions them in an allegorical relationship that shifts and changes. On the
one hand, just as he denies Mathewson divinity, Jackie denies his own status as
an artist in many conversations with his brother Arthur. On the other hand, he
accepts the title and role Mathewson gives him, as related by Fullerton: "He
showed me the rings you've done for him, yes, but he also said that you'd seen
him pitch every important game of his career . . . that you were . . . the
celebrant of his works" (195). While Deanne Westbrook sees Jackie as a
fan(atic), arguing that the first ring is his conversion to Mathewson and that
this conversion is his "spiritual catastrophe" (173), I see this celebration
leading to Jackie's affirmation of baseball as a spiritual and moral space. While
the title invokes the many references to baseball fandom, the word's
connections to the Christian priesthood and the celebration of the Eucharist
centers the Christ(y)an allegory. While Mathewson first applies the term
generically, as one who observes a solemn rite (his two no-hitters in this
instance), he eventually calls Jackie to be the priest who celebrates the
Eucharist, the apostle who knows the miracle, and the witness at the tomb who
records the pitcher's sacrificial atonement for baseball.

However, as Smith argues, "because of its moral base, allegory is doomed to an endless circularity in which its destruction of one morality and truth is followed by the realization that its own morality and truth belong in the same arena" (119). The circularity of the religious truths in *The Celebrant* turns on Jackie's function as Mathewson's "celebrant-in-chief" (196). While Jackie accepts this description and continues to celebrate the pitcher's glory with his art, Arthur makes clear that Mathewson is not God, the jewelry business "is not an abbey," and Jackie is "not a monk illuminating pages for the greater glory of God" (179). When the Hal Chase scandal comes to light, Mathewson, then managing Cincinnati, refuses to suspend him and is described as "the model of Christian forgiveness" (219), but Mathewson later figures his actions as other than Christian or forgiving. In the denouement, he describes seeking his true role and failing as a manager. He sees the Chase scandal as his failure and eventually locates his calling as that of the prophet who speaks the truth of the 1919 World Series. His desire for vengeance is foreshadowed by Jackie's deep anger at Eli's complicity in the Chase scandal. By writing Eli into that narrative, Greenberg adumbrates the older Jackie's ruin due to the Black Sox scandal. Jackie sees Eli's conspiracy with Chase, which included thrown games and large bets, as a betrayal of Mathewson and the sport. Furthermore, while Eli did not join the army to atone for his sins, Mathewson joined and expected to pay with his life for his failure to protect baseball (222).

Ultimately, *The Celebrant* denies its own Christian allegory and draws on Jackie's Judaism to reinstate its moral truths. While Greenberg's Christian references and allusions have garnered the most critical attention, Solomon argues that Jackie ultimately turns from "the convoluted, mock-Christian adoration of Mathewson in which he had been indulging" and returns to his Jewish roots (100). However, the novel relies on Jewish tropes and allusions throughout. For example, while Jackie comes close to admitting he worships Mathewson, he couches his hints as a Hebrew. When Eli teases that he is a "worshipper from afar," Jackie responds: "You don't crawl into the ark to worship *torah*" (42). While Jackie asserts that worship must be carried out with dignity, he contends that to worship Mathewson would be heresy, but it would be "a very American heresy" (42). The conversation leaves open and ambiguous just where Jackie's reverence lies: for the God of *torah* or the game of baseball. Jackie's two sites of worship are a constant; as noted above, he recalls occasions when he skirted his religious duties to go to a game, but he also buries himself in the synagogue to avoid a game (186). Throughout the novel his observation of Judaism is a constant, but so is his observation of baseball, as he concludes that he feels called to witness Mathewson (199), who in turn concludes that only through Jackie's bearing witness can his glory come to fruition; only Jackie's celebration makes his perfection real (263).

In the end, Mathewson is refigured as a prophet; a blend of the Christian messiah and the messiah of *torah*, he becomes the messiah of baseball, sacrificing himself in the fashion of Jesus, but demanding vengeance like an Old Testament prophet, damning the filth that corrupted the White Sox and promising to "allow them their full portion of loss" (262). Early on, Jackie describes Mathewson as bearing "the weight of a city's hopes" (129), and the pitcher in general as "standing at the axis of event" (128). However, he later defines the ballplayer's role according to the Old Testament, depicting the newest manager of the Cincinnati team as "a Joshua to Mathewson's Moses" (229). Yet the "world without grays, where all decisions were final" (128) becomes the site of the Merkle blunder and a game that is neither lost nor won.[4] In the midst of this catastrophe, though, when the game is still won, Jackie expresses his desire to confess his faith in Mathewson's presence (135). When a tie is called because of Merkle's failure to touch second, Jackie does not abandon his reverence for Mathewson or baseball. He refuses to cheapen the game, although he has learned that "the field of play was not exempt from life's injustices" (150). Jackie's reinscription of the diamond as a site of reverence is a subtle and often fraught process. Solomon characterizes the novel as "a moral event that demands justice—a traditional theme of Jewish writing" (105), and I agree that the flavor of the retribution at the end harkens to the Old Testament more than any other text. In many ways, the narrative denies the Christ(y)an myth that it seems to draw on as allegorical source, substituting in subtle and overt ways the myth of the Old Testament prophet. Mathewson's language becomes, rather than the Jesus narrative of forgiveness and doubts of self and of God, the language of a prophet sure of his visions and predictions. Fullerton suggests as much in noting that he is dying and "a dying man has a realm of thought the living never enter" (255). Both he and Jackie agree that Mathewson is the man to judge whether or not the Series is fixed (256). Like a prophet, Mathewson accepts that he is "not given to understand until [he has] reached the end" (261), and he contends in the final meeting with Jackie that justice has been served again and again in his career, in victory both won and denied. He intends to make retribution for his failure to rout out the gamblers when he managed Cincinnati. He suggests that he has been tempered by wins and losses for this final trial, that finally, he "alone could tell the truth of it" (262). Mathewson summarizes his career in a conflation of the roles of prophet and messiah. He figures his war injuries as death and his return in the terms of resurrection: "I rose from that death . . . I came to sit in judgment of those I'd walked among, to root out their sin and damn them for it" (262).

In the worldviews of both Jackie and Mathewson, baseball is a site of reverence. In an interview, Greenberg offers insight into his novel's vision of justice and morality on the diamond by contending that the Boston Red Sox are still being punished for selling Babe Ruth for "cash money": "[S]omehow baseball has contrived to not only deprive the Red Sox of ultimate victory ever since, but to make it hurt so much" (Nathan 16). Greenberg also contends, in the same interview, that the novel centers on "Jackie making a choice—between the old God and the new, between the Old Testament and the New, between Judaism and Christianity" (12). However, there is no choice made, or, rather, the choice becomes a choosing to keep baseball a place of justice, to restore it as a spiritual site. For example, Jackie recognizes that his only bet, a trivial wager for a quarter with his nephew, is a sin (244).

Throughout, the novel struggles to keep baseball a sacred space, above economic concerns, especially those of the gamblers. Early on, Jackie narrates a conversation between his sophisticated father-in-law and the equally erudite Mathewson that juxtaposes baseball's beginnings and what differentiates gambling, at the ballpark or the track, from the calculated risk of the stock market or the poker table. Mathewson sees gamblers as third parties, not directly involved in the competition: "I see no dignity in their occupation, and I fear their influence" (88). But where Mathewson separates the playing field from his life and becomes wealthy by selling his name for advertising, Jackie holds a deep disapproval of his family's purchase of Mathewson's endorsement for their jewelry business. That Jackie censures his brothers rather than Mathewson signals a moral opposition to bringing economic concerns into the game. At one point, when asking Jackie to phone Mathewson over money, Eli says that such actions merely make baseball look like the world (146). Conversations between Jackie and his younger, most ambitious brother Arthur bring to light Jackie's struggle to maintain the sacred space of baseball. Although Arthur fails to comprehend the sacredness of the diamond, he does understand what makes Jackie's work (and Mathewson's, for that matter) valuable. Arthur declares that the artist has value because "his work cannot be duplicated"; and while Jackie protests that his work is duplicated thousands of times in the family's machines, Arthur carries the point about the uniqueness of true talent (152). Where Arthur appreciates Jackie's artistry for its economic worth, Mathewson recognizes that the jeweler's unique talent is employed in the service of a ritual that honors the greatness of his own works in the sacred space of the diamond.[5]

The narrative draws on history to make clear the difference between players like Mathewson and Hal Chase, who contends of professional baseball, "you do it for money" (172). Chase's maxim fits well with Arthur's notion of ballplayers as he discusses making down payments on promising young pitchers (177). However, when Jackie sees himself as one of those who exploits rather than celebrates his hero (175), he stops looking to Mathewson for artistic inspiration and seeks the means for expression elsewhere. Jackie's turn to classical and popular art and away from the hero he celebrates fully undermines the messianic allegory as the celebrant priest reverts to the artist questing for inspiration. At the same time, Jackie retains reverence for baseball and describes the lawyers and merchants at the ballpark as "moneychangers" oblivious to the game and hardly knowing the final score (174). He clearly differs from Arthur and from Eli, who believes that "money makes all things possible" (245). While Jackie is outraged over Eli's complicity in Chase's conspiracy of gambling and fixed games and sees the deeper implications of gambling in the sport, both his brothers are completely oblivious to how the Chase scandal could damage Mathewson or baseball (222). On his way to lay off Eli's wagers on the 1919 World Series, Jackie ruminates on his brothers' faith in capitalism, how it now seems to rule the ballpark; but according to his brothers' ideology, "the structure of the game would not be threatened" (245).

However, Jackie ultimately disagrees, as he abides by Mathewson's spiritual and moral directives and refuses to participate in the corruption of the sport.

Like Jackie, Mathewson sees baseball as a site of "straight lines and clear decisions" (259), and he plays out the allegory of prophet-messiah to save the game as a sacred space. In his final scene, Mathewson brings to fruition the host of messianic portents and allusions embedded in the novel. He juxtaposes the perfection he achieved, celebrated by Jackie in stone, with his failure to protect the sport from gamblers in Cincinnati. He describes his punishment by mustard gas in the war and his new awareness that he has a greater role to play. After prophesying the truth about the Black-White Sox, Mathewson promises to "drive them from the temple" (262). Mathewson draws on the Christian narrative to explain why his celebrant cannot bet on the series; he describes the soldiers gambling for Jesus' robe while he suffered on the cross and asks if his celebrant will do the same while his hero is dying. Mathewson contends that Jackie will not (263). The witness to Mathewson's works, his high priest, Jackie closes their interview by gathering Mathewson's scattered rings, rings Jackie had made to pay homage to this god of baseball, and closing them within Mathewson's Bible. Richard Peterson suggests that this scene "runs dangerously close to surrendering the narrative to the most extreme form of hero-worship, [as] Jackie, after risking his own soul to save his brother from gamblers, is himself saved by Mathewson" (110), but I would suggest that there is more at play. Jackie has long denied that he worships Mathewson, just as his religious observance denies that he follows the Christian narrative. The novel relies on Christ(y)anity for resonance, but in the end, baseball is the thing upheld. Mathewson never ventures into eschatological terrain; heaven is moot here. Instead, he intends to drive the cheaters and moneychangers from the temple of baseball. The novel elevates "baseball to a sacred realm" as Mathewson both suffers for and avenges the sport (Hye 44).

As postmodern allegory, *The Celebrant* blocks the metaphoric nature of allegory, negates the earthly signs that might represent divinity, and severs the logocentric relationship between signs and ultimate meaning. Greenberg systematically draws his sources and their potentially divine signs back into baseball in a hermeneutic circle. Mathewson, in the end, is neither the Messiah nor God; Jackie finally celebrates the pitcher's works with the betrayal of his own brother, a betrayal that the narrative leaves ambiguous: Forty pieces of silver are transposed into forty thousand dollars and Eli's death, but the temple is also cleared of the moneychangers and the diamond, not money, remains as the site of worship. Madsen discusses allegory as an epistemological form because it responds to changes in cultural conceptions of the nature and availability of knowledge and makes "possible the comprehension of realities that cannot be apprehended literally" (5). Part of the American identity and dream, baseball has resonances and meanings that cannot be apprehended literally, and *The Celebrant* offers a means of interpreting the sport and its history. As allegorical source, the early history of the New York Giants and Mathewson's biography deny an authoritarian point of view and allow exposure of the ideological maneuverings of religion and capitalism—and racism, although that is not a concern of this essay—at play in the game and the country. In writing a postmodern and allegorical novel, Greenberg represents the repressive force of certain ideologies as totalizing explanations of the nature of reality without placing his work in a position above the discursive system that is the novel, in which no discourse is innocent, even the homage Jackie pays to Mathewson. Ultimately, Greenberg's Mathewson becomes beguiled by the fixed referent, his Bible. His subjectivity blocked, he is the Old Testament prophet, broken and bleeding, dying for his truth. As his celebrant, Jackie is denied ontological certainty; he stands a bereft priest and lone Jew, questing and requesting the interpretation with which he can live, including the meaning of baseball.

Throughout, *The Celebrant* offers baseball as a sacred space, not the garden—as made clear with the fall from innocence depicted graphically when Jackie sees two men fall to their deaths from the grandstand roof during a playoff game at the Polo Grounds—and not heaven, given the imperfection of the men on and surrounding the field. In his quest for meaning, Jackie likens baseball to his craft: The game welds its components into meaningful form with the pitcher as the gemstone (130). Craig Owens argues that allegory responds to a sense of estrangement and functions "in the gap between a present and a past which, without allegorical reinterpretation, might have remained foreclosed" (203). In part, *The Celebrant* revisits a dark period of baseball history and rescues from historical oblivion Mathewson's role in uncovering the corruption. Jackie's search for inspiration in Mathewson and for meaning in baseball becomes a quest to interpret his identity, as an American, a Kapinski, a Jew, a brother, and a celebrant. Before his final lament of "Eli, Eli!" (My God, my God), Jackie ruminates on the spiritual meaning baseball holds for him, likening the inspiration he received from Mathewson to the inspiration afforded a passing acquaintance by another pitcher, the Only Nolan. Throughout Jackie's narrative, the diamond is a temple, a site of reverence offered in the enduring, self-forgetting love of the fans, like Jackie, who offers his faith in stone, and like his nephew, who keeps meticulous records of all the teams. For Jackie, as for all the faithful, "the game was all" (15).

NOTES

1. The narrative is drenched with Christian references. John McGraw's coming is figured as the "advent" of Mathewson's greatness (50), Jackie is his "high priest . . . celebrant-in-chief" (196), and Mathewson sees him as the "voice of annunciation" (258). Bonehead Merkle's public ostracization is described as a "crucifixion" (150). Mathewson is figured as being in Gethsemane before one, and therefore before every, crucial game (197). When Jackie expresses his shock that Mathewson will fulfill his endorsement duties and attend the opening of a new jewelry store, his brother points out that "Christ walked among publicans and sinners" (179).

2. Another key figure in baseball's early history, Hal Chase (Prince Hal), although brilliant with both glove and bat, is now known largely as a primary source of

corruption in the sport. He began his career with the New York Highlanders in 1905 and was accused of throwing games as early as 1913. In 1918, he played for Cincinnati under Mathewson and was suspended for throwing games. Chase's involvement in the Black Sox scandal led to his permanent ban from baseball.

3. The narrative forces further similarities and connections on these men: Jackie's small daughter dies, and both men become the fathers of a solitary son; the aged and ailing Mathewson is reduced to seeking and speaking truth in a scorebook that becomes a counterpart to the sketchbook in which Jackie has long worked to express his own truths.

4. In a crucial game during the 1908 pennant race, Fred Merkle made a blunder that earned him the nickname Bonehead. Tied at 1 with the Cubs, the Giants had Moose McCormick on third and Merkle on first. Al Bridwell, the Giant batter, hit a single. McCormick crossed home plate, apparently scoring the winning run. Merkle, thinking the game was over, ran towards the Giant clubhouse without touching second base, wanting to avoid the fans converging on the field. The Cubs' second baseman, Johnny Evers, realized that a force out was still possible if he could get the ball and step on the bag before Merkle. Joe McGinnity, the Giants' third base coach, saw what Evers was planning and threw the ball into the stands, a ball that comes into Arthur's and then Jackie's possession in *The Celebrant*. The game was declared a tie, and the Cubs went on to win the pennant and the Series.

5. In so doing, Arthur denies Walter Benjamin's overarching argument in "The Work of Art in the Age of Mechanical Reproduction" that to mechanically reproduce art is to diminish its "aura," but he provides an example of Benjamin's conclusion that when the function of art is found outside ritual, it becomes based on another practice (224), in this case economics. For his part, Mathewson intuits Benjamin's contention that art "is never entirely separated from its ritual function" (223–224).

REFERENCES

Benjamin, Walter. *Illuminations*. Trans. Harry Zohn. New York: Schocken, 1969.

Greenberg, Eric Rolfe. *The Celebrant*. Lincoln: University of Nebraska Press, 1983.

Hye, Allen E. "The Baseball Messiah: Christy Mathewson and *The Celebrant*." *Aethlon* 7.1 (1989): 41–49.

Madsen, Deborah. *The Postmodernist Allegories of Thomas Pynchon*. London: Leicester University Press, 1991.

Nathan, Daniel A. "Touching the Bases: A Conversation with Eric Rolfe Greenberg." *Aethlon* 7.1 (1989): 9–19.

Owens, Craig. "The Allegorical Impulse: Toward a Theory of Postmodernism." *Art After Modernism: Rethinking Representation*. Ed. Brian Wallis. New York: Museum of Modern Art, 1984. 203–235.

Peterson, Richard. *Extra Innings: Writing on Baseball*. Urbana: University of Illinois Press, 2001.

Smith, Paul. "The Will to Allegory in Postmodernism." *Dalhousie Review* 62 (1982): 105–122.

Solomon, Eric. "'Memories of Days Past' or Why Eric Rolfe Greenberg's *The Celebrant* is the Greatest [Jewish] American Baseball Novel." *American Jewish History* 83.1 (1995): 83–107.

Westbrook, Deeanne. *Ground Rules: Baseball and Myth*. Urbana: University of Illinois Press, 1996.

"The Mob of Carefree Men and Boys": *Vanity of Duluoz* and Kerouac's Panoramic Consciousness

Matthew Kelley

In a short manuscript called *Football Novella* written when he was sixteen years old, Jack Kerouac tells the story of one Bill Clancy, a "football-hero-hobo"—a gifted college athlete who spends his time away from the football field reading novels and wandering the local railroad tracks. In the climactic seventh chapter of this short work, Kerouac shows Clancy on the stadium field, running through the pregame warmup in front of a packed crowd. Even though Clancy's team is on this day playing a school called Blaine, during the warmup the players are anticipating the next big game—a Thanksgiving Day showdown with "State College":

Nesmith Stadium was a scene of excitement. Just before game time, with the gridiron all spick and span, white lines and goal posts intact, the bands began to blare and crowds began to arrive. When the brilliant blue and white colors came out on the field, worn by two dozen husky football players, the roar went up from the stands. The cavernous maw which had enveloped the players in practice now seemed to be turbulent with life. "Wassamatter, Bill? Excited, nervous?" said the rangy tackle. "I dunno," muttered Bill, running his stubby hand through his brown hair. "It sure is a big crowd." "Wait till the rest of it arrives. As a matter of fact, wait till the big game of the year on Thanksgiving Day!" replied Martin. (Kerouac *Atop* 12–13)

Until the end of this chapter, Kerouac's narrative perspective shifts as through the lens of a camera opening with an establishing shot of the town itself, its streets filling with eager spectators, focusing finally on the stadium and then zooming in to capture the blues and whites of the gathering crowd in the stands. Within a few short sentences this universal panorama becomes so localized, so focused that the reader-spectator now hears the conversation of the players looking from field level up at the crowd and even beyond, predicting the next crowd for whom they will perform.

Though an apprentice, even juvenile work, *Football Novella*, and in particular this scene, introduces a motif and an accompanying narrative technique to which Kerouac will return again and again in his career—that of the crowd, its symbolic significance, and the narrative challenges it offers. A star football player for Lowell High School in Massachusetts and later at Horace Mann Preparatory and Columbia University, Kerouac revisits and rewrites this scene in his debut novel *The Town and the City* (1950) and again in his final novel *Vanity of Duluoz* (1968). Kerouac's use of crowd scenes and, more specifically, the implications of sports spectatorship—for him, young men undergoing heroic but anguished, highly publicized rites of passage—are presented early in his work quite simply. Football in particular, becomes a proving ground, a way for young men to attain public recognition, self-identity, and worth. These football players, a community of boys watched with great interest by a community of men—what Kerouac calls "mobs of carefree men and boys"—are an Ur-version of the male-male dynamics explored so intensely in much of the Beat literature that emerged by the late fifties. Yet by the end of Kerouac's career, when he has weathered the spoils and pain of universal fame, his sports crowds assume more sinister, complex positions. Many of the boys battling on the fields of Kerouac's late sports fiction do so while aware of the looming specter of World War II. And the spectators who gather to watch them play are constructed as a "mob" of a different sort—an audience or surrogate readership. As the crowd becomes an audience of readers, so too does the player become a writer.

Jack Kerouac is still known primarily to American readers as the author of *On the Road,* a novel that was heralded by the *New York Times* book critic Gilbert Millstein upon release in 1957 as an "authentic work of art" whose publication marked "an historic occasion" (qtd. in Theado 167). Though the book firmly put Kerouac on the literary and cultural maps, it was also Eisenhower America's most dramatic and sustained introduction to the Beat Generation. The Beats themselves emerged in an era defined by increasing anticommunist propaganda, fear and paranoia, mass industrialization, hydrogen bomb testing, the growth of television as the dominant medium, and the rise of the suburbs as an economic power. The Beats eloquently responded to these issues and the inevitable accompanying spiritual decay and malaise by pointing to a way out—through full-bodied honest confessional, heightened perception, and spiritual epiphany. However, "rather than seeing the goal of this, the public saw mainly the means—the frantic jazz scenes, fast cars, sex, and drugs. Initially, the Beats evoked fear and disgust, along with a general dismissal of their literary efforts" (Theado 17). Furthermore, Herb Caen of the *San Francisco Chronicle* coined the phrase "Beatnik"—a rank dismissal of the group of "unwashed bohemians" (3). Kerouac himself received enormous celebrity attention; stories of Kerouac "groupies," bacchanalian poetry jams, and loft parties abound. In his 1960 novel *Big Sur*, he meditates on the price of fame, telling of the seemingly endless letters and streams of young people vying for his attention, showing up unannounced on his lawn, wanting to party with the hero of *On the Road*. Yet *On the Road* was a book written by a much younger man—a semiautobiographical chronicle of his own journeys around America with his friend and muse Neal Cassady from 1947 to 1950. By the mid 1960s, Kerouac was burdened by a waning literary reputation, one littered with out-of-print books and by some severe alcohol-related symptoms that would contribute to his death in 1969 at the age of forty-seven.

Scholars of Kerouac typically divide his fiction into two groups. The first of these, the Lowell novels, variously recount his boyhood days in the industrial working-class town of Lowell, Massachusetts, and cover his life from roughly age three to the middle of his unfinished term at Columbia University. These books include *Visions of Gerard, Dr. Sax, Maggie Cassidy*, and *Vanity of Duluoz*. His other books are referred to simply as the "Road" novels, works that deal with Kerouac the writer interacting with his famous friends, traveling the roads of the world, gaining spiritual and physical experience (as in *On the Road, The Dharma Bums, The Subterraneans, Big Sur*, and *Desolation Angels*). The product of two decades of work and written and published out of chronological order, the novels make up a vast fictional autobiography, what he called "one enormous comedy" known as the Duluoz Legend. "In my old age," he wrote, "I intend to collect all my work and reinsert the pantheon of uniform names, leave the long shelf full of books there and die happy" (*Vanity* 1).

Before he became a Beat celebrity, Jack Kerouac was a football player, one of the best Lowell, Massachusetts, ever had. In his senior season at Lowell High he broke out as a running back star (most notably in a Thanksgiving Day football game, where he came off the bench to score two touchdowns), attracting the attention of coaches at Notre Dame, Boston College, and Columbia University most notably. This period is well chronicled in several of the Lowell books, as well as in his first novel, *The Town and the City*—a text heavily informed by the expansive, expressive epics of North Carolina writer Thomas Wolfe, Kerouac's first major writerly influence. Yet like all his fiction, *The Town and the City* was highly autobiographical. The novel itself is a chronicle of the changes of one family, the Martins, and as suggested by its title follows a very American literary tradition of contrasting the innocence, however stifling, of small town life with the destructive, depersonalized force of the big city. Kerouac transposes his working-class experience to the fictional town of Galloway in the novel, essentially "dividing himself into five characters who are the sons of George Martin" (Charters 64). For Ann Charters, Kerouac's first biographer, the author represents himself most clearly in the character of Peter Martin, thirteen years old in 1935, just as Kerouac himself was. Peter is a rising young football star, but one eager and restless to experience the world beyond the confines of provincial Galloway. One of the most feverishly dramatic and memorable moments in *The Town and the City* occurs during the Thanksgiving Football game anticipated in the early *Football Novella*.

This scene develops much as it does in *Football Novella*, but is dramatically attenuated, functioning finally as an extended meditation on Peter's very public coming of age. By the day of the big game, this time between Galloway and a team called Lawton, Peter, now sixteen, is under the increasing scrutiny of his coaches and his father in both practice and in games. There is seldom any meditation on the grueling physical demands of either practice or game time. We are told only that Peter grows comfortably and confidently in his physicality as "the awkward, shy, shambling movement of the novice on the football field gradually became the movements of a swift and knowing halfback" (*Town* 63). The "shambling, awkward" Peter later becomes "crafty," "deliberate," "assured," and "graceful" (63–64). His father watches him at practice nearly every day. Intriguingly, Kerouac presents these passages in limited third person: Peter runs here; Peter makes a tackle there, as if to allow the reader to function as a surrogate audience. The act of reading simulates the act of watching, and only when Peter becomes uncertain of his accompanying crowd or audience do we glimpse any first-person perspective. In fact, the introductory detail we are given in Peter's game debut concerns the crowd: "Before long he appeared in his first big game—considerably awed by the vast excitement of the stadium all around—but successful in making a favorable impression on everyone" (63). Prior to Kerouac's use of the adjectival "considerably awed" we are limited simply to watching Peter run here and there; now we are briefly but definitely allowed access to Peter's perspective before the point of view shifts back to the crowd and their "favorable impression" of his performance. At this point, the gathering crowds essentially prompt a moment of reflexivity and self-awareness.

The big Thanksgiving game scene is a narrative tour de force, four pages of intricate narration and dizzying shifts in point of view. Beginning with an aerial survey establishing the arriving crowds as they converge by highway and city streets onto the stadium site, Kerouac shifts immediately to focus on the Galloway team rushing out of the tunnel onto the field as "all around them the crowds roared and the bands drummed and blared, something in the air was like thunder and battle and glee" (76). Now at field level, the reader no longer "faces" the team coming out of the tunnel but follows their collective gaze towards the opposing Lawton team, the officials, and finally the packed stands: "[T]hey saw the whole mob-swarmed terrific stadium in a gray windswept blaze of vision" (77). The communal "they" by the very next sentence is limited immediately to Peter Martin's individual experience as he sees "the ball up in the air, wobbling and windswept, and [sees] it bouncing down before him. He was mortified with fear" (77). In the next sentence, Kerouac moves up to the crowd itself, zooming in on the Martin family and their attempts to identify Peter as he runs his plays. As Mr. Martin and younger brother Mickey "announce" the game, Mrs. Martin asks repeatedly, "'[w]hat's happening? Where is Peter?'" (77). The perspective expands from the family at this point to encompass the entire crowd's view, and Kerouac writes: "Down on the field the teams lined up, the linemen digging in low. . . . The cowbells clanked, someone shouted: 'Come awnnn, Gallo-wayyy!'" (77). These shifts in perspective and location continue in essentially the same pattern throughout: from the omniscient aerial view (Kerouac's prose equivalent of the Goodyear blimp camera shot) to the collective field perspective to Martin's view to the

Martin family in the stands and then to the crowd gazing onto the field. This approach allows Kerouac to challenge not only the local geography but the chronology of the scene as well; the family follows Peter as he runs his plays on the field where he ultimately makes the winning touchdown for Galloway, just as Kerouac himself did for Lowell High, ever aware of the roaring crowd. This simultaneity allows us to experience Peter viscerally at field level as a flesh and blood hero and at the same time as a dark, often unidentifiable figure seen from the stands above as the camera-eye narrator withdraws from the scene. Gerald Nicosia, the most richly encyclopedic of Kerouac's biographers, notes that Kerouac told Allen Ginsberg that one of his primary influences in writing this scene (one both writers agreed was one of the finest in the novel) was the end of the film *Children of Paradise*.

Kerouac saw *Children of Paradise* during a period of truancy from Horace Mann preparatory school in New York City, which he attended on a football scholarship. In *Vanity of Duluoz*, he describes the irresistible desire he had to "ride on down to Times Square and go see a French movie, go see Jean Gabin press his lips together saying 'Ca me navre' or Louis Jouvet's baggy behind going up the stairs" (76). This epic melodrama, directed by Marcel Carne and produced in Occupied France despite a film stock shortage, incessant power failures, Nazi curfews, and storms, is an 1820 period-piece that follows the life of a mysterious courtesan named Garance who arouses the passion and envy of the film's four male protagonists. The film is divided into a number of essential movements, all of which deal with Garance as she gains in experience and sorrow. The set piece is an enormous avenue in Paris called simply "The Boulevard of Crime." The film opens with a panoramic view of the Boulevard and its teeming throngs, zooming immediately onto a would-be suitor of Garance who comes upon her on the street, good naturedly attempts to seduce her, and then loses her in the crowd without knowing her contact information. The camera pans quickly across the crowd and then pulls back to the original panoramic survey of the street. Indeed, each major sequence is punctuated by a crowd scene on the "Boulevard of Crime," where just as the characters climactically merge, they lose each other to the seemingly infinite population—nothing is resolved in any sequence; rather only lost in the long streams of people. Kerouac and Ginsberg were fascinated by this technique, which they refer to in their letters as "panoramic consciousness."

This technique was one Kerouac and Ginsberg had long discussed and learned first from looking at the paintings of the Dutch artist Pieter Bruegel.[1] Many of Bruegel's canonical paintings are not only engaged with crowds, great movements of people and events, but are suggestive of simultaneity of experience. Oil paintings like *Hunters in the Snow* (1565) or *Landscape with the Fall of Icarus* (1558) afford the viewer conventional landscape vistas yet typically construct a "stage front" wherein a drama is unfolding to the degree that the vista becomes a background filtered through the experience of the foreground "frame" story. In *Landscape* we are conditioned to look at the distant ocean and skyline and foggy mountainous archipelago looming on the horizon. Guided by the Bruegel poems of Williams and Auden, we search for

Icarus's oversized kicking leg and sinking wings and the ship sailing calmly on, but we are distracted by the dark trail leading to the forest and the farmer and horse calmly plowing the field. In more frantic, hellish scenario paintings like *Dulle Griet* (1562) or *Procession to Calvary* (1564), Bruegel paints a landscape overloaded with series after series of self-contained vignettes—in one corner a rape scene, in another a fire, a theft, a flogging, a crucifixion, and so on. These are impossible to process with a limited fixed gaze as they demand a selectivity of vision and focus on one scene at a time at the expense of the painting's other elements. Interestingly, Kerouac's references to Bruegel represent one of the few instances where he acknowledges any stylistic debt to a visual artist. Many of Kerouac's close contemporaries (the Beat writers and their close affiliates the New York School of Poets and the writers of the San Francisco Poetry Renaissance) worked closely with or were influenced by painters, sculptors, and filmmakers. The freewheeling, associative, and spontaneous style that Kerouac is at least partly known for in his own work can be seen in the work of Willem De Kooning, Jackson Pollock, Robert Rauschenberg, Robert LaVigne, Jess, and others. Yet Kerouac, in his letters and essays, mentions these artists only as social acquaintances, never as aesthetic influences. Kerouac's mention of Bruegel is not to be compared to his friend and colleague Allen Ginsberg's debt to the art of William Blake (Ginsberg attributed much of his awareness and, indeed, his inspiration to a series of Blakean visions he had in his late twenties). However, in the "Essentials of Spontaneous Prose," published three years after *The Town and the City*, Kerouac consistently evokes visual terminology in his discussion of his own prose technique. Under a heading entitled "Set-Up," he writes, "the object is set before the mind, either in reality, as in sketching (before a landscape or teacup or old face) or is set in the memory wherein it becomes the sketching from memory of a definite image-object" (*Portable* 484). Such visual, even painterly, interests again stem largely from Kerouac's deep investment in the work of Wolfe, whom he described in a 1944 letter as "a panoramist, with a painter's eye for detail. Details are, after all, the life of the novel" ("To John Clellon Holmes" 115).

Yet Kerouac's use of a panoramic effect extends to suggest a kind of unity of experience within the narrative; all the parts contribute to a whole perspective. In *The Town and the City*, all the shifts in perspective are finally condensed into one shared experience. Peter Martin essentially validates his existence, becoming, in his own view, an important member of the family, his team, school, community, and the world. The Thanksgiving game scene builds to a single crescendo of sound—the blare of the band, the crashes of helmets on the field, and the roar of the crowd all dissolving into one sound rising skyward, "one vast whispering sigh" (*Town* 80). After *The Town and the City* was published, Kerouac told an admiring critic that he had wanted Peter's experiences in the novel to function as a "universal American story" ("To Yvonne Le Maitre" 227). That he uses the crowd as a living system of measurement, a barometer of his own acceptance in the world of American adulthood, is in many ways typical of the form of the athletic *bildungsroman*. Christian Messenger, in his study of sport narrative, posits that "the boys' school sports story offered a conventional genre of ritualized aggression where the individual submitted himself to assimilation with the team, the school, and by extension the values of American society in exchange for honor and influence in that society" (155). Yet for Kerouac, even in his relatively optimistic young novelist years, Peter's achievements and societal submissions are rather double-edged.

Though he does "submit" himself to the conventional trappings of success offered by the town-crowd-society because of his football skills, Peter recognizes that "to triumph was also to wreak havoc" (63). Though Peter's transformation into town hero is primarily redemptive, he recognizes himself as forever changed by this success as though by winning he has lost: "[H]e mourns the loss of his anonymity, wishing that he could proceed unnoticed like 'a prince disguised as a pauper'" (Jones 72). He feels he has "betrayed everyone he knew by having performed great feats that required their silence and their praise, their awe and embarrassment" (Kerouac *Town* 82). And so Peter is the haunted celebrity, the public man, the American success story—all of these roles Kerouac the famous writer would have to engage by the end of the 1950s and all are hallmarks of his final visitation to the trope of the crowd, realized most fully in his final novel, *Vanity of Duluoz*.

Ann Douglas notes that in the construction of the Duluoz legend project, Kerouac's personal mandate was one of complete honesty and frankness: "Kerouac makes the reader his confidant, taking her into his most private thoughts and experiences, into areas which the world sometimes seems to prohibit us from sharing with anyone" (17). *Vanity of Duluoz*, completed in May 1967 and published in 1968, is written from the point of view of the jaded yet sardonic Jack Duluoz, who is "speaking" to his wife in a laughably cruel but also teasingly self-parodic tone with tongue firmly in cheek. He tells her the story of his life from boyhood as he autobiographically runs the gauntlets of adolescence, football, war, and literary fame so she can understand his ironic discontent at being an established success. In this novel, Kerouac has come full circle, and in looking back he eschews the "road" legend of his "successful books" in favor of revisiting the events and themes of his early work in a now mature, cantankerous, more pessimistic style. Each "book" of the novel, subtitled "An Adventurous Education," begins with the direct address "Dear Wifey" and presents the events of his past using a simultaneously wistful and bitter tone. Using the full-bodied confessional "I" of his later work, Kerouac applies this narration to the story of *The Town and the City*, which had been written primarily using third-person point of view. In *Vanity of Duluoz*, "rather than create several characters to reveal in their actions and speech the widening consciousness of the world Kerouac wished to describe in the early work, Kerouac's Duluoz narrates the tale but acts also as an intrusive commentator on events" (Weinreich 152–153). The panoramic consciousness technique used in the earlier novel as a means of illuminating a collective, communal, town-family-team-crowd perspective is now complicated and immediately fixed to an essentially metaleptic narrative situation. Multiple consciousnesses are assumed by the form of Kerouac's competing identities in the novel—the young man about whom he is writing and the intrusive Duluoz narrator—both of whom have legitimate claim to the story that is being told, though the constant interaction of these consciousnesses with one another form a crowd all their own. We see now a prose informed by a more temporal kind of panoramic view, the consciousness of the old writer being imposed on the younger athlete-scholar-would-be writer of the past. Kerouac here uses panoramic consciousness not as a means of accessing a collective chorus of points of view but, rather, as a way of further fragmenting his own narrative self. Thus, Kerouac's use of the "I" pronoun allows him to represent both the young player-writer looking ahead and the older, less optimistic writer-former player looking back. Such an approach is directly informed by Kerouac's postmodern agenda and speaks to a central question in Kerouac criticism. Given the autobiographical nature of all the novels in the Duluoz legend (and often the repetition of the same events from book to book over three decades), are these stories best regarded as versions of the same evolving narrative or as an inspired postmodern revision of the picaresque and *bildungsroman* traditions (complete with the accompanying quest motif)? Kerouac's most famous novel, *On the Road,* deviates from the traditional *bildungsroman* in one central way: through a framing—a metanarrational—irony. We are told early in the novel that Sal (Kerouac's fictional stand-in) is a writer working on a big novel, and indeed each of the cross country trips he takes in the book throughout the later sections is punctuated by a mention of the novel he is writing (we see it grow in size until finally he finishes it during a long sojourn at home near *On the Road*'s conclusion). Given the actual chronology of the events in *On the Road* (roughly the years 1946–1950), it is clear that the novel Sal is writing is the fictional analogue of *The Town and the City.* Yet the novel also seems to function as a kind of logbook of Sal's travels throughout the book as though there is an actual *On the Road* book that exists within *On the Road,* the novel we read. So it is with the multiple stories, histories, and versions Kerouac revisits in *Vanity of Duluoz,* where one authorial self is allowed to respond to and even parody a previous self.

The postfame, postwar, postmodern Kerouac even writes the conventional crowd scenes differently. Throughout the text there is a rather consistent, if predicable, privileging of the past at the expense of the present. Though he promises "wifey" an account of his life from 1935 on, he deliberately stalls the text to address the audience (the readership) that overhears the dramatic monologue itself. As a reference to the widely panned prose style of his novels *Desolation Angels, Big Sur*, and *Dr. Sax*, Duluoz writes, "[i]nsofar as nobody loves my dashes anyway, I'll use regular punctuation for the new illiterate generation" (9). In recounting a college-boy dream he had of becoming a big-time gray-suited insurance executive waiting for the commuter train, Kerouac asks "wifey," and by proxy his readership, "[c]an you picture what this would be like today? What with the air pollution and all, and the ads in *Time Magazine*, and our nowadays highways with cars zipping along by the millions in all directions?" (16). Even when not making direct reference to the contemporary readership of the late 1960s, Kerouac presents the crowds in Duluoz's football past in a decidedly more complicated fashion than he did in the early work.

The first crowd scene we see in the book is reminiscent of the functional communal experience suggested in *The Town and the City*, where the small town is unified and vicariously empowered by the physical prowess of its young male athletes: "So here comes this mob of carefree men and boys too, even girls and quite a few mothers, hiking a mile across the meadow of the Dracut Tigers field just to see their boys of thirteen and seventeen play football in an up-and-down uneven field" (10). The mob of player boys is actually a tightly knit subcommunity Kerouac revisits again and again in his Lowell books. Many of them, like Kerouac, are sons of immigrant parents, representing a range of cultural backgrounds: Polish, Lithuanian, French-Canadian, and, most important, Greek. By the time the "team" moves from the playground to the high school practice field, the narrator is like any good backfielder thanking his front line, Kerouac-Duluoz giving "wifey" each player's name, weight, position, ethnic background, and ultimately some indication of what happened to each in later years. This breakdown of the team unfolds like a series of Homeric epithets, appearing as it does just before each game (which by now has assumed battle-like characteristics):

Let me say, though, first, we had a magnificent line: Big Al Swooda was right end, a 6 foot 4 Lithuanian or Pole strong as an ox and as mild. Telemachus Gringas at right tackle, nicknamed Duke and brother to great Orestes Gringas, both of them the toughest boniest and most honest Greeks to meet . . . Joe Mells center, a Pole of dynamic booming dramatic crewcutted tackles, later elected captain to next year's team and destined to play fullback and a good runner in track. (18)

Elsewhere in the novel, the players are elevated to hero status, like Greek warriors proving themselves dramatically in battle. Just as Peter Martin recognized, albeit briefly, the tragic implication of his achievement—that he has passed through his childhood through football success—the boys in *Vanity of Duluoz* are characters in a larger, more epic tragedy. Here the language is heightened and elevated almost in the style of the mock heroic. The narrator recalls sitting on the bench during a game and noticing "heroic Pietryka making sure to remove his helmet when he was helped limping off the field so everyone could see his tragic hair waving" (19). Kerouac-Duluoz, as a frustrated bench player at first, refers constantly to the starters as "the great starters," in quotation marks this time, and later as "heroes," also in quotation marks. As the season progresses, the games are referred to as "big tests" (all in quotations). as though this kind of achievement is somehow hollow and contrived.

Much of the motivation for this tonal shift must be attributed to the narrator's own frustration at being ultimately ill used as a football player, despite his obvious gifts. The Duluoz narrator, like his real and fictional analogues, does go to New York to play football; and yet instead of reveling in his success, he reflects negatively on his position. The redemptive Thanksgiving game itself is only vaguely referred to in this book. The narrator, instead of being a part of the action, tells the tale not from inside the stadium, using the dizzying narrative angles of the other texts, but rather from a distance. In fact, he doesn't even play; it is rather the "'heroes' [again in quotation marks] who have their day on the radio with eighteen thousand watching" (22) while he occupies the bench. At no point are we allowed into the scene itself. Intriguingly, Kerouac was much maligned as a fictional autobiographer, dismissed by the press (see Truman Capote's televised statements that Kerouac was a typist, not a writer) because he simply reported the base inanities of his life. Yet if all of the fiction is simply autobiographical, which Thanksgiving game is true and which is fantasy?

Whatever his motivations in changing the fabula of the Thanksgiving Day game, the truncated version of the later novel is provocative and in keeping with the cynical, postfame tone he embraces. Interestingly, though *The Town and the City* is generally called Kerouac's exercise in Wolfean derivation, the perception of the crowd and the self-loathing it prompts in *Vanity of Duluoz* is more akin to crowd references in Wolfe than anything in the earlier novel. In *Look Homeward Angel*, the protagonist, Eugene Gant, is constantly aware of crowds as a negative force. On the playground as a schoolboy, "he feared and hated the recess period, trembled before the brawling confusion of the mob and playground" (Wolfe 72). Eugene is himself not much of an athlete except in the field fantasies he conjures for himself as a baseball hero. But even though his athletic prowess is largely imaginary, when he breaks out of the fantasy, "all the misery of his life was revealed . . . he remembered the countless humiliations, physical and verbal, he had endured at the hands of school and family, before the world" (Wolfe 169). But Kerouac's mission in the final book is not to dwell simply on schoolboy angst and ambition. Instead, he claims "this is a story of the techniques of suffering in the world which includes football and war" (*Vanity* 76). The war haunts this novel; practically all the boys on the Lowell, Horace Mann, and Columbia teams are enlisted by the end of the novel, lending some palpable implications to their on-field success. We literally see them training for the war and metaphorically falling down and dying in the world's arena. The narrator, in fact, uses the war as an excuse to quit football by the end of the book and to become a writer, claiming "I had chosen football at that time when it would no longer matter to anybody" (64) and later stating, "football, schmootball . . . the war must have been getting in my bones" (87). Though Kerouac-Duluoz sees limited military action—he is discharged from the Navy because he feigns mental illness and is only intermittently a Merchant Marine—the larger issue here is that football success, seen as futile in wartime, is comparable to Kerouac's success as a novelist which was fleeting and, by the time of this novel, hardly remembered. The bittersweet end-of-game triumph of Peter Martin is now manifest in a writer flinging his book and by proxy his life into the void. The crowd itself is finally America, a group of would-be readers, an "America that has become such a potboiler of broken convictions, messes of rioting and fighting in the streets, hoodlumism, cynical administration all gone into the mosaic mesh of Television" (103).

Crowd scenes in American fiction are of course nothing new, and in general are affixed with a certain sinister quality—from the angry, provincial mobs pursuing the King and the Duke and the lynch mob on the heels of Huck and Jim in Twain's *Adventures of Huckleberry Finn* to Nathanael West's chilling peroration of *The Day of the Locust* as Tod Hackett screams his way through the mysterious Los Angeles riot at the end of the novel to, more recently, Don DeLillo's chilling introduction to the 1991 novel *Mao II* that "the future belongs to crowds" (16). At the end of *Vanity of Duluoz*, the optimistic athlete has become the ranting Swiftian misanthrope, railing at the teeming world. The novel does not end on a "high note"; it is not a euphoric victory, but Kerouac's dedicated and tireless revision of these scenes, his willingness to revisit the crowds of his life over and over again, indicates that he is definitely worth watching and even occasionally cheering for.

NOTE

1. In a series of Ginsberg-Kerouac letters from 1945, both writers discuss the need for a "New Vision" in writing and art, which started with a letting go of their provincial small-town selves and culminated in a view of themselves as small but a part of an infinite universe. "We must see ourselves as a part of a panoramic consciousness, like being part of one of Bruegel's otherwordly nightmare paintings. To see from ourselves and toward ourselves all at the same time. We must look at the open sky above, to see the city and the earth hanging in space, of a perishable world within a permanent void." ("To Allen Ginsberg" 124).

REFERENCES

Caen, Herb. "The Unwashed Bohemians." *The San Francisco Chronicle* 4 Apr. 1958: 3+.

Charters, Ann. *Kerouac: A Biography*. New York: St. Martins, 1994.

Children of Paradise. Dir. Marcel Carne. Criterion, 1945.

DeLillo, Don. *Mao II*. New York: Penguin, 1991.

Douglas, Ann. "'Telepathic Shock and Meaning Excitement': Kerouac's Poetics of Intimacy." *College Literature*. 27.1 (2000): 8–22.

Kerouac, Jack. *Atop an Underwood: Early Stories and Other Writings*. Ed. Paul Marion. New York: Penguin, 1999.

———. *The Portable Jack Kerouac*. Ed. Ann Charters. New York: Viking, 1995.

———. "To Allen Ginsberg." 9 Dec. 1945. *Kerouac and the Beats: A Primary Sourcebook*. Eds. Arthur and Kit Knight. New York: Paragon House, 1988. 124.

———. "To John Clellon Holmes." 22 Sept. 1944. *Kerouac and the Beats: A Primary Sourcebook*. Ed. Arthur and Kit Knight. New York: Paragon House, 1988. 115.

———. "To Yvonne Le Maitre." 8 Sep. 1950. *Selected Letters 1946–1950*. Ed. Ann Charters. New York: Penguin, 1995. 227.

————. *The Town and the City*. New York: Harvest, 1970.

————. *Vanity of Duluoz: An Adventurous Education 1935–1946*. New York: Penguin, 1994.

Messenger, Christian. *Sport and the Spirit of Play in American Fiction*. New York: Columbia University Press, 1981.

Millstein, Gilbert. "On the Road." *The Beats: A Literary Reference*. Ed. Matt Theado. New York: Carroll and Graf, 2003.

Nicosia, Gerald. *Memory Babe: A Critical Biography of Jack Kerouac*. New York: Grove Press, 1983.

Theado, Matt. *The Beats: A Literary Reference*. New York: Carroll and Graf, 2003.

Weinreich, Regina. *The Spontaneous Poetics of Jack Kerouac: A Study of the Fiction*. New York: Marlowe, 1995.

Wolfe, Thomas. *Look Homeward, Angel*. New York: Simon and Schuster, 1929.

"And That's the Ball Game!": Cognitive Linguistics, the LIFE IS A GAME Metaphor, and the Late Twentieth-Century Southern Novel

Suzanne Disheroon-Green

For the better part of two decades, cognitive linguists have investigated the ways in which conceptual metaphors structure language use. Conceptual metaphors, it has been argued, provide the basic and essential structure of language, causing individual speakers and listeners to understand the messages they receive because they unconsciously perceive and process the larger concepts underlying those messages. As George Lakoff and Mark Johnson have demonstrated, "metaphor is pervasive in everyday life, not just in language but in thought and action. Our ordinary conceptual system, in terms of which we both think and act, is fundamentally metaphorical in nature" (3). The linguistic implications of conceptual metaphors "serve to reveal aspects of higher-level mental representation" (Sweetser and Fauconnier 1). Michael Blasenstein has noted that

[c]onceptual metaphors have become so commonplace in our everyday language that they pass unnoticed by the average speaker. Their transparency in daily life invisibly influences the way we think and speak about most subjects. Indeed, this influence often leads us to take certain concepts for granted, as if they could not possibly be thought about in any other way. However, conceptual metaphors have meaning only through some sort of shared experience between speaker and listener underlying the discourse. (par. 1)

Furthermore, Lakoff and Mark Turner have argued that "basic conceptual metaphors are part of the common conceptual apparatus shared by members of a culture" (51). To a significant extent, conceptual metaphors can transcend ethnic, and even national, boundaries in ways that allow generalized concepts, as well as their specific linguistic manifestations, to be understood cross-culturally.

Cognitive theorists have identified a multitude of specific conceptual metaphor systems. These metaphors range from the commonplace examples that speakers hardly recognize as metaphoric to others that appear more closely aligned with the conventional definitions of poetic metaphor articulated by Aristotle than with those offered by contemporary metaphor theory. Conceptual metaphors such as LIFE IS A JOURNEY or ARGUMENT IS WAR generate commonplace phraseology that we hear every day: "He took a wrong turn"; "She's on a one-way road to trouble"; "He shoots down every point we make"; "She made an indefensible claim." A great deal of scholarly attention has been focused on identifying these metaphor systems and articulating the ways in which they provide the structure of our daily language. Lakoff and Johnson, in their groundbreaking study *Metaphors We Live By* (1980), demonstrated both the breadth of concepts that we conceive of in metaphorical terms and the multitude of linguistic manifestations of these concepts that populate our daily language.

If we accept the premise that conceptual metaphors provide the foundation of human language usage, and hence of communication, it stands to reason that the linguistic foundation provided by conceptual metaphors serves as the basis for literary texts as well. Late twentieth-century southern novels provide fertile ground for investigating the function of conceptual metaphor in literature, in large part because of the frequent recurrence of a metaphor system that is universal yet simultaneously reflective of the southern experience—the LIFE IS A GAME conceptual metaphor.

Despite the fact that it evokes many common linguistic uses, the LIFE IS A GAME metaphor has generated little discussion. This metaphor is the foundation of many syntactic structures, and the situations in which they arise are widely arrayed. They range from the sexual ("he's a switch-hitter," or "she's batting from the other side of the plate") to the corporate ("she's a team player," or "he took one for the team"), and from commentary on the successes or failures of others ("he's a bench warmer," or "her idea was a home run") to requests for particular types of treatment for an individual ("give him a slow soft one down the middle" or "we're going to have to call in some bench strength to finish the project on time").

The fact that the LIFE IS A GAME conceptual metaphor is a rich linguistic source is useful in itself from the perspective of understanding the sources of language, but this metaphor is also of interest because of its frequent occurrence in literary texts. In looking at conceptual metaphor in the context of literary works, we must realize that its occurrence is an unconscious phenomenon, and precisely because it is an unconscious phenomenon, conceptual metaphor can yield a great deal of insight not only into the workings of an author's thought processes but into mental constructs undergirding the culture by which the author was influenced, through the discourse of the characters. As Donald C. Freeman, Margaret Freeman, and Monika Fludernik have argued, during the latter half of the twentieth century, our understanding of metaphor has become increasingly complex as we have "moved away from traditional conceptions of poetic language as somehow being sublime" (384–385). Our understanding of the orientation of metaphor has, according to Mark Turner, moved "in quite the opposite direction, [focusing on] the intrinsic linkage between linguistic processes in general and the more specific literary instances of them" (xi).

The LIFE IS A GAME conceptual metaphor frequently crops up in the late twentieth-century southern novel. I argue that the prevalence of this particular conceptual metaphor results from the complexities of southern history as exemplified by the intensity with which the "good old boy"—the powerful, white, landowning male—has persisted as a major character in both fact and fiction. This powerful segment of the region's population has perpetuated the disenfranchisement of women, people of color, and the poor. Sports and games are cornerstones of Southern culture in all walks of life—outdoor sports such as hunting and fishing, as well as the arguably rabid interest of many southerners in team sports such as football and baseball—so representing life itself, as well as the attitudes of the South's inhabitants in terms of gaming and the rules of games, is a natural outgrowth of the southern world view. Southern culture is rule-driven to a significant extent, with propriety dictating clearly defined ground rules: Smile and play nicely in public, but when pitching—when someone forgets his or her place, steps out of line, disregards commonly accepted behavioral standards—throw inside with the heat and strike the other guy out swinging. Perhaps nowhere else in the United States can be found such overt acceptance of this double standard of behavior—of the social acceptability of duplicity between the public and the private face.

To demonstrate both the significance and the cultural connotations of the LIFE IS A GAME conceptual metaphor, I offer examples from several late twentieth-century novels, each of which derive from a different southern subculture. Dorothy Allison's *Cavedweller* (1998) presents poor whites and relates the stories of women who on the surface seem to have little interest in sports or gaming, yet the LIFE IS A GAME metaphor system frames the narrative. Ellen Douglas's *Can't Quit You Baby* (1988) is narrated by an upper-class white woman attempting to come to terms with the relationships that define her life, especially the one with her long-time African American domestic assistant. As the novel is largely set in the home—specifically, the kitchen—of the upper-class woman, the reader's expectation might again be that sports and gaming would be of little interest, yet the metaphoric constructions nonetheless prove pervasive, speaking to the unconscious nature of conceptual metaphor and the ways in which women's domestic roles are perceived. Alice Walker's *The Third Life of Grange Copeland* (1970) is set in a black sharecropping community characterized by random violence, gambling, carousing, and drinking; and metaphoric constructions positing LIFE IS A GAME form the framework for the text. The lives of these protagonists are posited as games that must be played by strictly codified rules—rules that govern both public behavior and private relationships. The language of these texts reinforces cultural expectations that are conceptualized at a cognitive level so basic that they structure the very language with which they are described. These novels share a common theme that highlights the oppressed and undervalued status of the disempowered minorities controlled by privileged white society.

Dorothy Allison's second novel, *Cavedweller*, derives its structure from the LIFE IS A GAME metaphor system. Early in the novel, Delia Byrd describes her life as "swimming a mud tide" (4) and her best friend Rosemary parallels life with sports like rafting and canoeing, evoking LIFE IS A GAME: "Life sweeps you away like a piss river" (173). Evoking images of water sports like swimming and rafting, Allison subconsciously draws upon the LIFE IS A GAME metaphor system, depicting life as a wild ride that is beyond the control of its players. Throughout the novel, Allison makes much of the dangers inherent in caving, and Delia's daughter Cissy makes repeated references to being swept away by an underground river or being caught in a "sink" from which many spelunkers never emerge. In fact, swimming in mud and being swept away by forces beyond control become central ideas in the novel, both literally and metaphorically. Cissy becomes fascinated with spelunking the caves of rural Georgia; and on a metaphoric level, the LIFE IS A GAME conceptual system encapsulates the position in which Delia and her three daughters find themselves. Members of the lower-class South by birth, they are in many ways prototypical white trash, freely exhibiting alcohol problems, insensitivity to behaving badly in public, and cavalier disregard for the appearances resulting from their relationship exploits.

Each of Allison's women exhibits the devastating results of poverty that spans generations and the persistent challenges of living in a society dominated by class prejudice. Theirs is a world inhabited by "Neanderthal jocks who just want us to crawl ahead of them so they can look at our butts" (272)—Allison's description of the redneck good old boys who populate much of contemporary southern fiction. This attitude causes sexual intimacy to be viewed as a game between two people in which only one may emerge victorious. Even the women's physical attributes are described in the context of gaming, as in the case of Cissy's "pinball eyes" (169). The lives of Delia, her daughters, and her friend are a physically and emotionally trying sport, and their trials are reinforced by the LIFE IS A GAME conceptual metaphor that provides the foundation of the narrative.

The LIFE IS A GAME metaphor system is particularly apparent in the descriptions of caving which are both literal and metaphorical. Caving is a game in itself, a "nonlucrative occupation, a pastime for ex-jocks and the kind of intense skinny youths who can be seen doggedly swimming laps or race walking while others pursue team sports. There are no medals for this hobby, no trophies but the regard of other experts" (270). Cissy becomes obsessed with caving, finding the danger with which it is fraught to be one of its most seductive attractions: "Caving is not a sport but a dare, more a trial than an excursion" (250). She is repeatedly described as sliding through mud on her belly: Often Cissy "crawled head down through three miles of mud and gravel, mapped a passage where no one has been . . . [so that later cavers could] discover her secret life" (270). Conversely, Rosemary, Delia's best friend, suffers a "curse in the belly" (170)—the same body part that literally swims through mud in Cissy's case. While she attributes this curse to herself, it metaphorically extends to Delia because of the dysfunctions suffered by each of her three daughters, dysfunctions that Rosemary has come to help Delia alleviate. The LIFE IS A GAME conceptual metaphor recurs in the depictions of Cissy's experiences with spelunking, which she describes as testing "the nerves, the muscles, the survival instincts, but the risk is awful" (250). Yet caving also represents Cissy's escape from the unhappiness of the game of life, from the realities of a father dead too soon, a mother's seemingly incomprehensible decisions, and a search for completeness that is not fulfilled any other way. Suffering the disdain and disillusionment that are the result of their poverty and the moral code associated with poverty by those with more money and power, Delia and her family engage in games fraught with struggle and violent potential, mirroring the realities of their day-to-day existence.

Similarly, Ellen Douglas's *Can't Quit You Baby* delves into the nature of relationships while focusing closely on the ways in which race and the layers of oppression implicit in it can influence the development or stagnation of relationships. The interactions between the two protagonists, Cornelia, a rich, white woman, and Tweet, a poor African American domestic worker, which take place over the course of most of their adult lives, are confined to the domestic sphere, a sphere from which men are notably absent but one that would not exist but for the largesse of privileged men. Tweet and Cornelia's relationship and their activities are contextualized by recurring manifestations of the LIFE IS A GAME conceptual metaphor, underscoring Cornelia and Tweet's mutual positions as disempowered and undervalued members of a culture that places little value on their efforts. Although each woman must play according to socially acceptable rules, the games that define Cornelia's life are to a large extent of her own choosing while Tweet must play the hand that she is dealt if she is to maintain her quality of life. Accordingly, the manifestations of the LIFE IS A GAME metaphor system when describing Tweet's experiences encompass more practical metaphors deriving from games and sports than those associated with her privileged employer, who is more often associated with artistic and solitary sporting activities.

In the first scene of *Can't Quit You Baby*, the women are making fig preserves together, going "to a great deal of trouble to keep them whole, so that in the jars they will swim in all their shapely beauty, surrounded by cartwheels of golden lemon curls" (3). Their activity represents the types of work in which they routinely engage, yet the description could also be viewed as a symbolic description of their entire lives. They are contained in a relatively small sphere with definite, transparent boundaries; Cornelia's role requires her to create, with Tweet's able assistance, a beautiful environment that can withstand and even enjoy the scrutiny of her husband and family. Cornelia and Tweet swim together in this environment, surrounded by activities and light but separated from the realities of life. The LIFE IS A GAME metaphor informs this description, with Douglas positing their work as light-hearted play, describing the end result of their labor in terms of insignificant and elusive childhood games—swimming and cartwheels.

Unlike Tweet, whose livelihood is tied to Cornelia's need to maintain the game, Cornelia's life is a game in which she asserts an aloof independence: She is a "dancer, a skier—skimming calmly over the surface of her life as if it were a polished floor or a calm summer lake" (127). Her husband's business acumen allows her to play better, and more solitary, games than those that Tweet's finances can support: Cornelia has years in which she can "sail and fly . . . swim and fish" (13), although she had to prevail in a game with more challenging rules to arrive at this seemingly carefree point in her life. After meeting her future husband, a man whom Cornelia's mother found an unsuitable prospect, the two women find themselves "locked in [a] combat" so intense that they had to "retire to consider the next move" (83). Cornelia's relationship with her mother is a brutal game, described as an ongoing boxing match between two unequally matched opponents. When Cornelia's beau prepares to help her escape from the bedroom where her mother has imprisoned her so she will consider her error in judgment, she tells him that she has been "climbing trees and swinging on ropes all my life" (92). The man himself is described as athletic, with a "light, ballet dancer's walk" (90), further reinforcing the game metaphors. Cornelia's entire life is constructed around the various attributes of games, their rules, and their elements, extending to life-altering decisions about whom she will marry and to what extent she will defy her mother.

Cornelia's personal game, however, is played out through her willful deafness, which becomes a symptom of her unwillingness to hear unpleasant, unpalatable, or uninteresting things about the people around her. She suffers from progressive physiological deafness beginning in her twenties; but rather than representing a tragic loss of communication with her family, Cornelia's physical symptoms serve to highlight the intentional ignorance of the lives and concerns of those seemingly closest to her. Her physical deafness allows her to play games with those around her. She often seeks a reprieve from those who bore her, choosing play as a means of escape. She clicks off her hearing aid—or takes it out altogether—and she "swims laps three times a week . . . [living] for a while in a silence that does not strive either to hear or to give the appearance of hearing" (15). Cornelia's deafness becomes a game that allows her to play at listening to some people and to shut out the rest in silence. As she ages and her children grow up, she is confronted with all that her family has kept from her over the years. Her family knows "well enough how complicated their lives would be made by confession" (130), making them complicit in Cornelia's game of willful ignorance. At first, she feels betrayed because they have excluded her from their emotional ranks, but by the novel's end she comes to realize that her isolation from those closest to her is the result of her quiet, stubborn resistance to emotional intimacy with them.

The games that define Tweet's life, on the other hand, demonstrate her social position as both a poor woman and a person of color. In addition to the expectations placed on women to handle the domestic chores efficiently, as a woman of color, Tweet must exist in a world that offers her few choices. The traditional crafts and foodways that Tweet learns as a child are often belittled as unworthy forms of expression that do not measure up to the standards of art. In Southern culture, folk traditions for many years were denigrated as childish pursuits or games, especially those folk activities associated with the poor or with people of color. Accordingly, the skills Tweet is taught as a child—"to make a split oak basket, rob a bee tree, skin a catfish"—evoke the LIFE IS A GAME conceptual metaphor through the direct references to outdoor activities such as fishing and hunting. Whereas Cornelia's games are those generally reserved for the rich and privileged by virtue of the expense of participating in them and the training they require, Tweet's activities are practical yet oddly more sportsmanlike because of their proximity to nature and the player's intention to use nature's resources as they were intended. The games in which Tweet engages are those that serve to enhance—and in many cases sustain—her life. Tweet's life is described as a metaphorical game, but the game becomes literal as she avoids being "outfoxed" (21) by Cornelia and by a social system that is heavily invested in keeping her in her place. Ironically, Tweet knows the game that Cornelia plays, and in fact she is the only person in the novel who "raises her voice and tells Cornelia what is really going on" (129), regardless of whether she wishes to hear it or not.

Cornelia is outfoxed, however, and must come to terms with what she has missed throughout her life because of the games she plays with her deafness. The perfect game that is Cornelia's life begins to crumble unexpectedly, and the events that precipitate her examination of her relationships with her husband, her children, and even Tweet are heralded by an extended sporting story Cornelia recalls that mirrors the LIFE IS A GAME conceptual metaphor. A young woman is water-skiing; and as she is pulled behind the boat, she is dragged into a nest of water moccasins. In the few seconds it takes the driver of the boat to reach the girl and pull her out, she dies of multiple snakebites. The coda of this story relates that "a tangle of water moccasins lies in wait for the skier. Always, always true" (131). Cornelia has spent her life skimming across the top of the water, effortlessly, untouched by pain and refusing to admit a "flaw into her perfect kingdom" (129), but Douglas's novel demonstrates the many potential dangers aimed at those who are oppressed, who are pulled along behind the boat at the mercy of the environment and the driver.

The issue of life's dangers is also apparent in *The Third Life of Grange Copeland*, for it relates the redemption of the degraded and frustrated title character, positing his life as a game with ruthless rules and painful penalties for the losers. The lives depicted in this novel become little more than an endless sporting event, an ongoing boxing match where the knockout punch is never mercifully delivered. Grange articulates this concept when he explains his resistance to voting, saying that he does not want Ruth and the other "children" to know the despair "when you finds out the fight can't be won" (Walker 241). The only relief is found through running—either to the North, which offers the only potential escape from the poverty suffered by the sharecroppers who populate Grange's world—or through drowning the ability to think in alcohol, women, and violence. Running, drowning, being hunted by powerful landowners, as demonstrated through Grange's death at the novel's end—these literal events characterize the rules of the game for the pawns who must play it, rules embodied by the LIFE IS A GAME system of conceptual metaphors. Grange, his family members, and their acquaintances live in utter squalor, the depths of which can be altered in a moment at the whim of the white community, who, as a result of their ownership of the land which the predominately black sharecroppers farm, hold power over them. These sharecroppers are often described as pawns in a game: Quincy, the young man who comes to Grange's farm to convince Grange to register to vote, describes himself as the "little joker used to trail along behind Sister Madeline" (237); Josie, the barmaid who gives Grange's son Brownfield a job, recalls being ridden by a witch (a witch who, in reality, was her father's disappointed expectations) as a jockey might ride a horse; and Brownfield calls himself the "grand prize pawn" (47). The players in the game often become tired, as when Brownfield needs "a little chance to catch his breath" (32) after spending days on the road, running away from home. The rules of the game are well known to all who play it, and ironically, those who sought to escape suffered more bitterly than those who accepted their lot. Mem, Brownfield's long-suffering wife, quietly worked to save money so that they might improve their situation, but "all her moves upward and toward something of their own would be checked by him" (58), equating life with a chess game in which one player must achieve complete victory over the other. The LIFE IS A GAME conceptual metaphor recurs in Walker's depiction of the sharecroppers' lives, demonstrating the pervasive nature of this metaphor system as a function of conceptualizing the lives of poverty-stricken, oppressed populations.

Even in the face of death, the LIFE IS A GAME conceptual metaphor recurs, demonstrating that the game continues ad infinitum—the pawns are interchangeable and are easily replaced. Despite the many misdeeds and abuses meted out by Grange throughout his life, he dies heroically, attempting to shield his granddaughter from an angry group of whites. His death is described in terms associated with hunting animals for sport. Grange is first tracked and then shot dead, and he is described as something akin to the prey of a sportsman. After speaking his piece to the angry group, he "raced" home, and after leaving Ruth in a relatively safe place, he "took off in a trot through the woods" as police cars "circled" the house (246). Grange's death at the hands of white sportsmen, under the guise of meting out justice due him for lawless behavior, reveals the LIFE IS A GAME metaphor. Dying under a tree from the gunshot wound "seemed appropriate, as a drink is an appropriate end to a long dry poker game" (246–247). The manner of Grange's death evokes metaphors of sporting as an integral function of life, especially among the empowered white males to whom Grange and his family are beholden for their entire lives. Grange is shot down in the woods in the same manner as a deer or a rabbit, and he dies quietly under a tree even as he hears the "rustle of footsteps creeping near" (246). The oppression suffered by poor sharecroppers in the rural South is implicit in the hunting metaphor that structures the description of Grange's death.

The common thread in these three seemingly disparate novels is the conceptual metaphor system that frames them. The southern predisposition toward gaming and sporting, as embraced by the prototypical "good old boy" and all of his contradictions, is unconsciously spoken in the Southern voice. The cultural influence of games and their rules—whether outdoor sports such as hunting and fishing, team games like baseball and football, or individual activities like swimming or skating—is intrinsically coded into the language of the literary artists of the region. The LIFE IS A GAME conceptual metaphor elucidates key elements of the culture and frequently highlights long-standing deficiencies found in it, as illustrated by the persistent manifestation of this metaphor system in the works of the region's writers. Members of traditionally marginalized groups—women, people of color, poor people—most often function as the objects of the game, playing because they have no choice. Precisely because conceptual metaphor is an unconscious linguistic phenomenon, its prevalence in literary texts serves to draw attention to the roles of these populations of undervalued people.

REFERENCES

Allison, Dorothy. *Cavedweller*. New York: Dutton–Penguin, 1998.

Blasenstein, Michael. "Shapes and Reflections: Conceptual Metaphors as Sculptor and Mirror of Thought." 3 Nov. 1998. 2 Oct. 2003 <http://home.earthlink.net/~meb9/school/metaphor.htm>.

Douglas, Ellen. *Can't Quit You, Baby*. New York: Penguin, 1988.

Fludernik, Monika, Donald C. Freeman, and Margaret H. Freeman. "Metaphor and Beyond: An Introduction." *Poetics Today* 20.3 (1999): 383–396.

Lakoff, George, and Mark Johnson. *Metaphors We Live By*. Chicago: University of Chicago Press, 1980.

Lakoff, George, and Mark Turner. *More than Cool Reason: A Field Guide to Poetic Metaphor*. Chicago: University of Chicago Press, 1989.

Sweetser, Eve, and Gilles Fauconnier. "Cognitive Links and Domains: Basic Aspects of Mental Space Theory." *Spaces, Worlds, and Grammar*. Eds. Gilles Fauconnier and Eve Sweetser. Chicago: University of Chicago Press, 1996. 1–28.

Turner, Mark. *Reading Minds: The Study of English in the Age of Cognitive Science*. Princeton, NJ: Princeton University Press, 1991.

Walker, Alice. *The Third Life of Grange Copeland*. New York: Harcourt Brace Jovanovich, 1970.

Selected Bibliography

Anthologies

Aymar, Brandt, ed. *Men in Sports: Great Sports Stories of All Time from the Greek Olympic Games to the American World Series*. Toronto: Crown Publishing Group, 1995.

Bandy, Susan J., and Anne S. Darden, eds. *Crossing Boundaries: An International Anthology of Women's Experiences in Sport*. Champaign, IL: Human Kinetics, 1999.

Battista, Garth, ed. *The Runner's Literary Companion*. New York: Breakaway Books, 1994.

Bjarkman, Peter C., ed. *Baseball and the Game of Life*. New York: Vintage Books, 1991.

Blaustein, Noah, ed. *Motion: American Sports Poems*. Iowa City: University of Iowa Press, 2001.

Buchwald, Emilie, and Ruth Roston. *This Sporting Life: Poems about Sports and Games*. 2nd ed. Minneapolis: Milkweed Editions, 1998.

Byrne, Robert, ed. *Byrne's Book of Great Pool Stories*. New York: Harvest Books, 1995.

Dawidoff, Nicholas, ed. *Baseball: A Literary Anthology*. New York: Library of America, 2002.

Early, Gerald Lyn, ed. *Body Language: Writers on Sport*. St. Paul: Graywolf Press, 1998.

Graber, Ralph S., ed. *The Baseball Reader*. New York: A. S. Barnes, 1951.

Halberstam, David, ed. *The Best American Sports Writing of the Century*. Boston: Houghton Mifflin, 1999.

Hallberg, William. *Perfect Lies: A Century of Great Golf Stories*. Garden City, NY: Doubleday, 1989.

Holtzman, Jerome, ed. *Fielder's Choice: An Anthology of Baseball Fiction*. New York: Harcourt Brace Jovanovich, 1979.

Horvath, Brooke, and Tim Wiles, eds. *Line Drives: 100 Contemporary Baseball Poems*. Carbondale: Southern Illinois University Press, 2003.

Houston, Pamela, ed. *Women on Hunting*. Hopewell, NJ: The Ecco Press, 1995.

Jennings, Jay, ed. *Tennis and the Meaning of Life: A Literary Anthology of the Game*. Collingdale, PA: Diane Publishing, 2000.

Knudson, R. R., and May Swenson, eds. *American Sports Poems*. New York: Orchard Books, 1988.

Madden, W. C., comp. *Baseball Stories for the Soul: 50 Stories, Poems and Other Soulful Inspirations about America's Favorite Pastime*. Fishers, IN: Madden Publishing Co., 2000.

McNally, John, ed. *Bottom of the Ninth: Great Contemporary Baseball Stories*. Carbondale: Southern Illinois University Press, 2003.

Morris, Holly, ed. *Uncommon Waters: Women Write about Fishing*. 2nd ed. Seattle: Seal Press, 1998.

Nauen, Elinor, ed. *Diamonds Are a Girl's Best Friend: Women Writers on Baseball*. Boston: Faber and Faber, 1994.

————, ed. *Ladies, Start Your Engines: Women Writers on Cars and on the Road*. Boston: Faber and Faber, 1996.

Plimpton, George, ed. *The Norton Book of Sports*. New York: W.W. Norton, 1992.

Riordan, James, ed. *The Young Oxford Book of Sports Stories*. New York: Oxford University Press, 2001.

Sandoz, Joli, ed. *A Whole Other Ballgame: Women's Literature on Women's Sport*. New York: Farrar, Strauss and Giroux, 1997.

————, ed. *Whatever It Takes: Women on Women's Sports*. New York: Farrar, Strauss and Giroux, 1999.

Scannell, Vernon. *Sporting Literature: An Anthology*. Oxford: Oxford University Press, 1987.

Schinto, Jeanne, ed. *Show Me a Hero: Great Contemporary Stories about Sport*. New York: Persea Books, 1995.

Seybold, David, ed. *Seasons of the Angler: A Fisherman's Anthology*. New York: Atlantic Monthly Press, 1998.

Silverman, Al, and Brian Silverman, eds. *The Twentieth Century Treasury of Sports*. New York: Viking, 1992.

Stadohar, Paul D., ed. *Baseball's Best Short Stories*. Chicago: Chicago Review Press, 1995.

Starrs, James E., ed. *The Literary Cyclist*. Halcottsville, NY: Breakaway Books, 1997.

Streker, Trey, ed. *Dead Balls and Double Curves: An Anthology of Early Baseball Fiction*. Carbondale: Southern Illinois University Press, 2004.

Trudell, Dennis, ed. *Full Court: A Literary Anthology of Basketball*. Halcottsville, NY: Breakaway Books, 1996.

Wiebusch, John, and Brian Silverman, eds. *A Game of Passion: The NFL Literary Companion*. Atlanta: Turner Publications, 1994.

Wimmer, Dick. *The Schoolyard Game: An Anthology of Basketball Writings*. New York: Simon and Schuster, 1992.

Reference

Burns, Grant. *The Sports Pages: A Critical Bibliography of Twentieth-Century American Novels and Stories Featuring Baseball, Basketball, Football, and Other Athletic Pursuits.* Metuchen, NJ: Scarecrow Press, 1987.

Deardorff, Donald L., II., *Sports: A Reference Guide and Critical Commentary, 1980–1999.* Westport, CT: Greenwood Press, 2000. Especially chapter 6 "Sport and Literature" and chapter 8 "Sport and Popular Culture."

Dinan, John. *Sports in the Pulp Magazines.* Jefferson, NC: McFarland, 1998.

Orodenker, Richard, ed. *American Sportswriters and Writers on Sports. Dictionary of Literary Biography.* Vol. 241. Farmington Hills, MI: Gale Group, 2001.

———. *Twentieth Century American Sportswriters.* Detroit: Gale Research, 1996.

Shannon, Michael. *Diamond Classics: Essays on 100 of the Best Baseball Books Ever Published.* Jefferson, NC: McFarland, 1989.

Wise, Suzanne. *Sports Fiction for Adults: An Annotated Bibliography of Novels, Plays, Short Stories and Poetry with Sporting Settings.* New York: Garland Publishing, 1986.

Scholarly Studies

Aethlon: The Journal of Sport Literature. Johnson City: East Tennessee State University Press. Continues (1988–) *Arete: The Journal of Sport Literature.*

Baker, Aaron. *Contesting Identities: Sports in American Film.* Champaign: University of Illinois Press, 2003.

Berman, Neil David. *Playful Fictions and Fictional Players: Games, Sport and Survival in Contemporary Fiction.* Port Washington, NY: Kennikat Press, 1981.

Candelaria, Cordelia. *Seeking the Perfect Game: Baseball in American Literature.* Westport, CT: Greenwood Press, 1989.

Dodge, Thomas. *A Literature of Sports.* Lexington, MA: D.C. Heath, 1980.

Higgs, Robert J. *Laurel and Thorn: The Athlete in American Literature.* Lexington: University of Kentucky Press, 1981.

Horvath, Brooke K., and William J. Palmer, eds. *Modern Sports Fiction.* Issue of *Modern Fiction Studies* 33.1 (1987).

Messenger, Christian K. *Sport and the Spirit of Play in American Fiction: Hawthorne to Faulkner.* New York: Columbia University Press, 1981.

———. *Sport and the Spirit of Play in Contemporary Fiction.* New York: Columbia University Press, 1990.

Morris, Timothy. *Making the Team: The Cultural Work of Baseball Fiction.* Champaign: University of Illinois Press, 1997.

Nathan, Daniel A. *Saying It's So: A Cultural History of the Black Sox Scandal.* Champaign: University of Illinois Press, 2003.

Oriard, Michael. *Dreaming of Heroes: American Sports Fiction, 1868–1980.* Chicago: Nelson-Hall, 1982.

———. *King Football: Sport and Spectacle in the Golden Age of Radio, Newsreels, Movies and Magazines, The Weekly and The Daily Press.* Chapel Hill: University of North Carolina Press, 2001.

———. *Sporting with the Gods: The Rhetoric of Play and Game in American Culture.* Cambridge: Cambridge University Press, 1991.

Orodenker, Richard. *The Writer's Game: Baseball Writing in America.* New York: Twayne, 1996.

Rivers, Jacob F., III. *Cultural Values in the Southern Sporting Narrative.* Columbia: University of South Carolina Press, 2002.

Umphlett, Wiley Lee, ed. *The Achievement of American Sports Literature: A Critical Appraisal.* Cranbury, NJ: Associated University Press, 1991.

Vanderwerken, David L., and Spencer K. Wertz, eds. *Sport Inside and Out: Readings in Literature and Philosophy.* Fort Worth: Texas Christian University Press, 1985.

Westbrook, Deeanne. *Ground Rules: Baseball and Myth.* Champaign: University of Illinois Press, 1996.

Index

About the Editors and Contributors

LISA ABNEY is the Director of the Louisiana Folklife Center and an Associate Professor of English at Northwestern State University. She directs the Natchitoches/NSU Folk Festival and the public programming of the Louisiana Folklife Center, a division of NSU. Dr. Abney has coedited *Songs of the New South: Writing Contemporary Louisiana* and *Songs of the Reconstructing South: Building Literary Louisiana, 1865–1945.* She has also coedited the 21st Century American Novelists volume in the *Dictionary of Literary Biography* series. Dr. Abney continues work on the Linguistic Survey of North Louisiana and research into grave, burial, and memorial traditions in the Ark-La-Tex region. She is currently working on a manuscript "The Last Respects: Grave Digging by Hand in Northern and Central Louisiana." She serves as an Associate Editor for the Longman anthology of Southern literature, entitled *Voices of the American South,* and has written over thirty articles regarding linguistics, folklore, and literature of the American South. She has written over fifteen funded grants.

GREG AHRENHOERSTER earned his Ph.D. at the University of Wisconsin–Milwaukee, writing about sport in twentieth-century American fiction for his dissertation. He has published articles in *Aethlon* about the use of sports references by William Faulkner and Ralph Ellison. A long-time fan of William Shakespeare and the Milwaukee Brewers, Greg is an expert on tragedy. He currently teaches English at the University of Wisconsin–Waukesha.

RYAN K. ANDERSON is a Ph.D. candidate in U.S. History at Purdue University. His research interests center on social and cultural topics including gender, youth, popular culture, and the history of the book. He wishes to thank Professors Randy Roberts, David Welkey, and Michael Butler for their assistance in early drafts of this piece, as well as Jim Buss and Scott Randolph, for their comments on later drafts.

SUSAN J. BANDY earned a B.A. in literature and physical education at Berry College (1970), an M.Ed. in physical education at the University of Georgia (1972), and a Ph.D. in sport studies at Arizona State University (1982). Before joining the Program on Gender and Culture at the Central European University in 2000, she taught at San Diego State University, United States International University, and East Tennessee State University and was the Assistant to the Manager of the Women's Institute for Continuing Education in Paris. Her expertise is in the cultural study of sport, with particular emphasis on the participation of women in sport and gender and the body. She has edited two books—*Coroebus Triumphs: The Alliance of Sport and the Arts* and *Crossing Boundaries: An International Anthology of Women's Experiences in Sport*—and one monograph devoted to women, sport, and literature, as well as a special issue of *Aethlon: The Journal of Sport Literature*. Her most recent book is *The Viking Tradition: 100 Years of Sport at Berry College*. She was a Fulbright Scholar to the Hungarian University of Physical Education from 1997 to 1999 and a visiting professor in the Faculty of Physical Education and Sport Science, Semmelweis University, Budapest, from 1999 to 2002. At present she is a visiting professor at the Department of Gender Studies, Central European University, and an associate professor in the Department of Sport Science at Aarhus University in Aarhus, Denmark.

STEPHEN J. BURN teaches at Northern Michigan University. He is the author of the first book devoted to Wallace's fiction, *David Foster Wallace's Infinite Jest: A Reader's Guide* (2003), and his work has appeared in the *American Book Review, James Joyce Quarterly*, the *Review of Contemporary Fiction*, and the *Times Literary Supplement*.

MICHAEL COCCHIARALE is Assistant Professor of English at Widener University, where he teaches American literature, creative writing, and composition courses. He holds a Ph.D. from Purdue University. In addition to sports literature, Cocchiarale's research interests include the short story cycle and Christianity in literature.

A. FLETCHER COLE is currently part of the English Department at the University of Maryland at College Park. His specialty is autobiography and life-writing in nineteenth-century American literature.

TRACY CURTIS hails from Cleveland, Ohio, where she first began to appreciate basketball as played on blacktop. She, however, is not athletic at all. Her most recent writing has been on the experience of race in graduate school and on the perils of the health care system. Her current projects include studies on the impact of visual culture on African American women's autobiography, performed poetry, and African American women's conceptions of themselves as citizens in the 1930s, as well as a short story collection. She lives in sunny, smoggy Los Angeles.

SUZANNE DISHEROON-GREEN serves as Associate Professor of American Literature and Director of Graduate Studies in English at Northwestern State University in Natchitoches, Louisiana. Her research interests include the works of southern writers, especially as they are influenced by race, class, and gender; Louisiana writers; women's writing; and turn-of-the-century American literature. She is coauthor of four books: At Fault *by Kate Chopin: A Scholarly Edition with Background Readings* (2001); *Kate Chopin: An Annotated Bibliography of Critical Work* (1999) with David J. Caudle; *Songs of the New South: Writing Contemporary Louisiana* (2001); and *Songs of the Reconstructing South: Building Literary Louisiana, 1865–1945* (2002) with Lisa Abney. Her work has also appeared in journals such as *Southern Quarterly* and *Southern Studies*. Disheroon-Green is the general editor of Longman's *Voices of the American South*, a comprehensive anthology of Southern literature; she has recently completed editing a volume in the *Dictionary of Literary Biography* series titled "Twenty-first Century American Novelists" with Lisa Abney. She is currently working on a book-length study entitled "Understanding Kaye Gibbons" for the University of South Carolina Press.

DAVID C. DOUGHERTY directs the Graduate Program in Liberal Studies and is a Professor of English at Loyola College in Maryland. He has chaired that department and has served as a technical writing consultant for many firms and governmental institutions. A Woodrow Wilson Dissertation fellow at Miami University, he is the author of book-length studies of poet James Wright (1927–1980) and novelist Stanley Elkin (1930–1995) and editor of a casebook on Elkin's *The Dick Gibson Show*. His journal and reference book essays treat many American and British writers, most recently Toni Morrison, John Dos Passos, Thomas Hardy, Elkin, Saul Bellow, W. D. Snodgrass, and John Updike. He recently completed mini-biographies of professional athletes Bob Gibson, Ernie Banks, and Jerry West, as well as the introduction to the forthcoming Dalkey Archive of Elkin's *A Bad Man*. His current research is toward a biography of Elkin.

SCOTT D. EMMERT earned his Ph.D. in American literature from Purdue University. In addition to sport literature, his research interests include American realism and naturalism, the short story, and the fiction and film of the American West. An Assistant Professor of English at the University of Wisconsin–Fox Valley, he is indeed a stranger in a strange land: a fan of the Minnesota Vikings residing in the heart of Green Bay Packers' country.

MARK S. GRAYBILL is Assistant Professor of English at Widener University, where he also serves as Assistant Provost. A graduate of the doctoral program in English at the University of South Carolina, his scholarly interests include Southern fiction, postmodern literature and culture, and literary theory. He has published refereed journal articles on Shakespeare, Walker Percy, Barry Hannah, Bobbie Ann Mason, and Josephine Humphreys. Hypermasculinity notwithstanding, he remains an inveterate baseball fan.

ROXANNE HARDE holds a doctorate in American Literature from Queen's University and is currently a postdoctoral fellow at Cornell University. She has published several book chapters, and her articles have appeared in *Legacy, Critique, Mosaic,* and *The Journal of the Association for Research on Mothering.* While her research focuses primarily on American women's religious writing and feminist theology, she makes frequent trips to the ball diamond in her teaching and research.

MATTHEW KELLEY is an Assistant Professor at the University of Michigan where he is a Faculty Fellow of the Sweetland Writing Program. He has published articles and reviews in *Clio, Modern Fiction Studies, Shofar,* and most recently in *Poetry's Poet: Essays on Allen Grossman* (2004). He is also the author of *Literature through Art: A Guidebook* (2002).

DIEDERIK OOSTDIJK completed his dissertation, "Karl Shapiro and *Poetry: A Magazine of Verse* (1950–1955)," a literary-historical analysis of the magazine's second flowering, in 2000, and has since published articles in books and magazines on Middle Generation poets and their relationship to American culture. He taught at the University of Nijmegen in the Netherlands and as a guest lecturer at the University of Iowa and is currently Assistant Professor at the English Department of the Free University in Amsterdam.

RON PICARD earned his Ph.D. from Purdue University and works as an Instructor at Naugatuck Valley Community College. His specialties include twentieth-century American literature, contemporary theory, multicultural literature, professional writing, and rhetoric and composition. He developed this essay from his dissertation, which is titled "Bridging the Post/Modern Divide: Reading High Modern and Multicultural Postmodern Works Side by Side."

ANDREW J. PRICE is a Professor in the English Department at Mount Union College, where he holds the Mary W. and Eric A. Eckler Professor in American Literature and also directs the Gender Studies program. He teaches courses in American literature, gender studies, and critical theory. His current research has focused on body studies, gender, and whiteness.

DEREK PARKER ROYAL is an Assistant Professor of English at Texas A&M University–Commerce. His essays in late nineteenth- and twentieth-century literature have appeared in such journals as *Modern Fiction Studies, Studies in the Novel, Shofar, Studies in American Jewish Literature, Texas Studies in Literature and Language,* and *Critique.* He is currently completing a book on narrative and identity in Philip Roth's later fiction, tentatively titled *More Than Jewish Mischief*, editing a collection of new essays on Roth for Greenwood Publishing, and serving as a guest editor for upcoming issues of *Shofar* and *Studies in American Jewish Literature*. He is also the founder and current president of the Philip Roth Society.

When **CHRIS YORK** was hit by his own coach in little league batting practice, he realized that his life journey would be outside the lines. He is currently a journeyman academic who has published in the fields of baseball literature, popular culture, and student retention. He currently teaches at Winona State University.